Picture Credits:

Brian Bennett
Gary Bettmann
Bruce Bennett Studios/C. Anderson, Rick Berk,
M.Desjardins, M.Di Giacomo, J. Di Maggio, H. Dirocco,
A. Foxall, D. Giacopelli, J.Giamundo, P. Laberge, J. Leary,
Scott Levy, R. Lewis, R.McCormick, Jim McIsaac,
Layne Murdoch, L. Redkoles, W. Robers, Rick Stewart,
J. Tremmel, Nick Welsh, B. Winkler
Hockey Hall of Fame

Published in the United States by
Benchmark Press
601 South LaSalle Street, Suite 500
Chicago, Illinois 60605,
in association with
Carlton Books Limited, 1998

ISBN 1-892049-04-X

Printed in Italy

This book is available in quantity at special
discounts for your group or organization.
For further information, contact:
Benchmark Press
601 South LaSalle Street, Suite 500
Chicago, Illinois 60605
Tel (312) 939-3330
Fax (312) 663-3557

NHL HOCKEY

AN OFFICIAL FANS' GUIDE

THIRD EDITION

John MacKinnon

Benchmark
PRESS

Contents

Top Notch: Avalanche goaltender Patrick Roy (left)
solidified his position as one of, if not the, best
netminders in hockey with another stellar season
for Colorado.

INTRODUCTION

The transformation of the National Hockey League from a parochial league into an organization with a global vision began with the 1972 Summit Series between Canadian stars and the great national team of the Soviet Union—the Big, Red Machine.

After years of seeing their understaffed team whipped by the Soviets at the Olympics and World Championships, Canadians were finally given the chance to see their best players, their professionals, the stars of the NHL, supposedly deliver an overdue lesson to the big, bad Russians. It didn't work out quite that way.

The Canadians won, but it took some desperate, last-minute play and a goal by Paul Henderson with 34 seconds remaining in the final game to give Canada a 6-5 victory in the game and a slender series triumph—four games won, three lost, one game tied. The Canadian-invented sport—and the NHL—would never be the same.

NHL teams soon began to copy the superior Russian training methods, to blend their intricate, purposeful drills into often unimaginative North American practices, to pay more attention to the game's technical aspects.

The Russians, and other European teams, grafted the North Americans' never-say-die competitiveness and physical courage onto their highly skilled brand of hockey.

As the NHL expanded, first from six to 12 teams, then to 14, then 18, then 26 and now, with the granting of franchises to Nashville, Atlanta, Columbus and St. Paul, Minnesota, to 30 teams by the turn of the century, teams have to cast their nets wider and wider in search of major-league talent. The talent search has hauled in US high-schoolers and collegians, Russians, Finns, Swedes, Germans, Czechs, Slovaks and Polish-born players.

The NHL, dominated for its first half-century by Canadian stars like Frank McGee, Howie Morenz, Aurel Joliat, George Hainsworth, Maurice (Rocket) Richard, Gordie Howe, Glenn Hall, Bobby Hull, Bobby Orr and Frank Mahovlich, was adjusting to an influx of European talent.

NHL fans grew to admire players like Borje Salming, Anders Hedberg, Ulf Nilsson, Peter, Anton and Marian Stastny and, in the 1990s, Sergei Fedorov, Pavel Bure, Jaromir Jagr and Teemu Selanne.

As the NHL moves toward the 21st Century, it has blossomed from a six- to a 30-team league. By 2000 there will be teams in 16 US states, as well as the District of Columbia and four Canadian provinces. Along with its traditional strength along the Eastern Seaboard and in the Northeast and Midwest, the NHL has planted its pennant in such previously unlikely spots as North Carolina, Tennessee, Georgia, Texas, Florida and Arizona.

The cliché that the NHL appeals merely to regional interests in the US simply does not apply any longer.

In the fall of 1996, the inaugural World Cup of Hockey was held, a joint venture involving the NHL and the NHL Players' Association. Team USA beat Canada in a best-of-three final series, stunning the favored Canadians in the process.

The 1998 Olympic hockey finals was a triumph for the sport and enabled millions worldwide to watch some of the NHL's greatest stars in action. They reveled in the exploits of Wayne Gretzky, Joe Sakic and Patrick Roy of Canada; Finland's Teemu Selanne and Saku Koivu; Pavel Bure and Alexei Yashin of Russia; Brian Leetch, Keith Tkachuk of Team USA and, of course, the incomparable Dominik Hasek and Robert Reichel of the Czech Republic. The finals also showed that the once dominant North America stranglehold had weakened to such an extent that neither the USA or Canada took a medal home with them. The Czech Republic's stunning victory against Russia in the Final was proof that hockey was truly a global game.

The NHL has come a long way indeed since Henderson's legendary goal on a cold September night in Moscow in 1972. The ongoing progress should be great fun.

Growing Center: With Wayne Gretzky and Mark Messier at the end of brilliant careers, and Mario Lemieux in retirement, Eric Lindros' time to emerge as the dominant player in the NHL is at hand.

BIRTH OF A HOCKEY LEAGUE

The whole world was not watching when a small cluster of men met in a downtown Montreal hotel on November 22, 1917 and formed the National Hockey League. The National Hockey Association, a forerunner of the NHL, had suspended operations, so the heads of the Montreal Canadiens, Montreal Wanderers, Ottawa Senators and Quebec Bulldogs attended a founding meeting and formed a new league.

A single reporter—Elmer Ferguson, of the *Montreal Herald*—reported on the somewhat shaky launch. For starters, the Bulldogs, a poor draw in Quebec City, decided not to operate in the NHL's first season, so the Toronto Arenas were admitted to the league as a replacement.

The league was down to three teams early into the first season, though, after the Westmount Arena, home to the Montreal Wanderers, burned down. With nowhere to play, the Wanderers, too, dropped out. The NHL, then, featured the Original Three for most of its initial season, not the Original Six, a term that would gain common usage years later.

The first president of the NHL was Frank Calder, a soccer-playing British émigrée to Canada who had grown to love the Canadian game of hockey. His name would eventually be etched onto a trophy given annually to the best first-year, or rookie, player in the NHL.

In that first season, the league held the first of many dispersal drafts to distribute the players from the Bulldogs, including their scoring star, Joe Malone, who was chosen by the Canadiens.

In one of two opening-night games for the new league on December 19, 1917, Malone scored five goals as the Canadiens defeated Ottawa 7-4. Malone went on to score 44 goals during the 22-game regular season, easily winning the scoring title and setting a scoring pace never equalled in NHL history. The new league had its first superstar.

The league suffered its first major setback the following season, 1918-19. An influenza epidemic enfeebled many of the players on both finalists in the Stanley Cup playoffs—the Montreal Canadiens and Seattle Metropolitans of the Pacific Coast Hockey Association. Joe Hall, one of Montreal's star players died of the disease and so many players were stricken that the series was cancelled with no winner declared.

Building a Following

Interest in NHL hockey grew appreciably through the 1920s and 1930s, but the popularity curve was far from smooth.

In 1919, the Mount Royal Arena was built as the home of the Montreal Canadiens and five years later, the Montreal Forum was constructed to house the Maroons, the other NHL team in that hockey-mad city. In Ottawa, Frank Ahearn built a 10,000-seat arena called the Auditorium in 1923. And in Toronto, Maple Leaf Gardens was completed in 1931.

When Ottawa met the Canadiens in the 1923-24 playoffs,

11,000 jammed into the Auditorium to see the Canadiens, with Howie Morenz, defeat the Senators 4-2. The Canadiens went on to defeat Vancouver to win the Stanley Cup, the first of 24 they would win in the NHL's 80 years.

The Forum, the Canadiens' home for most of the century, was actually built as the home of the Maroons. But a warm spell spoiled the natural ice at the Mount Royal Arena in the fall of 1924, so the Canadiens asked to play at the Forum, which had artificial ice. So it was that the Canadiens opened the Forum on November 29, 1924, whipping the Toronto Maple Leafs 7-1.

The 1924-25 season witnessed the first labor-management dispute when the players of the Hamilton Tigers, where the Quebec Bulldogs had shifted in 1920, went on strike before the playoffs. They wanted to be paid an extra $200 Cdn. per player for work during the playoffs, a seemingly reasonable request since Hamilton had made a record profit.

Fans' Target: NHL president Clarence Campbell enraged Montreal fans in March 1955 when he suspended their hero, Maurice (Rocket) Richard.

League president Calder, though, acted in support of the owners, in the belief that giving in to the players would put at risk the owners' "...large capital investment in rinks and arenas, and this capital must be protected."

Accordingly, Hamilton was disqualified from the playoffs, and the players were suspended and fined $200 Cdn. each. The Hamilton players' stand on playoff pay would be echoed in a similar stand later in the century by all NHL players, but at the time it seemed a minor obstacle on the league's pathway to success.

By the 1927-28 season, the NHL had grown from three teams to ten, split into two divisions: the Canadian and American. The Canadian division included the Toronto St. Patricks, the Ottawa Senators, the New York Americans, the Montreal Maroons and Montreal Canadiens. The American division consisted of the Boston Bruins, the New York Rangers, the Pittsburgh Pirates, the Chicago Blackhawks and the Detroit Cougars. This two-division alignment remained intact for 12 seasons, although this era was hardly immune from franchise shifts.

After winning the Stanley Cup in 1927, the Ottawa Senators, increasingly cashstrapped as the Great Depression approached, slid downhill. In 1930, the Senators sold star defenseman Frank (King) Clancy to the Toronto Maple Leafs for $35,000 Cdn., the largest sum ever paid for a hockey player. But even that cash infusion couldn't staunch the financial hemorrhage and, after suspending operations for the 1931-32 season, the Senators moved to St. Louis. The Eagles, as they were called, staggered through one season, before folding. Franchises also sprung up, struggled and folded or moved, in Pittsburgh and Philadelphia.

There was no shortage of star players in this era, which featured the scoring exploits of Nels Stewart, Cy Denneny, Aurel Joliat, Babe Dye, Montreal's incomparable Morenz, Harvey (Busher) Jackson, Charlie Conacher, Bill Cook and Cooney Weiland.

The game was evolving, finding itself, through the NHL's early days. Forward passing of the puck was not permitted at all until the 1927-28 season, when a rule change legalized this radical change in the defensive and neutral zones. When another rule change in 1929-30 gave players the green light to pass the puck ahead to a teammate in all three zones, goalscoring doubled. Ace Bailey led the league with 22 goals in 1927-28, compared to 43 goals for the league-leading Weiland the following season.

Play in the NHL was often vicious in the early days, but no incident horrified fans quite like Eddie Shore's attack on Ace Bailey on December 12, 1933 at the Boston Garden. Shore had been bodychecked into the boards by Red Horner and got up seeking revenge. He skated up to Bailey, who had his back to him, and knocked his feet out from under him. Bailey's head smacked against the ice and he went into convulsions. Horner responded by knocking Shore out with one punch, opening up a seven-stitch cut. Surgeons had to drill a hole in Bailey's skull to remove a blood clot that had formed near his brain. He remained unconscious, near death for 15 days and never played again.

The NHL of the 1930s produced many sublime evenings, also, but none like the Longest Game, a playoff encounter that began March 24 and ended March 25 in 1936.

That night, the Montreal Maroons and the Detroit Red Wings faced off in a Stanley Cup semifinal series opener that lasted 176 minutes 30 seconds. The only goal was scored by Detroit's Modere (Mud) Bruneteau at 16:30 of the sixth overtime period, provoking momentary stunned silence among the 9,000 fans at the Montreal Forum, followed by a huge ovation of relief. The game that began at 8:34 pm had ended at 2:25 am the following morning and all in attendance were utterly exhausted. None deserved a rest

more than Detroit goaltender Norm Smith, a Maroons castoff, who stopped 90 shots in his first NHL playoff game.

The Forum was also the scene for one of the saddest days in NHL history—the funeral of Canadiens great Howie Morenz on March 10, 1937. Morenz had died from complications arising from a broken leg. More than 25,000 fans filed past the coffin at center ice in the Forum.

As the 1930s progressed, teams began to die as well, as the NHL shrank from a ten-team, two-division league to a one-division league with seven teams by 1940.

The War Years

In the early 1940s, a rule change introduced a center red line to the NHL ice surface. The idea was to speed up play and reduce offside calls. The change marked the onset of the league's so-called Modern Era.

As the NHL moved into this new phase, one player dominated the transition—Maurice (Rocket) Richard. Playing

Mr. Hockey: Gordie Howe's marvellous career stretched over five decades. His legendary longevity permitted him to play in the NHL with his sons, Mark and Marty.

Russian Bear: Anatoli Tarasov has been called the father of Soviet hockey. In fact, he studied the hockey writings of Toronto's Lloyd Percival.

Rubbing salt in the fans' wounds, he replaced Drillon with Don Metz, a raw rookie, putting him on a line with Nick Metz, his brother, and Dave (Sweeney) Shriner. The trio dominated the rest of the series as the Leafs, who got spectacular goaltending from Turk Broda, did the seemingly impossible and won the Stanley Cup. Drillon never played for the Leafs again.

Many NHL stars of this era enlisted in the Canadian armed forces and served in the war, including Broda, Syl Apps, Bob Goldham, the Metz brothers, Jimmy Orlando, Sid Abel, Mud Bruneteau and Bucko McDonald. The league operated throughout the wartime era, but the quality of competition was thinned by military service.

It was in the 1940s, too, that the NHL stabilized as a six-team league, its constituent members coming to be known as the 'Original Six.' The general managers, the sporting architects of those teams, became as legendary as the players: Frank J. Selke in Montreal; Toronto's Smythe; Jack Adams, who built the great Detroit Red Wings teams of the 1950s; Tommy Ivan with the Chicago Blackhawks.

The Richard Riot

Sports journalist Rejean Tremblay once said: "The Rocket once told me that when he played he felt he was out there for all French Canadians."

Accordingly, all of French Canada was outraged in March 1955 when NHL president Clarence Campbell suspended Richard from the final three regular-season games and the entire playoffs for slugging a linesman in a fracas during a game in Boston.

Campbell, who embodied Anglophone dominance for many French-Canadians, attended the Canadiens' next game, against Detroit, at the Montreal Forum and quickly became a target for the irate Montreal fans seeking revenge for what they perceived as unjustly severe treatment of their hero.

At the end of the first period, a young man approached the NHL executive, extending his hand. But when Campbell held out his for an expected handshake, the man slapped his face. Moments later, a tear-gas bomb was set off behind one of the goals and soon after, the city's fire chief stopped the game, which was forfeited to Detroit.

The 15,000 fans filed out onto Ste-Catherine Street and a procession of pillaging unfolded along the street for several blocks.

The next day, Richard went on radio and television to appeal for calm in Montreal. The incident resonates to this day in Quebec. Many cite it as the spark that touched off the so-called Quiet Revolution, a period of profound and peaceful social change in the early 1960s.

right wing with center (Elegant) Elmer Lach and left winger Hector (Toe) Blake, Richard was the scoring star for the Montreal Canadiens, a symbol of competitive excellence for all French-Canadians and one of the most fiery, combative athletes ever to play any professional sport.

In the 1944-45 season, Richard scored 50 goals in 50 games, setting the standard for scoring brilliance for years to come. Lach (80 points), Richard (73) and Blake (67) finished 1-2-3 in the scoring race, earning the nickname, the 'Punch Line'.

Richard set a single-game scoring record that season, too, by scoring five goals and adding three assists as the Canadiens whipped the Red Wings 9-1 in Montreal on December 28.

The Stanley Cup highlight of the World War II period had to be the Toronto Maple Leafs' dramatic comeback victory in 1942, the only time in NHL history that a team overcame a 3-0 deficit in games to win a seven-game final series.

The Maple Leafs, second-place finishers during the 48-game regular season, found themselves in that predicament against the Detroit Red Wings, who had finished fifth in regular-season play.

At that point in the series, Maple Leafs' manager Conn Smythe, the man who built Maple Leaf Gardens and whose hockey credo was: "If you can't beat 'em in the alley, you can't beat 'em on the ice," took extreme measures.

Smythe benched right winger Gordie Drillon, the Leafs' top scorer, provoking outrage among Maple Leafs' supporters.

The league entered the 1950s with its depth of talent restored, its membership rock solid and the quality of play impressive.

The Rocket and Mr. Hockey

If the overall quality of play was high, two teams stood out head and shoulders above the pack—the Detroit Red Wings and the Montreal Canadiens. Between them the Red Wings and Canadiens won ten of 11 Stanley Cups from 1950-1960. From 1951 through to 1960, the Canadiens made the Stanley Cup finals ten straight times, winning the Cup six times, including five in a row from 1956-60.

Beginning with the 1948-49 season and ending with the 1954-55 campaign, the Red Wings finished first in the regular season seven straight times, topping things off with a Stanley Cup victory four times during that run of excellence.

The Red Wings were constructed around Gordie Howe—Mr. Hockey, a prolific scorer and physically powerful player with a legendary mean streak he often expressed by delivering a pile-driver elbow to an opponent.

The Canadiens' leader was Maurice (Rocket) Richard, a passionate star with a burning desire to win at all costs. Richard's eyes, it was said, lit up like a pinball machine as he crossed the opposition blue line and homed in on the net to score.

In the Stanley Cup semifinals against Boston in 1952, Richard scored one of his most memorable goals. After a thunderous check by Boston's Leo LaBine, Richard left, semi-conscious, for the Forum clinic to have a nasty gash to the head stitched. He returned to the game late in the third period, with the score tied 1-1. His head bandaged, still groggy, Richard fashioned an end-to-end rush that he completed by fending off defenseman Bill

---

Quackenbush with one hand and shovelling a one-handed shot past goaltender Sugar Jim Henry.

With two spectacular stars like Howe and Richard, the NHL's popularity soared, and television broadcasts of NHL games only added to its appeal.

It was a period of consistently fat profits for the club owners: Conn Smythe in Toronto; the Norris family, which owned or controlled the Detroit Red Wings, Chicago Blackhawks and New York Rangers; Weston Adams in Boston; and the Molson family in Montreal.

Some of the players, notably Ted Lindsay of Detroit and Doug Harvey of Montreal, did some figuring and estimating and concluded that they were reaping a small slice of a revenue pie that was much larger than the owners let on.

In 1957, Lindsay was the driving force behind the formation of the National Hockey League Players' Association. The group wanted to take control of the players' pension fund, and channel broadcast revenues from the All-Star game directly into the fund.

The owners were, to say the least, hostile to the players' efforts. Jack Adams, the Red Wings' GM, traded Lindsay and goaltender Glenn Hall, both first-team All-Stars, to the Chicago Blackhawks. The Canadiens, unwilling to lose their best defenseman, waited three years before trading Harvey to the New York Rangers. Ownership battled the players every step of the way and in 1958 the players dropped their attempt to form a legally recognized association.

The exciting on-ice wars between the Red Wings, Canadiens, Bruins and Maple Leafs obscured the decade-ending labor-management skirmish. Far more prominent in the public imagination was the dominance of the Canadiens, who won a record five straight Stanley Cups to close the decade.

The Canadiens of that era were so proficient on the power play they forced a rule change. In 1956-57, the NHL ruled that a penalized player could return to the ice if the opposing team scored a goal in his absence. Previously, a player had to sit out the full two minutes, during which time the potent Canadiens power-play unit sometimes scored two or even three times.

As the league moved into a new decade, Richard retired, but another brilliant player emerged with the Chicago Blackhawks—Bobby Hull. Actually, it was Bernie Geoffrion, one of Richard's ex-teammates, who became the second player to score 50

The Fog: Fred Shero coached the Philadelphia Flyers to two straight Stanley Cups in the 1970s but couldn't rekindle that magic as coach of the New York Rangers.

Skill Set: Along with Hedberg, Hull and Lars-Erik Sjoberg, the flashy Winnipeg Jets had plenty of skill and helped change the way hockey is played in North America.

ICE TALK

"THERE IS NO WAY (THE CANADIENS) CAN BEAT US WITH A JUNIOR B GOALTENDER,"

GEORGE (PUNCH) IMLACH, TORONTO MAPLE LEAFS' GENERAL MANAGER AND HEAD COACH ON ROOKIE MONTREAL GOALIE ROGATIEN VACHON ON THE EVE OF THE 1967 STANLEY CUP FINAL SERIES

goals in a season. Of course, Geoffrion recorded the feat in the 1960-61 season, a 70- not a 50-game season. Hull recorded the first of his five 50-plus goal seasons the following year.

Hull and teammate Stan Mikita were at the top of an impressive list of 1960s scoring stars that included Frank Mahovlich, the still-impressive Howe, Jean Beliveau, Andy Bathgate, Red Kelly, Alex Delvecchio, Rod Gilbert, Ken Wharram, John Bucyk and Norm Ullman.

The Toronto Maple Leafs supplanted the Canadiens as the dominant team in the early 1960s, winning three straight Stanley Cups from 1962-64, but the Canadiens won four in five years from 1964-69. They might have won five straight, except for Toronto's stunning upset victory over Montreal with an aging team in 1967.

That Stanley Cup final was truly the last of an era, because the NHL was preparing for unprecedented growth as the decade wound down.

A Victory for the Aged—Toronto's 1967 Stanley Cup Win

The Montreal Canadiens had won two straight Stanley Cups and seemed a solid bet to win a third as they prepared to meet the Maple Leafs in the final pre-expansion final series.

The Maple Leafs, third-place finishers during the season, had surprised lots of people by knocking off the first-place Chicago Blackhawks in the semifinals, but the younger, speedier Canadiens had swept the New York Rangers in four games, going with rookie goalie Rogatien Vachon.

The Maple Leafs' lineup had an average age of more than 31 years that included 42-year-old goalie Johnny Bower, and 41-year-old defenseman Allan Stanley. Twelve members of the roster were over 30—seven of them over 35.

When the Canadiens won Game 1, 6-2, with Henri Richard recording the hat-trick and Yvan Cournoyer scoring twice, it seemed to confirm the experts' analysis—the younger, quicker Canadiens were simply too good for the aging Leafs.

Then the ageless Bower went out and shut out the Canadiens as Toronto won Game 2, 3-0. The Leafs won Game 3 in overtime 3-2, with Bower brilliant again, making 60 saves. But when he strained his groin in the Game 4 pre-game warm-up, Maple Leafs' coach Punch Imlach had to insert Terry Sawchuk in goal.

The Canadiens seemed to solve Sawchuk, winning 6-3 to even the series 2-2. But Sawchuk only gave up two goals in the final two games—as Toronto stunned the hockey world by winning the series 4-2. The ageless wonders had turned back the clock and rediscovered their prime.

"I felt sick for a month afterwards," said Montreal defenseman Terry Harper. "To lose the Stanley Cup, that was horrible, but to lose to Toronto and have to live in Canada afterwards, oh man—everywhere you'd go you'd run into Leafs' fans, well, that was like losing twice."

So Long, Original Six, Hello Expansion

The success—artistic and financial—of the Original Six had attracted interested investors as early as the mid-1940s. In 1945-46, representatives from Philadelphia, Los Angeles and San Francisco had applied for franchises. The Original Six owners, jealously guarding their rich profit margins, were hostile to the notion for years.

But envious of the lucrative TV contracts U.S. networks were signing with the National Football League, American Football League and Major-League baseball, and recognizing that such riches were definitely beyond the grasp of a six-team, Canadian-

Broad Street Bounty

"We take the shortest distance to the puck and arrive in ill humor." That was the Philadelphia Flyers credo, as enunciated by head coach Fred Shero. He wasn't kidding.

The Flyers were constructed around a core of stellar players: goaltender Bernie Parent; defensemen Jim Watson and Bob Dailey; centers Bobby Clarke and Rick MacLeish; and wingers Bill Barber and Reggie Leach.

The supporting cast included some honest checkers like Bill Clement, Terry Crisp and Ross Lonsberry and a platoon of enforcers like Dave (The Hammer) Schultz, Bob (Houndog) Kelly, Don (Big Bird) Saleski, Jack McIlhargey and Andre (Moose) Dupont.

The blend of goaltending brilliance, team defense, toughness and scoring punch helped make the Flyers the first expansion club to win one Stanley Cup, let alone two.

Shero was nicknamed 'The Fog' by his players because he was given to cryptic sayings.

On the day of Game 6 in Philadelphia's Stanley Cup victory over the Boston Bruins in 1974, Shero wrote this message on the chalkboard in the dressing room: "Win together today and we'll walk together forever."

The Flyers won, and carved their names into the Stanley Cup.

based league, the league governors decided to proceed with expansion. The decision was spurred, in part, by aggressive efforts by the Western Hockey League, a development league, to push for major-league status.

The NHL governors received 15 applications for new franchises and in February, 1966, granted teams to Los Angeles, San Francisco, St. Louis, Pittsburgh, Philadelphia and Minnesota. The new franchises cost $2 million U.S. each.

The new teams were grouped together in the West Division, which enabled them to be competitive amongst themselves, even if they weren't really competitive with the six established teams in the East Division. The first three years of expansion, the St. Louis Blues, coached by Scotty Bowman, and staffed with aging stars like Glenn Hall, Jacques Plante, Doug Harvey, Dickie Moore and others, advanced to the Stanley Cup final. Each year, the Blues lost in four straight games.

The third of those three four-game sweeps of the Blues was administered by Bobby Orr and the Boston Bruins. Orr had become the first defenseman in NHL history to record 100 points in 1969-70, when he scored 33 goals and added 87 assists for 120 points to win the scoring championship. Many thought it was the first Stanley Cup of a Boston dynasty, but Orr's career was foreshortened by a series of knee injuries. He left the NHL before he was 30, with just two Stanley Cup rings—1970 and 1972.

Expansion coincided with the establishment of the NHL Players' Association—ten years after Ted Lindsay's effort had failed. A Toronto lawyer named Alan Eagleson had helped striking players on the minor-league Springfield Indians win their dispute with Eddie Shore, the club's miserly, ogre-like president and manager.

That victory helped him win the players' support when, led by a core group of Toronto Maple Leafs players, the association was established in 1967, with Eagleson as its executive director.

King of Kings: After Wayne Gretzky was traded to Los Angeles in 1988, it suddenly became chic to be seen at an NHL game in La-La Land.

Players' salaries, kept artificially low for decades, were about to increase dramatically, but it was a rival league—the World Hockey Association—far more than the Eagleson-led NHLPA that would be responsible.

The Winnipeg WHA franchise provided instant credibility for the rival league by signing Bobby Hull for $1 million Cdn. Then they borrowed Hull's nickname—The Golden Jet—to name their own club. Other high-profile players who followed included J.C. Tremblay, Marc Tardif, Gerry Cheevers and Derek Sanderson.

Many clubs signed players to lucrative contracts rather than lose them to WHA teams.

To combat the upstart league, the NHL kept on expanding, adding Vancouver and Buffalo in 1970. That year, the great Gilbert Perreault was the prize available for the expansion club fortunate enough to choose first in the entry draft. To decide between the Sabres and Canucks, the league brought in a wheel of fortune apparatus, the kind popular at country fairs. The Sabres were assigned numbers one through ten, with the Canucks getting 11-20. The wheel was given a spin and came to rest at the number 1—or so it seemed. Clarence Campbell, the league president announced that the Sabres had won, prompting elation among the Buffalo supporters. But the wheel had stopped at 11. Campbell stepped back to the microphone and uttered this phrase: "A mistake has been made."

Perreault played 17 seasons for the Sabres and scored 512 goals, while Dale Tallon, selected by the Canucks, had a solid, but unspectacular career with Vancouver, Chicago and the Pittsburgh Penguins. Expansion continued in 1972, when Atlanta and the New York Islanders were added, and in 1974 the Kansas City Scouts and the Washington Capitals joined the league. The NHL had tripled in size in just seven years, severly depleting the talent base.

The dilution was made more apparent by the 1972 Summit Series between Canada and the Soviet Union. Canadians expected their pros, who had been banned for years from competing in World Championships or Olympic competitions, to drub the Soviets, but were stunned when the Soviets beat Canada 7-3 in the opening game at the Forum. The Soviet game, with legendary coach Anatoli Tarasov directing its development, had caught up to and, in many areas, passed the Canadian style. That realization stunned a country which prided itself on producing the best hockey players in the world.

Canada, playing on pride, guts and determination, won a narrow series victory with four victories, three losses and one game tied. But the game had changed forever.

On the expansion front, meanwhile, not all the franchises took root where they were first planted. The California Golden Seals moved to Cleveland in 1976, then merged with the struggling Minnesota North Stars in 1979. The Kansas City Scouts moved to Denver, Colorado in 1976 and then in 1982 to East Rutherford, New Jersey, where they remain as the Devils.

In the early expansion days, Montreal general manager Sam Pollock took advantage of expansion to build a 1970s dynasty in Montreal. The Canadiens, rich in solid talent throughout their farm system, swapped good young players, and sometimes established but aging players, to talent-starved expansion clubs for high draft picks.

Swedish Import: Anders Hedberg was Bobby Hull's linemate in his WHA days with the Winnipeg Jets, but he became a Ranger when the Jets entered the NHL in 1979.

In this fashion, the Canadiens obtained Guy Lafleur, Steve Shutt, Bob Gainey, Doug Risebrough, Michel Larocque, Mario Tremblay—the building blocks of the six Stanley Cup champions during the 1970s.

Many complained that the rapid expansion drastically diluted the talent in the NHL. The Philadelphia Flyers, the first post-expansion club to win the Stanley Cup, certainly weren't overloaded with talent. Their canny coach, Fred Shero, made the most of a small nucleus of excellent talent, led by goalie Bernie Parent, center Bobby Clarke, and wingers Bill Barber and Reggie Leach, and a belligerent style of play that intimidated the opposition.

That formula led the Flyers to back-to-back Stanley Cup championships in 1974 and 1975. By 1976, the Canadiens load of drafted talent—particularly Guy Lafleur—had matured, and Montreal rolled to four straight Stanley Cup championships to close out the 1970s.

ICE TALK

"I REALLY LOVED EDMONTON. I DIDN'T WANT TO LEAVE. WE HAD A DYNASTY HERE. WHY MOVE?"

WAYNE GRETZKY, ON HIS BEING TRADED TO THE LOS ANGELES KINGS IN 1988, A TRANSACTION THAT SENT ALL OF CANADA INTO A STATE OF MOURNING

The turn of the decade also saw the ten-year war with the WHA resolved, when the only four surviving teams from the rival league—the Quebec Nordiques; Hartford Whalers; Edmonton Oilers; and Winnipeg Jets joined the NHL. The teams were stripped of the talent they had recruited, often in bidding wars with NHL clubs, and denied access to TV revenue for five years after joining the NHL.

As a result, the Jets lost stars Anders Hedberg and Ulf Nilsson, both of whom played for the New York Rangers thereafter. The Oilers were permitted to keep Wayne Gretzky, who had signed a personal services contract with Oilers owner Peter Pocklington. And the Whalers iced a lineup that included 50-year-old Gordie Howe, playing with his sons, Mark and Marty.

The Nordiques' response was be to creative in its recruiting efforts. Club president Marcel Aubut arranged for Slovak stars Peter and Anton Stastny to defect from Czechoslovakia, and the pair were joined one year later by older brother Marian. The Stastnys, especially Peter and Anton, became the scoring stars on the rebuilt Nordiques.

The success of the Stastnys helped convince NHL managers that there were rich veins of talent in Europe that had to be tapped. Communism was one major obstacle to doing so immediately, however.

There were few large impediments to importing Scandinavian talent, though, as the New York Islanders found out. They won four straight Stanley Cups, beginning in 1980, with some talented Scandinavians, like Tomas Jonsson, Stefan Persson, Anders Kallur and Mats Hallin, playing important roles.

The European influence really took hold in the NHL, though, with the Edmonton Oilers, who supplanted the Islanders as the NHL's pre-eminent team in 1984, when they won the first of five Stanley Cups in seven years.

Glen Sather, the Oilers' general manager and coach, sprinkled some talented Europeans like Jari Kurri, Esa Tikkanen, Reijo Ruotsalainen, Kent Nilsson and Willy Lindstrom around the Edmonton lineup, with good results.

But Sather went one step further, borrowing much from the flowing, speed-based European style and adapting it to the NHL.

Sather once described the Oilers' style as the Montreal Canadiens (of the 1970s) updated for the 1980s.

The style of play—executed by great players like Gretzky, Mark Messier, Glenn Anderson, Paul Coffey and Kurri—helped Sather construct a Canadiens-like 1980s dynasty.

Thinking Globally

As the NHL moved toward the 1990s the governors began to develop a larger vision. This was not an easy process. The traditions and mind-set of the Original Six had continued to dominate the league well after expansion had transformed a small, regional league into a continental one, albeit a weak sister compared to major-league baseball, football and basketball.

The NHL had evolved into a 21-team league but was controlled by the triumvirate of league president John Ziegler, Chicago Blackhawks owner Bill Wirtz and NHLPA executive-director Alan Eagleson.

The league had traditionally been gate-driven, dominated by shrewd entrepreneurs like Smythe, the Norrises, the Wirtz family and the Molsons, who owned their own arenas and knew how to fill them but had little feel for or interest in marketing the league as a whole.

A series of linked events began to change this. By the summer of 1988, Wayne Gretzky had led the Edmonton Oilers to four Stanley Cups and established himself as the best player in hockey. But to Oilers owner Peter Pocklington he was a depreciating asset whose value had peaked.

Pocklington traded Gretzky to the Los Angeles Kings—sending Edmontonians, and Canadians in general, into mourning, and stunning NHL ownership.

Bruce McNall, then the Kings' owner, promptly raised Gretzky's salary. He reasoned that Gretzky would generate far greater revenues for the Kings, both at the gate and through advertising and he was proved right.

Two years later, the St. Louis Blues used similar logic when they signed Brett Hull, their franchise player, to a three-year contract. Then they signed restricted free agent defenseman Scott Stevens to a four-year deal.

While salaries were rising, there were other parts of the hockey business taking off as well. In the United States more people watched NHL hockey on Fox and ESPN than ever before. In Canada, Saturday became a double dream as *Hockey Night in Canada* began running doubleheaders. And in the U.S. and Canada the NHL found success in five new markets. Anaheim, Ottawa, San Jose, Miami Florida and Tampa Bay all greeted the game with excitement and big crowds. The value of an NHL franchise rose and the level of people wanting to own a team grew.

As the economics of major professional hockey changed, the NHL realized that the old, gate-driven model would not work anymore. Hockey entrepreneurs began to build new, larger arenas, which featured scores of so-called luxury suites, hotel-plush boxes designed to enable corporate executives and guests to enjoy a game in high style.

Merger Man: Quebec Nordiques president Marcel Aubut was a key player in the NHL admitting four former WHA franchises to the NHL in 1979.

Labor Man: Under executive-director Bob Goodenow, the NHL Players' Association has become more proactive about getting its share of the NHL revenue pie.

New forms of advertising opportunities—on scoreboards, rink boards, even on the ice itself—were deployed to generate more money. And the NHL, long a marketing luddite among major professional leagues, got into the merchandising business in a concerted way.

As the hockey business grew more sophisticated, the players became more assertive about their interests, also. Dissatisfaction with the now-disgraced NHLPA executive-director Alan Eagleson's autocratic, company-union style had been growing and, in 1990, the players selected former agent Bob Goodenow, the man who had negotiated Brett Hull's blockbuster contract, as their new director.

At the end of the 1992 season, the players staged an 11-day strike, demanding, among other things, the marketing rights to their own likenesses. They wanted a chunk of the revenue pie, in other words, and were prepared to fight to get it. The players also sought more relaxed free agency guidelines enabling them to sell themselves on the market.

As the league adjusted to a new economic and labor reality, it sought new leadership capable of achieving peace with the players and the league's on-ice officials, and proactively directing its newly ambitious business aspirations.

In 1992, a search committee selected Gary Bettman, a lawyer and former executive with the marketing-slick National Basketball Association to become the league's first commissioner.

Early in his tenure, Bettman made a business statement by recruiting two powerful new partners to set up NHL franchises—the Disney Corporation and Blockbuster Entertainment.

Michael Eisner, the Disney CEO, named his company's team the Mighty Ducks of Anaheim, after a commercially successful movie of the same name. Wayne Huizenga, head of Blockbuster,

established a second team in Florida, the Panthers, based in Miami.

It had long been a cliché that pro sports was an entertainment business, but recruiting the likes of Eisner and Huizenga suggested that NHL head office had actually begun to believe this maxim.

One team—the Ottawa Senators—misread the market and grossly overestimated the promotional opportunities available to young stars when they signed untried No. 1 draft pick Alexandre Daigle to a five-year contract in June 1993. The deal included a marketing component that was unrealistically generous for an unproven rookie.

If the Gretzky, Hull and Stevens contracts had lifted the salary ceiling, the Daigle deal significantly raised the entry level and helped cause an ownership backlash. The notion of a rookie salary cap took hold and a second owner-player showdown in three years loomed.

The result was a lockout that cancelled 468 games from October 1, 1994 to January 19, 1995, shrinking the regular season to 48 games with no inter-conference play. The deal finally struck included a rookie salary cap and provided somewhat greater freedom of movement for older players.

The new, five-year deal couldn't help franchises stuck with outmoded arenas, however, and two Canadian teams, the Quebec Nordiques and Winnipeg Jets, moved south to Denver and Phoenix, respectively—Quebec for 1995-96, Winnipeg for the 1996-97 season. The move proved successful for Colorado when they won the Stanley Cup in their first year.

The Next One

Eric Lindros was so dominant as a junior hockey player that he was dubbed 'The Next One'—Wayne Gretzky being 'The Great One'—well before he was drafted No. 1 overall by the Quebec Nordiques in 1991.

He was also supremely confident in his ability and secure in the knowledge that his extraordinary skill and potential as a marketing vehicle gave him unprecedented leverage to negotiate.

He warned Nordiques president Marcel Aubut, with whom he did not get along, not to draft him, saying he would refuse to report if he were selected. Sure enough, Quebec drafted him and Lindros, true to his word, did not report. He played another year of junior and for Canada's Olympic team at the 1992 Olympics in Albertville, France.

In June 1992, Aubut invited a bidding contest for Lindros and thought he had made a blockbuster deal with the New York Rangers. But the Philadelphia Flyers also had an offer on the table that included $15 million U.S., six players and two first-round draft picks.

An arbitrator was called in and he awarded Lindros to the Flyers in one of the most bizarre transactions in NHL history.

Going For Gold

The 1997-98 season was an historic one for the NHL, which, for the first time ever, suspended operations to enable the stars from all participating countries to join their respective national teams to compete at the 1998 Winter Olympics in Nagano, Japan.

The so-called Dream Teams concept was the result of years of negotiating among the NHL, NHLPA, the International Ice Hockey Federation and its member federations, and the International Olympic Committee. The result was the first-ever best-on-best men's hockey tournament at the Winter Olympics which saw the Czech Republic beat Russia 1-0 to take gold.

The Olympic Games gave the NHL a great chance to move further away from its parochial Original Six mentality and further establish itself as a major force in the international sporting market.

As the league's vision continues to expand globally, it has granted expansion franchises to four more cities: Atlanta, Nashville, Columbus, Ohio and St. Paul, Minnesota, which has been without a franchise since the Stars moved to Dallas. Unlike previous expansion efforts, the NHL, under Bettman, is deploying its considerable marketing forces not just to ensure that individual franchises succeed, but to implant a hockey culture across the United States. The proof will come in the 1998-99 season, as the new Nashville Predators franchise takes to the ice.

Through its state-of-the-art website, grassroots programs such as the NHL's involvement with In-Line and Street hockey, as well as its growing involvement with women's hockey, the league is, in fact, raising the profile of the NHL as well as the sport of hockey itself.

As the NHL heads into the next century, the marketing momentum is building; the league and the sport are growing. Its future has never been more exciting.

Mightiest Duck: Disney Company CEO Michael Eisner transposed cinematic marketing techniques to help sell the sport of hockey in Southern California.

TEAMS IN THE NHL

With the growth of the National Hockey League in North America and the influx of bright international stars like Jaromir Jagr, Sergei Fedorov and Peter Forsberg, the NHL is showcasing more individual talent in the 1990s than it ever has. Yet the team concept continues to endure as the bedrock principle of the sport. It's a cliché in hockey that no player—no matter how spectacular his contribution—is bigger than his team.

Consider Eric Lindros, whom many regard the heir apparent to the mantle of the greatest player in the NHL, now that Mario Lemieux has retired and Wayne Gretzky's brilliant career is drawing to a close.

Lindros entered the NHL with Philadelphia in the 1992-93 season, loaded down with achievements. He had helped the Oshawa Generals win the Memorial Cup as Canada's best junior team, helped Canada's National Junior Team win the World Junior Hockey Championship, helped Team Canada win the 1991 Canada Cup (now the World Cup of Hockey) tournament, and helped Canada's Olympic team win a silver medal at the 1992 Winter Olympics in Albertville, France.

He has continued to pile up awards in the NHL, winning the Hart Trophy as the league's most valuable player in 1995. But Lindros and his growing number of followers had to wait while the Flyers surrounded their awesomely talented star with the right supporting cast before seeing their hero lead Philadelphia into the Stanley Cup Finals for the first time in his era in 1997.

The ultimate standard

Successful hockey teams are an amalgam of coaching acumen, solid team defense, great goaltending, timely scoring, leadership, fan support and the most elusive factor of all—team chemistry.

Coaches set the tone for success and none was more successful than Hector (Toe) Blake, the legendary coach of the Montreal Canadiens in the 1950s and 1960s.

In his first meeting with his team, in October 1955, Blake told his players: "There are some guys in this room who play better than I ever did. I have nothing to teach them. But what I can show you all is how to play better as a team."

Blake obviously succeeded. In 13 years as coach of the Canadiens, the team finished first in the regular season nine times and won eight Stanley Cups, including five straight from 1956-60.

Scoring titles and individual awards may be the measure of a

Doom Trooper: Big, offensively skilled John Leclair was a key part of Philadelphia's Legion of Doom line, along with Eric Lindros and Michael Renberg, until the latter was traded to Tampa Bay.

player's excellence, but NHL teams are measured by one standard only—their ability to win the Stanley Cup.

An entire generation of Toronto Maple Leafs fans has grown to adulthood without seeing their club win the Cup, yet the legend of an aging Leafs club that did win it in 1967 lives on.

In the early 1970s, the New York Islanders entered the NHL as an expansion club and were carefully crafted into a formidable group by general manager Bill Torrey. The validation of Torrey's genius in drafting Denis Potvin, Mike Bossy, Bryan Trottier, Clark Gillies and others was the four straight Stanley Cups the Islanders won, beginning in 1980.

As great as those stars were, though, the Islanders championship chemistry didn't click until Torrey traded for Butch Goring, a speedy, gritty, centerman. Goring checked the opposing team's top center and, a keen student of the game, designed the Islanders' penalty killing system.

The Edmonton Oilers of the 1980s were loaded with offensive firepower, boasting the likes of Wayne Gretzky, Jari Kurri, Glenn Anderson, Paul Coffey and Mark Messier. But they didn't become champions until coach Glen Sather had taught them to play solid, if not necessarily brilliant, team defense.

Mario Lemieux, the game's best player, led Pittsburgh to two straight Stanley Cup triumphs in the early 1990s, but a key member of both teams was Trottier, who brought invaluable playoff experience to those Pittsburgh teams.

New York fans of a certain age have fond memories of stars like Jean Ratelle, Rod Gilbert and Vic Hadfield, the famous GAG (Goal-a-game) line of the 1970s. But none of those players ever won a Stanley Cup.

The Rangers faithful had to wait until 1994, after Messier, who learned how to be a champion with the Oilers, had moved to New York and instilled team values in his new teammates.

Fair Trade: When Colorado Avalanche traded Owen Nolan to the San Jose Sharks for defenseman Sandis Ozolinsh they acquired one of the most offensively talented defensemen in all of the National Hockey League.

Saving goals

And no team can succeed without great goaltending: the Islanders' Billy Smith; Grant Fuhr of the Oilers; the Rangers' Mike Richter; Tom Barrasso of the Penguins.

No goalie can boast a Stanley Cup performance chart quite like Patrick Roy of the Colorado Avalanche. He led the Canadiens to a Stanley Cup as a rookie in 1986 and backstopped them to another in 1993, when he cooly closed the door on the opposition as Montreal won 10 games in overtime.

In 1996, Roy's stingy netminding was central to Colorado winning the Stanley Cup. In that four-game sweep of the Florida Panthers, Roy gave up just four goals total—one per game.

In 1995-96, the talent-rich Red Wings won a record 62 regular-season games, breaking the old record for most victories in a season (60) set in 1976-77 by the Canadiens. But that Montreal team was in the process of winning four straight Stanley Cups.

The Red Wings' berths in the 1997 and 1998 Stanley Cup finals were, for them, further chances to measure themselves against the other great teams in NHL history by the only yardstick that matters—Stanley Cup championships.

MIGHTY DUCKS OF ANAHEIM

The changing of the guard at the Mighty Ducks during the 1997-98 season saw coach Ron Wilson pack his bags.

The 1997-98 season was a big headache for the Mighty Ducks of Anaheim. The main reason was the delicate cranial condition of one of the team's two superstars. Paul Kariya, who many considered the best player in the NHL going into the season, did not play after suffering a concussion on February 1 and the Ducks finished out of the playoffs for the fourth time in five seasons.

Teemu Selanne did his best to carry the load alone. The man nicknamed the 'Finnish Flash' tied for the League lead in goals with 52 and he was one of three finalists for the Hart Trophy as the NHL's MVP. Not only did Selanne have to play without his linemate and good friend Kariya to end the season, he was also without Kariya for the first 32 games, when Kariya was sidelined during the prolonged contract negotiations that he was caught up in.

The Ducks' offensive woes were highlighted by the fact that Kariya's 17 goals tied him for second on the team with Steve Rucchin and Kariya played just 22 games. The team's defensive woes were illustrated by the fact that Anaheim goaltenders Guy Herbert and Mikhail Shtalenkov ranked second and third in the NHL in average shots against. Both faced slightly more than 30 shots per night, a few tenths of a shot behind what Buffalo Dominik Hasek saw on a nightly basis.

Wilson waves goodbye

Kariya wasn't the only familiar face absent in 1997-98. During the '97 off-season, the team parted ways with Ron Wilson, the only coach the franchise had ever known. Wilson, who wound up behind the bench for the Washington Capitals and guided the team to the Stanley Cup Finals, was replaced by veteran coach Pierre Page, who was relieved of his duties shortly after the Ducks finished the 1997-98 season with the second-fewest points (65) in the Western Conference. His replacement is Craig Hartsburg, himself a firing victim in Chicago in spring 1998.

There were some bright spots on which the Ducks can hope to build over the coming months. Travis Green came over from the New York Islanders late in the season and he is a talented, young player. Jason Marshall developed into a solid defenseman for the team and rookie center Matt Cullen was one of the Duck's best players down the stretch.

Celluloid birth

The NHL's Mighty Ducks probably wouldn't exist if it hadn't been for Emilio Estevez and a rag-tag bunch of skaters who turned a low-budget Disney production into a celluloid success.

"The movie was our market research," recalls Disney chairman Michael Eisner, who approached the NHL about an expansion franchise after the screen version of the Mighty Ducks

Finn Teemu Selanne had to shoulder much of the burden of keeping the Ducks afloat after injury plagued teammate Paul Kariya.

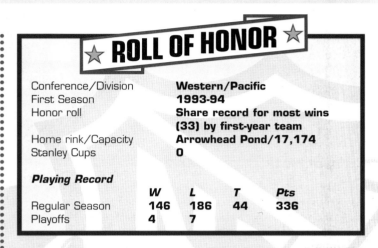

ROLL OF HONOR

Conference/Division	**Western/Pacific**
First Season	**1993-94**
Honor roll	**Share record for most wins (33) by first-year team**
Home rink/Capacity	**Arrowhead Pond/17,174**
Stanley Cups	**0**

Playing Record

	W	L	T	Pts
Regular Season	146	186	44	336
Playoffs	4	7		

grossed almost $60 million.

In the fall of 1993, the real-life Mighty Ducks became the NHL's third California-based member, joining the Los Angeles Kings and San Jose Sharks, and were the league's big surprise that first year, tying an NHL first-year team record with 33 victories, including 19 road wins, the most ever by a first-year club.

In the strike-shortened 1994-95 season, they developed their first star players, such as Kariya and defenseman Oleg Tverdovsky, who was then traded, along with center Chad Kilger, to obtain the high-scoring Selanne from the Winnipeg Jets on February 7, 1996. Selanne and Kariya provide the Mighty Ducks with a formidable 1-2 offensive punch.

The Mighty Ducks are equally powerful at the marketing and merchandising level. Their logo—a goalie mask resembling an angry duck—and team colors of purple, jade, silver, and white are big sellers well beyond the Magic Kingdom.

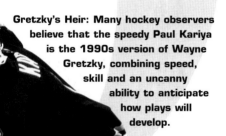

Gretzky's Heir: Many hockey observers believe that the speedy Paul Kariya is the 1990s version of Wayne Gretzky, combining speed, skill and an uncanny ability to anticipate how plays will develop.

Rock bottom in 1996-97, the Bruins launched a huge revival last season that put a smile back on their supporters' faces.

Talk about a turnaround. After sitting out the playoffs for the first time in nearly three decades in 1997, the Bruins went from worst record in the League to fifth seed in the Eastern Conference playoffs. A young, talented roster didn't know it wasn't supposed to do that well.

Not only did the team emerge, but so did one of its players. Jason Allison came to Boston as part of a big trade with the Washington Capitals toward the end of the 1996-97 season. The former player of the year in junior hockey finally reached his potential in the NHL, finishing with 33 goals and 83 points for ninth place in the NHL scoring race.

Coach Pat Burns did nothing to hurt his reputation as one of the game's most astute and cunning coaches, not to mention his skills as a quick-fix expert. He leaned on Allison to become an offensive leader and got the usual solid production superstar defenseman Ray Bourque has been providing at both ends of the rink. Burns also got Byron Dafoe to develop into a legitimate No.1 goalie and had his team play disciplined enough hockey to rank second behind the Ottawa Senators in fewest penalty minutes per game.

The consolation for finishing last in the League in 1996-97 was the No.1 pick in the draft, which the Bruins used to select Joe Thornton, who many considered to be the next Eric Lindros. While Thornton struggled as an NHL rookie, the player the Bruins selected seven spots behind him made an immediate splash: Sergei Samsonov, the little dynamo from Russia, earned the Calder Trophy as rookie of the year after leading all rookies with 22 goals

Disallowed dismay

This was a good first step in getting back to the Finals for the first time since 1990. The Bruins lost in the first round of the 1998 playoffs to eventual Eastern Conference champions Washington. Three of the games went to overtime (two to double overtime) in a series that could have gone either way, but eventually went 4-2 to the Caps. Bruins fans will never forget the overtime goal that was disallowed in game 3 when it was determined Boston forward Tim Taylor had his skate in the crease. The Caps won that game in double OT.

Awesome Orr

Boston's last Cup triumph was in 1972. That Cup, like the one in 1970, featured the uplifting play of a young defenseman named Bobby Orr, who first arrived on the scene in 1966-67, after the Bruins had missed the playoffs for six straight seasons of a streak

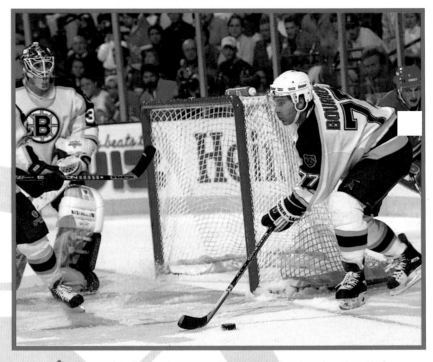

After the disappointment of not qualifying for the playoffs in 1997, Ray Bourque and the Bruins bounced back in 1998.

that would eventually reach eight years.

On May 10, 1970, Orr, arguably the best defenseman ever until his knees gave out after ten years with Boston, left his personal imprint on the team's first Cup win in 29 years, scoring the winning goal against St. Louis Blues netminder Glenn Hall.

Founder members

One of the original six NHL teams, the Bruins started play in the 1924-25 season. They were fortunate to have had several glittering performers grace their roster in ensuing years—notably the tough guy defenseman Eddie Shore, right winger Dit Clapper and center Milt Schmidt. But despite these talents they had only three Stanley Cups to their credit before Orr, slick center Phil Esposito and (Chief) Johnny Bucyk combined their talents for the two Cups in the early 1970s.

Orr was the first NHL defenseman to win the scoring championship, achieving the feat in 1969-70. Esposito won five scoring titles in just over eight seasons with Boston. In 1968-69, he became the first NHL player to compile more than 100 points in a single season.

Byron Dafoe (right) developed throughout the season to become the number one goalie.

BUFFALO SABRES

Czech Republic goaltender Dominik Hasek started the 1997-98 season slowly but finished as the NHL's outstanding talent.

The year of 'The Dominator' almost had a fairy tale ending for the second time. The Buffalo Sabres' all-world goaltender, Dominik Hasek (aka The 'Dominator'), pulled off one miracle in February when he led the underdog Czech Republic team to the gold medal in the Winter Olympic hockey tournament. Hasek then nearly got his little-fancied Sabres side into the Stanley Cup Finals.

The Sabres advanced to the Eastern Conference finals before losing to the Washington Capitals, 4 games to 2. Three of Washington's wins came in overtime, including the last two. Hasek was in unbelievable form despite starting the season under a cloud.

The goalie was booed in his own building back in October because fans were unhappy with his comments about popular coach Ted Nolan, the 1997 Jack Adams award-winner as coach of the year who, controversially, was not brought back for the 1997-98 campaign. But Hasek eventually won back the hearts of the Sabres' fans back with a series of brilliant performances. He set an NHL record with six shutouts in December and he led the league in save percentage for the fifth straight season. No less an

Peca performance: Buffalo's 1997-98 captain Michael Peca won the 1997 Selke Trophy and was a finalist for the award in 1998.

expert than the legendary Wayne Gretzky called him the best player in hockey. Hasek was rewarded with his second straight Hart Trophy as league MVP and his fourth Vezina Trophy as the best goaltender. Even better news for Sabres' fans was the announcement in March that Hasek had agreed terms on a multi-year contract. "I really believe," said Sabres chairman of the board John Rigas, "that with Dominik's presence, and the team we have assembled...I think we have the makings of a team that can compete for the Stanley Cup."

New Year success
Like Hasek, Buffalo started the season slowly, but turned in the best record in the NHL after January 1. Lindy Ruff, a former Sabres captain, did an outstanding job in his rookie season as coach, helping restore calm to the most turbulent franchise in the league. The team lacked offensive punch and the leading scorer, Miroslav Satan, had just 46 points, but seemed to get timely contributions from a wide variety of players. Michael Peca, the 1997 Selke Trophy winner as best defensive forward and a 1998 finalist for the award, settled into the captaincy nicely. Defenseman Alexei Zhitnik improved to the point where he could be a Norris Trophy candidate as top defenseman in the near future,

Flashy past
The Sabres were once one of the NHL's flashiest offensive teams. The franchise scored a major coup months before it took to the ice for the first time in the 1970-71 season. Through a stroke of luck — the spin of a numbered wheel — the Sabres got the first draft pick ahead of their expansion cousin, the Vancouver Canucks.

George (Punch) Imlach, the wily former Toronto Maple Leafs coach who was the Sabres first coach and general manager, plucked a rangy, swift-skating magician named Gilbert Perreault from the junior ranks. The high-scoring center was an anchor for more than a decade, especially when teamed with youngsters Rick Martin and Rene Robert to form the French Connection line. Perreault and Martin still rank 1-2 in club history for goals scored, with 512 and 382, respectively. The trio powered the Sabres to the Stanley Cup final in 1975, where they lost to Philadelphia in six games: a sobering end to their best season — they had a franchise-high 113 points in winning their first Adams Division title.

The Sabres have never got closer to a Stanley Cup title, despite the promise of the Scotty Bowman era in the early 1980s.

Bowman did however become the winningest NHL coach while in Buffalo. He surpassed Dick Irvin's 690 career coaching wins on December 19, 1984.

The Dominator: Dominik Hasek, the Czech Republic's Olympic Games hero, won back-to-back Hart Trophies as the league MVP.

CALGARY FLAMES

The Flames hopes of improving on their 1996-97 form were extinguished when they missed the playoffs once more.

It was not a season the Calgary Flames will look back upon with a great deal of fondness. The Flames missed the playoffs for the second straight season, the first time that had happened in franchise history. Among the other lowlights of 1997-98 were the lowest-ever winning percentage (.408) and the fewest points (67) in a non-shortened season since the team arrived in Calgary in 1980. Then there were also the road woes that included the fewest road wins (eight) and points (25) in franchise history.

In amongst the doom and gloom, the brightest spot for first-year coach Brian Sutter was the form of rookie defenseman Derek Morris, who may have been a finalist for the Calder Trophy as rookie of the year if he had played in a bigger market or on a winning team. The 19 year-old blueliner made an impact at both ends of the ice and should hopefully be a cornerstone for many years to come. Another cornerstone, forward Jarome Iginla, suffered through a sophomore slump in 1997-98. He's being counted on to re-discover the form — and ideally exceed it — that made him a Calder Trophy finalist as a rookie.

Forward Jarome Iginla suffered a slump in form after an outstanding 1996-97 season.

Fine Fleury

Star forward Theo Fleury had another fine offensive season. His 78 points tied him for 11th in the league scoring race. He also experienced the thrill in February of being selected for Canada's Olympic team in Nagano, Japan, only to then feel the bitter disappointment and shock of finishing out of the medals. Cory Stillman was another gem up front, finishing tied for the team lead in goals (27) after coming into camp without a contract.

Goaltending is a priority for the team's future and the management addressed that need by trading for Ken Wregget in the 1998 off-season. Wregget is relishing the chance to be the undisputed No.1 goalie after feeling he was always just a fill-in in previous stops. Flames' fans can therefore rest assured that motivation won't be a problem for Wregget.

Heading South

Exciting was a word used in 1972, when the Flames' franchise got its start—in Atlanta. It was a bold move by the NHL, as it was their first venture into the Deep South of the United States, an experiment that lasted seven years after Georgia businessman Tom Cousins was granted a franchise.

Former Montreal Canadiens star and legend Boom Boom Geoffrion, served as coach and showman in the early years, wooing fans in their thousands in an accent every bit as sweet as a Georgia peach. Excited fans would flock to the 15,000-seat rink known as 'The Omni' to watch Geoffrion direct a stunning ice symphony with awesome performers such as dynamic goaltender Daniel Bouchard

and flashy forwards Jacques Richard, Eric Vail and Guy Chouinard.

Moving Flames

Alas, the novelty soon wore off. Geoffrion was gone by 1975, and so was the franchise five years later, purchased by Vancouver real-estate magnate Nelson Skalbania, and transferred to Calgary.

It was a humble beginning in the Flames' new abode, the 7,000-seat Stampede Corral, where the club remained until moving into the 20,000-seat Saddledome in 1983.

The Flames would win one Stanley Cup, two Conference titles and two best-overall crowns over the next 15 years. (Badger) Bob Johnson arrived from the University of Wisconsin to coach the Flames in 1982. Johnson, who coined the phrase, "It's a great day for hockey," took the Flames to the Stanley Cup final in 1985-86.

Three years later, with wisecracking Terry Crisp at the helm, Calgary won its first Cup, becoming the first visiting team to do so against the Canadiens at the venerable Montreal Forum.

Fittingly, it was the final bow for Lanny McDonald, the bushy-lipped co-captain who had come to epitomize the heart and soul of the team.

Mighty Mite: Theoren Fleury is the league's smallest player but he may well have the biggest heart also.

After a change in location, the Hurricanes are hoping they can build a loyal fan base by turning in some outstanding displays.

A change in venue didn't do anything to immediately change this franchise's fortunes. In the club's first season in North Carolina, the former Hartford Whalers missed the postseason for the sixth straight season. A 1-7-2 start while adjusting to a new home set the tone for a season that saw the Hurricanes finish ninth in a conference that sends eight teams to the playoffs.

The Hurricanes lack a big-name superstar player, but management made a bid to change that when it offered restricted free agent forward Sergei Fedorov of the Detroit Red Wings a $38 million contract that had incentives designed to dissuade the Red Wings from matching it. The Red Wings did match the offer sheet, however.

One of Fedorov's former Detroit teammates, Keith Primeau, is Carolina's cornerstone. The big centreman was one of Canada's best players in the 1998 Olympics and showed signs that he can be Carolina's main man up front. He had 26 goals and 63 points, identical stats to another Hurricanes forward who will be a player the team can build around. Sami Kapanen nearly doubled his career point total of 34 with his 1997-98 output.

Kidd come of age

Another bright spot for the Hurricanes was the form of goaltender Trevor Kidd, the former Calgary Flames mainstay. Kidd's .922 save percentage and 2.17 goals-against average were not only personal bests, but franchise records.

The Hurricanes played to some intimate home crowds in their first season — largely due to the fact that they play in Greensboro, approximately 90 miles away from their 1999-2000 home of Raleigh — so the likes of Primeau, Kapanen and Kidd will be important components over the coming years in helping build a fan base in this new market

Gary Roberts will be hoping the Hurricanes can go one better in 1998-99 and make the playoffs for the first time in seven seasons.

★ ROLL OF HONOR ★

Conference/Division	**Eastern/Southeast**
First season	**1979-80 (as Hartford Whalers)**
Honor roll	**Adams Division title, 1986-87**
Home rink/Capacity	**Greensboro Coliseum/21,500**
Stanley Cups	**0**

Playing Record

	W	L	T	Pts
Regular Season	567	750	185	1319
Playoffs	18	31		

Frustrating misses

Hartford was one of four WHA teams who joined the NHL in 1979 — Winnipeg, Quebec and Edmonton were the others.

While Hartford had a core of fans which were loyal to the end, the lack of a winning tradition was often a source of frustration. The club finished first in its division only once — in 1986-87 — and, that season aside, it never ended higher than fourth place. When the Whalers were eliminated on the final weekend of their last season in the city, it marked the 10th time in their 17 years in Hartford that the team missed the Stanley Cup playoffs and the eighth straight time it finished below .500. Only once did they advance beyond the first playoff round.

Hartford's first NHL season featured the awe-inspiring Howe family — the legendary Gordie and sons Mark and Marty — whom the Whalers had signed to a WHA contract two years earlier. Gordie, a 50-year-old grandfather, played in all 80 games in 1979-80, scoring 15 goals and collecting 41 points, inspiring his young and adoring teammates to a playoff berth before retiring at the end of the season.

The player who has most marked the Whalers' history is center Ron Francis. He spent all of the 1980s with the club and remains the leader in most of the franchise's offensive categories. Francis collected 821 points and 264 goals in 714 games as a Whaler.

The Compuware group had a successful formula with their youth and junior hockey operations, and they have been trying to adhere to the same blueprint with the Hurricanes.

General manager Jim Rutherford and head coach Paul Maurice were both members of that Compuware program. In fact, it was Maurice who became the youngest head coach in professional sports when he replaced Paul Holmgren behind the Hartford bench in November 1995. He had been highly successful with the Detroit Junior Red Wings, where he compiled a 86-38-8 record in two years.

Child's play: Trevor Kidd set personal and franchise records in 1998

The Blackhawks' 28-year streak of reaching the playoffs was one short of the NHL record. But in 1997-98 it came to an end.

The streak finally ended. After 28 straight trips to the NHL playoffs, the Chicago Blackhawks found themselves five points shy of the last postseason berth in the Western Conference. It was the end of an era, and the end of Craig Hartsburg's tenure as Hawks coach.

There was plenty of off-season speculation that superstar St. Louis Blues forward Brett Hull, an unrestricted free agent, might sign with the Blackhawks. The talk made sense, even beyond the sentimentality of signing the son of one of the franchise's truly legendary figures, Bobby Hull. In the end, Hull signed with Dallas. The Chicago offense managed just 192 goals in 82 games in 1997-98, besting only the Tampa Bay Lightning in that scoring category. The defense allowed the eighth-fewest goals against in the league and goaltender Jeff Hackett emerged as a bona fide No.1 goalie.

Captain's burden

While the Hawks boasted two 30-goal scorers in Eric Daze and Tony Amonte — a rare feat in a season when goals league-wide were down — the team lacked a No.1 center who could create offensive chances on a regular basis. And future Hall of Famer Chris Chelios didn't deliver his usual goods. As captain of Team USA in the Olympics, Chelios had the added burden of making public restitution for some unnamed teammates' well-publicized mischief in the Olympic Village in Nagano, Japan. The pressures heaped upon Chelios's broad shoulders undoubtedly affected his performances for the Blackhawks. Chicago filled the void in the middle in the offseason by signing New Jersey's free-agent center Doug Gilmour.

The search for a replacement for Hartsburg seemed to drag on well into the off-season before former Blackhawks star Dirk Graham was finally installed as coach. Graham has plenty of challenges to keep him busy in the coming season as he attempts to restore pride to the Blackhawks after the shattering of their proud and treasured run of postseason appearances.

Despite their playoff streak, actually getting their hands on the Stanley Cup has been a different proposition for the Blackhawks. Victories have been few and far between for the Chicago Blackhawks, who joined the NHL way back on September 25, 1926.

At the time, their first head coach was a man named Pete Muldoon, who would lose the job after one only season in charge. However, it was a season spiced with intrigue. Muldoon was fired after a woeful display by the Blackhawks. But he didn't go gently. He is alleged to have placed a curse on the team, saying it would never finish first because it had treated him so ignominiously.

Hawks' Eric Daze (left) managed to score over 30 goals despite a season in which goals league-wide were down.

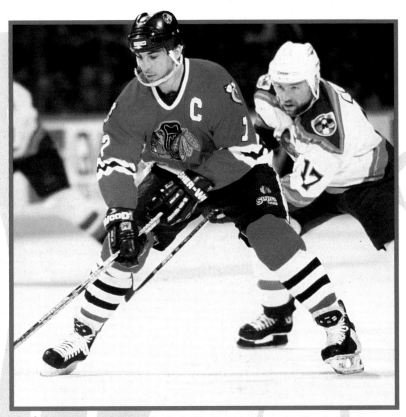

Best in the Business: Chris Chelios has won the Norris Trophy as the NHL's best defenseman with both the Montreal Canadiens and Chicago Blackhawks.

The Muldoon curse lasted 40 years, as Chicago didn't finish first until the 1966-67 season. In Stanley Cup play, the Blackhawks have managed to escape the curse only three times — when they won in 1934, 1938 and 1961.

Talent vs curse

Yet, it is a franchise which has been blessed with some wonderful talent who, before moving into the spacious United Center in the 1994-95 season, played at raucous Chicago Stadium.

Bobby Hull, the 'Golden Jet' who shellshocked goaltenders with his patented slap shot, became the first NHLer to score more than 50 goals in a season, in 1966. Stan Mikita, the gifted center immortalized in the Hockey Hall of Fame, sparkled for 21 seasons, scoring 541 goals, second to Hull's 604. Both Hull and Mikita are regarded as the unofficial 'inventors' of the curved stick.

Then there was 'Mr. Goalie', Glenn Hall, who introduced the butterfly style of goaltending much in vogue today.

After Hall, it was Tony (O) Esposito making some history — his 15 shutouts in 1969-70 are a modern-day single-season NHL record.

★ ROLL OF HONOR ★

Conference/Division	Western/Northwest
First Season	1979-80 (Quebec); 1995-96 (Colorado)
Honor roll	107-point season in 1996-97
Home rink/Capacity	McNichols Sports Arena/ 16,061
Stanley Cups	1996

Playing Record

	W	L	T	Pts
Regular Season	642	674	196	1460
Playoffs	64	62		

COLORADO AVALANCHE

Center Peter Forsberg was in awesome form for the Avalanche, but unfortunately his teammates couldn't follow his example.

As a player in the Swedish Elite League, Peter Forsberg was known as the best player not in the NHL. Now he's one of the best players in the league.

Star forwards Joe Sakic and Peter Forsberg should have realized it wasn't their year when they both departed the Winter Olympics in February without a medal, even though Sakic's Team Canada and Forsberg's Team Sweden were two of the pre-Games favorites to contend for a gold medal in Nagano.

Out of luck

Their luck didn't change in the Stanley Cup playoffs. Even though the Colorado Avalanche finished first in the Pacific Division for the third straight year, the Avs season ended disappointingly in the first round with a loss at home in game 7 against the Edmonton Oilers, who were two games below .500 during the regular season. Oilers goaltender Curtis Joseph was in great form and limited the high-powered Colorado offense to just one goal in the last three playoff games.

The Avs entered the playoffs with a limp, going 2-6-1 down the stretch amid rumors of ailing team chemistry. The game 7 loss to Edmonton was Marc Crawford's last as Avs coach. He was replaced by the franchise's top minor league coach, Bob Hartley.

Fantastic Forsberg

Despite falling short of of his Stanley Cup aspirations, it was another banner year for Peter Forsberg, whom many consider to be the best all-round center in the game at the moment. A late-season groin injury might have derailed his bid to win the Art Ross Trophy as the NHL scoring leader, but his 91 points ranked second behind the Pittsburgh Penguins' Jaromir Jagr, who had 102. None of the other high-profile players could match Forsberg's performances. Sakic missed nearly a quarter of the season, playing in just 62 games.

Checkered history

This is NHL Part 2 in Colorado, and, it's been a spectacular sequel thus far. Unlike 1976-77, when Colorado inherited the mediocre Kansas City Scouts, the region managed to entice the Quebec Nordiques, a rising NHL power, whose owners felt they could no longer financially survive without a revenue-generating new rink in Quebec City.

Nordiques president Marcel Aubut and his ownership group sold the franchise to COMSAT, an entertainment company headed by Charlie Lyons, in the summer of 1995. That returned the NHL to Colorado, without a franchise after the Rockies moved and they became the New Jersey Devils in 1982.

One of four World Hockey Association teams absorbed by the NHL in 1979, the Nordiques made the playoffs for seven straight years after their initial season. But as star players aged and key draft picks failed to deliver the goods, lean times arrived

Quiet Superstar: Joe Sakic quietly, unassumingly accumulates his points every season, like clockwork.

for the Nordiques. The club missed the playoffs for five straight seasons much to the chagrin of the fans.

In 1991, No. 1 draft pick Eric Lindros refused to sign with Quebec, setting off a year-long battle that culminated in the Nordiques' trading him to both the New York Rangers and Philadelphia Flyers. An arbitrator had to intervene, awarding him to the Flyers.

The trade was seemingly a turning point for the franchise. Among the players Quebec acquired was Forsberg, who pledged his future to the Avalanche last season and signed a long-term contract, ensuring that he will be as much a part of the Colorado scenery as the Rocky Mountains.

DALLAS STARS

Commitment and dedication saw Dallas win the President's Trophy in a season when injury plagued the Stars throughout.

Perhaps the most overworked member of the Dallas Stars in 1997-98 was the team trainer, yet despite the setbacks, the Stars still shone brightly. Key contributors such as forwards Mike Modano, Greg Adams, Bob Bassen, Benoit Hogue and Dave Reid and defensemen Derian Hatcher and Shawn Chambers all played fewer than 70 games. Still, the Dallas roster was deep enough and good enough and the team was committed enough to coach Ken Hitchcock's defensive philosophy to finish the season with 109 points and win the President's Trophy for having the most points in the NHL during the regular season.

The Stars seemed to finally be healthy as the playoffs began, but star forward Joe Nieuwendyk was injured in the first playoff game and unavailable for the rest of the postseason. Nieuwendyk was a key component to a power play that ranked No.1 in the league during the regular season. His 39 goals were the seventh most in the NHL, and his absence was felt in the playoffs, even though the team made it to the Western Conference finals and stretched eventual Stanley Cup champions Detroit to six games.

Highs and lows
The Stars went from being one of the highest scoring teams during the regular season to being one of the lowest-scoring teams ever to advance so far in the playoffs (2.4 goals per playoff game). Dallas power-play efficiency dropped nearly in half, from 20 per cent in the regular season to 10.5 in the playoffs.

That left Ed Belfour little room for error. He proved, however, that he was up to the task for the most part, helping the team break a 70-year old record by holding opponents to two goals or less than 10 straight postseason games. Belfour had been spectacular in most of his first season in Dallas. The former Chicago Blackhawks two-time Vezina Trophy winner led the league in goals-against average at a stingy 1.88. He is part of the core of the team that will be intact to make another run at Lord Stanley in 1999. Joining that core is newcomer Brett Hull; the former St. Louis sharpshooter signed as a free agent in the summer.

Tragic start
The franchise, which has operated in Dallas since 1993, burst on the NHL scene in 1967-68, along with five other expansion brethren. It was the Minnesota North Stars way back then, but

Lone Star Star: In Mike Modano, the Dallas Stars have a capstone player; now both they and he have a dependable supporting cast.

Sergei Zubov was part of a Dallas side affected by injury throughout the season, yet which still showed great character to make it deep into the playoffs.

an early on-ice tragedy would make star-crossed a more appropriate description.

On January 13, 1968, about halfway through the North Stars' inaugural season, a helmetless Bill Masterton struck his head violently on the ice and died in hospital from brain injuries two days later. It was the first and, thankfully, to this day, the only NHL on-ice death.

Bill Goldsworthy was the North Stars' first big goal-scorer. He was the first player from a post-1967 team to score 250 goals, 48 of which came in the 1973-74 season.

On the move
The North Stars made the Stanley Cup final in both 1981 and 1991, losing to the New York Islanders and Pittsburgh Penguins, respectively. The North Stars' tremendous playoff run in 1991 temporarily revived lagging fan interest in Minneapolis but in 1993 Norm Green, who had become the team owner three years earlier, moved the franchise to Dallas.

Dropping the North from their nickname, the Stars were the first NHL club in Texas and the sixth in the United States 'Sun Belt'.

After their 1997 Stanley Cup win, the Detroit Red Wings decided they wanted more of the same and repeated the feat in 1998.

When the Detroit Red Wings won the Stanley Cup in 1997 and ended a 42-year-old pursuit of hockey's top prize, it was more a sense of relief for the players than anything. At last, the jinx was lifted. But when the Wings repeated the 1997 triumph by winning the Cup again in 1998, it was pure, unadulterated joy. The second Stanley Cup was for two people in particular: Vladdy and Sergei.

Vladimir Konstantinov was one of the most feared players in the league when he helped Detroit win the 1997 Stanley Cup. He was a punishing hitter and a finalist for the Norris Trophy as the NHL's best defenseman. Sergei Mnatsakonov was the team masseur, the one whose hands helped the Red Wings players recover from the bruises, bumps and abraisions that are part and parcel of hockey.

Six days after the Wings won the 1997 Cup, the two were seriously injured when a limo in which they were passengers, along with Wings defenseman Slava Fetisov, collided with a tree with horrific force.

The Wings players rallied around their injured colleagues. Konstantinov was on hand for the clinching game 4 of the Stanley Cup Finals against the Washington Capitals and captain Steve Yzerman put the cup in Vladdy's wheelchair at the end. It was an emotional climax to a season that placed sport in its proper context.

Double whammy

The Wings became just the second team of the 1990s to win consecutive Stanley Cups, following in the skates of the Pittsburgh Penguins who collected two cups in 1991 and 1992.

But with four straight conference finals appearances, three Stanley Cup Final appearances in four years and two straight Cups, the Wings have staked their claim to being the top team of the '90s.

They did it with one of the most complete team efforts in recent memory. Eleven players scored double-digit goals in the regular season, not including superstar Sergei Fedorov, who had six in 21 games after missing most of the season due to protracted and intense contract negotiations.

Even in the playoffs, the players spread it around. Forward Tomas Holmstrom, who scored five goals all year, turned in a star performance during the playoffs with an incredible seven goals.

To many observers, the Red Wings were a team of destiny and nothing was going to stop them getting their hands on the Stanley Cup once more. What is worrying for their opponents is that the team returns in 1998-99 virtually intact and seeking that magical three-in-a-row.

Red hot past

The Red Wings were the NHL powerhouse in the first half of the 1950s, winning four Stanley Cups in six years.

That was the era of the Production Line of (Gordie) Howe,

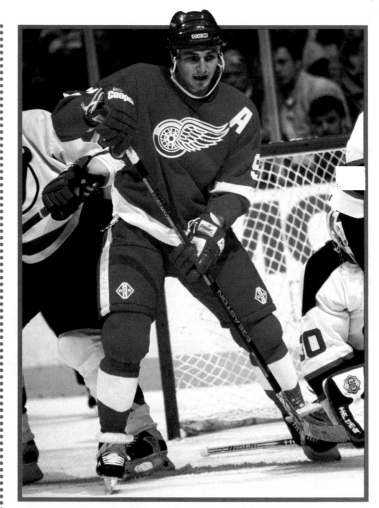

First Among Equals: The flashiest player on Detroit's roster is undoubtedly Sergei Fedorov, a two-way superstar.

(Ted) Lindsay and (Sid) Abel, defensive stalwarts Red Kelly and Bob Goldham, icy-veined Terry Sawchuk in goal and Jolly Jack Adams at the managerial helm.

Until Wayne Gretzky came along a few decades later, Howe was the NHL's leading career goal-scorer with 801, all but 15 of them coming with Detroit. His linemate Lindsay is regarded by many as the toughest customer of all time. Abel, who went on to coach the Red Wings, was the set-up man on the line.

Sawchuk was impenetrable in goal, recording 85 shutouts with Detroit and an NHL record 103 in his career. The numbers brought Sawchuk an election to the Hall of Fame, one of 46 people associated with the Red Wings who have earned such an honor.

Stevie Y: Yzerman is the elder statesman of the superb Red Wings, with a career points-total second only to Gordie Howe.

☆ ROLL OF HONOR ☆

Conference/Division	**Western/Central**
First season	**1926-27 (Cougars); 1930-31 (Falcons); 1932-33 (Red Wings)**
Honor roll	**Seven straight regular-season titles (1948-49 to 1954-55)**
Home rink/Capacity	**Joe Louis Arena/19,275**
Stanley Cups	**9 (1936, 1937, 1943, 1950, 1952, 1954, 1955, 1997, 1998**

Playing Record

	W	L	T	Pts
Regular Season	2072	1998	728	4902
Playoffs	222	207	1	

With a hardcore of young talent, the Oilers are hoping to build on last season's shock defeat of Avalanche.

The biggest victory for the Edmonton Oilers in 1997-98 was not the first round playoff upset of the Pacific Division champions Colorado Avalanche. No, the Oilers' biggest victory was avoiding the fate of the team Colorado was before it relocated in 1995 — the Quebec Nordiques. The Nordiques were one of four teams to enter the NHL in 1979 from the old World Hockey Association.

Small market economics caught up to the franchise in 1995 when it moved to Colorado. The next year, the Winnipeg Jets met the same fate, moving to Phoenix to become the Coyotes.

In 1997, the Hartford Whalers became the Carolina Hurricanes. That left just one of the four WHA teams in its original city — the Edmonton Oilers. And for much of the season, it looked like Edmonton might be next to follow suit. But the team dug deep and dug wide, and eventually found a new local ownership with a $70 million US offer from the Edmonton Investors Group Ltd. And with that taken care of, they found their old magic in the playoffs. The Investors' faith in the Oilers was paid back in full when they met the season ticket goal for the third consecutive year. "It is clear a very high level of interest exists for Oilers hockey," said Investors Group spokesman Jim Hole, "and I would like to pay tribute to all the individuals and corporations who helped us reach this goal."

Golden Glen

With a core of young, talented players, not to mention one of the best goalies in the league in Curtis Joseph, the Oilers were seen as an up-and-comer at the beginning of the 1997-98 season. The team never caught its stride, however, and appeared aimless and drifting before GM Glen Sather grabbed matters by the scruff of the neck and proved his craftiness once again by making trades to bring in such key players as defensemen Janne Niinimaa and Roman Hamrlik and forward Bill Guerin.

Edmonton dethroned the Colorado Avalanche in seven games, with Cujo allowing just one miserly goal in the final three games. It was all rather reminiscent of 1997, when the Oilers knocked off Central Division champions Dallas Stars in the first round.

Center Doug Weight was voted team MVP by the fans after leading the team in scoring for the fifth straight season.

With new players such as Josef Beranek — back for a second spell at the Oilers — and goaltender Tim Thomas replacing the Toronto-bound Joseph during the summer, new faces should inspire the side.

Camelot on ice

The Edmonton franchise didn't join the NHL until 1979—one of four World Hockey Association franchises to do so—but it surely made up for lost time. In five years, the Oilers built a powerhouse

that produced five Stanley Cups in seven years, between 1983-84 and 1989-90. They were successful because a superb nucleus of players came of age together, and a coach and Sather displayed a green thumb in developing the vast talent on hand. "In the 1980s it was Camelot," recalls Oilers owner Peter Pocklington. "It was almost surreal. We were always on a roll."

The supporting cast sometimes changed but the main actors did not. There was Wayne Gretzky, arguably the finest player to lace on skates, menacing Mark Messier, crafty Jari Kurri, multi-dimensional Glenn Anderson, the steady Kevin Lowe on defense and the unflappable Grant Fuhr in goal.

The shock trade of Gretzky to the Los Angeles Kings in 1988 signalled the impending demise of Camelot, it wasn't the end of the Oilers' spring skate with the Stanley Cup. Messier, Anderson, Kurri, Fuhr and Lowe were around for one last hurrah, in 1989-90.

Carrying his Weight: On the post-dynasty Oilers, Doug Weight is the scoring star.

Oiler on the Rise: Jason Arnott's enormous potential is only one piece in Edmonton's strategy of resilience.

★ ROLL OF HONOR ★

Conference/Division	**Eastern/Southeast**
First season	**1993-94**
Honor roll	**Most points (83) by first-year team (1993-94)**
Home rink/Capacity	**Broward County Arena/19,088**
Stanley Cups	**0**

Playing Record

	W	L	T	Pts
Regular Season	153	158	67	373
Playoffs	13	14		

FLORIDA PANTHERS

The 1997-98 season was one of big disappointment for the Florida Panthers. Big improvements are needed for 1998-99.

The good news for the Florida Panthers was that they were not the worst team in the state of Florida. The bad news was that, in terms of points, they were the second-worst team in the league.

Only the cross-state Tampa Bay Lightning managed fewer points than the Panthers' 63. Doug MacLean, the former Jack Adams award winner as a coach of the year, did not last the season in South Florida, being shown the door as early as November 1997. He was replaced by the man who fired him, GM Bryan Murray, who did not fare much better. After the season, Murray himself stood down and hired his brother Terry to take over as bench boss. Terry Murray had coached the Philadelphia Flyers to the Stanley Cup Finals in 1997, but he had lost his job after Philadelphia was swept aside by the Detroit Red Wings.

Despite his firing by Philadelphia, Terry Murray has the total confidence of brother Bryan, who said. "Terry is an experienced, successful, no-nonsense coach who has a history of working well with young players.

"Originally I worried about the perception of hiring my brother. But I felt an obligation to hire the best available candidate. I believe Terry will do a fine job."

Turning tide

For a team that made it to the Stanley Cup Finals on defense in 1996, the tide sure turned for the Panthers. Only Vancouver, Tampa Bay and Anaheim allowed more goals than Florida. The offense wasn't much better, either, ranking a dismal 20th out of the 26 in the league.

Despite all the losses, the season did have some bright spots. Ray Whitney, who was claimed off waivers from the Edmonton Oilers early in the season, tied the Panthers record for goals in a season with 32. Center Viktor Kozlov was acquired from the San Jose Sharks and showed why he has been so highly touted with strong play down the stretch.

The Panthers continued trading after the season closed with defensemen Chris Allen, Peter Ratchuk and Curtis Doell in early June, as well as forward Tero Lehtera from the Finnish Elite League. The team needs as many attractions as it can get. After all, this season it moves into a brand new, $185 million building in Broward County.

Brash rats

Owned by Wayne Huizenga of the Blockbuster Video empire, the Panthers were something of a blockbuster themselves in 1993-94, the season they joined Tampa Bay as the NHL's expansion entries from the Sunshine State. Under renowned hockey tactician Roger Neilson the Panthers became the most successful first-year NHL

The Stopper: Great goaltending from John Vanbiesbrouck helped the Florida Panthers play respectable hockey from Year 1.

Once again Slovakian defenseman Robert Svehla was a rock for the Panthers.

team, collecting 83 points and narrowly missing a spot in the Stanley Cup playoffs.

The Panthers came achingly close to a playoff berth in the strike-shortened 1994-95 season, adhering to the same smothering style and solid goaltending by Vanbiesbrouck, the first pick in the 1993 expansion draft. But Panthers management, headed by Bill Torrey, who shaped the New York Islanders' dynasty in the early 1980s, decided a coaching change was required and Neilson was replaced by MacLean, a product of the Detroit Red Wings system.

MacLean modified the neutral-zone trap during the 1995-96 season, favoring a mix of offense and defense, and it vaulted the Panthers to a dramatic seventh-game Conference final triumph over Pittsburgh and a hard-fought six games before succumbing to Colorado in the final.

LOS ANGELES KINGS

The Los Angeles Kings are improving with a 1997-98 playoff place that augurs well for the future.

There's always plenty to do in Los Angeles in the springtime. Since 1993, going to a Kings game hadn't been one of them. The Kings made it to the Stanley Cup Finals in 1993 and then missed the next four postseasons. That painful drought was finally broken in 1998 with a blissful rain of success. Unfortunately, the relief didn't last long and the long-awaited playoff run soon dried up. The Kings earned the fifth seed, but were the only playoff team to get swept in the first round, falling to St.Louis in four straight.

The playoff exit was also laced with a heavy dose of controversy that had the ice buzzing. A five-minute major penalty in game 3 in which the Blues scored all four of their goals in a 4-3 win will rapidly become a moment cloaked in infamy and recrimination.

Despite the early playoff exit, the season was one to build on and improve morale within the Kings camp. For one thing, the team's star defenseman, Rob Blake, returned to form with a bang that caught opponents unawares. Plagued by injury in previous seasons, Blake was back to his awesome best. He led all NHL defensemen with 23 goals and won the Norris Trophy, given to the league's best defenseman.

Stumpel's surprise

Blake wasn't the only bright spot for the Kings. Center Jozef Stumpel made a big impact after coming over from the Boston Bruins, in the process giving the Kings a top-notch first-line playmaker. Even though he struggled some down the stretch, Stumpel finished 10th in the league in points with a total of 79. Glen Murray led the Kings in goals with 29. The club also had a stellar tandem of young and able goalies in Stephane Fiset and Jamie Storr.

The Kings have unveiled a new logo and colors for the 1998-99 season, and undoubtedly the new look will bring with it fresh expectations from the supporters that a more consistent playoff run can be cobbled together.

The Kings are still without a crown, almost 30 years after Canadian-born entrepreneur Jack Kent Cooke engineered the NHL's West Coast expansion by establishing a franchise in Los Angeles. The crown almost materialized in 1993, when the Kings imbued their fans with a fever reminiscent of the California gold rush by reaching the Stanley Cup final for the first time. Alas, they fell in five games to the Montreal Canadiens.

LA stars

The franchise has had its share of jewels. One of them was Marcel Dionne, a diminutive but Houdini-like center who was acquired in a trade with Detroit after the 1974-75 season. He skated his way into the Hall of Fame, scoring 550 of his 731 career goals—third-best in NHL history—as a member of the Kings. Along the way, Dionne inherited Charlie Simmer and Dave Taylor as linemates, and the Triple Crown Line, as they were

Center Jozef Stumpel (right) proved an inspired playmaker for the Kings after arriving from the Boston Bruins.

dubbed, were the scourge of the league for several seasons.

The Dionne era ended in 1987, when he was dealt to the New York Rangers. But in true Hollywood fashion another superstar arrived on the set just over a year later — Wayne Gretzky. The NHL's marquee player arrived from Edmonton in a blockbuster trade. While Gretzky revived sagging hockey interest in Los Angeles, the Kings got no closer to their first Stanley Cup triumph than the dramatic 1992-93 final against Montreal.

Rob Blake (below) was back to his brilliant best leading the NHL defensemen with 23 goals in the 1997-98 season.

⭐ ROLL OF HONOR ⭐

Conference/Division	**Western/Pacific**
First season	**1967-68**
Honor roll	**Reached Stanley Cup final 1992-93**
Home rink/Capacity	**Great Western Forum/16,005**
Stanley Cups	**0**

Playing Record

	W	L	T	Pts
Regular Season	951	1128	361	2263
Playoffs	55	91		

MONTREAL CANADIENS

All eyes will turn to the Canadiens' goaltending in 1998-99 after the retirement of Andy Moog left a big hole in their armory.

The Montreal Canadiens' season ended unlike any in the team's eight decades. The final game was a loss at home that completed a playoff series sweep. The Canadiens had been swept in best-of-seven playoff series three times before the Buffalo Sabres did the trick in May, but none of the previous sweeps ended on Montreal's home ice.

The deciding factor in the Canadiens' second-round loss to the Sabres was goaltending. Buffalo played in fornt of the great Czech Republic goalie Dominik Hasek and the Habs had a trio that simply couldn't match his tremendous efforts.

Andy Moog, who compiled some of the best stats in NHL history during his illustrious career, retired after the season ended. That means the two youngsters — Jocelyn Thibault and Jose Theodore — should get the chance they've both been waiting for and prove they can be a No.1 goalie in the NHL.

Special agents
The smallish Canadiens played an entertaining brand of hockey in coach Alain Vigneault's first season.

Vigneault had come in at the beginning of the season to replace previous coach Mario Tremblay. Tremblay had resigned after just one complete season in the job and, as a parting shot, he launched a stinging attack on some of the media adversaries who had made his spell an uncomfortable one. Tremblay became the fifth coach in 12 years to depart the pressure of guiding the fortunes of a franchise under intense media scrutiny.

Only the Philadelphia Flyers scored more goals in the Eastern Conference, and the Habs had the third-best power play in the league thanks to power-play stalwarts such as Mark Recchi and Shayne Corson. The team had 13 free agents to keep them occupied during the off-season, including Recchi, Saku Koivu, Brian Savage and Martin Rucinsky.

The team also wanted to get captain Vincent Damphousse locked up to a long-term deal in the off-season.

Great expectations
No team has to deal with higher expectations from its loyal followers than the Canadiens—and that's because of the winning tradition of the Club de Hockey Canadien. With 24 Stanley Cups, they are the most successful major professional sports franchise. By comparison, the New York Yankees have won 23 World Series and the Boston Celtics have 16 National Basketball Association crowns. The Canadiens have 11 more Cup triumphs than their closest pursuer, the Toronto Maple Leafs.

Saku Koivu was one of 13 free agents plying their trade for the Canadiens last season.

Leading Man: A native Montrealer, Vincent Damphousse is the on-ice leader for the young, harassed Canadiens.

Torch of Glory
Little did J. Ambrose O'Brien realize when he founded the team on December 4, 1909 that it would gain world-wide renown for its hockey prowess—in fact, he sold the club a year later. But by 1926 Canadiens players such as Newsy Lalonde, Aurele Joliat, Joe Malone, Georges Vezina and Howie Morenz were stars.

The late 1950s saw an unmatched five consecutive Stanley Cups, as the team responded to an excerpt from the John McRae poem *In Flanders Fields*—"To you from failing hands we throw the torch. Be Yours to Hold it High" which has been a fixture in the dressing room since 1952. No one grabbed the torch with as much gusto as Maurice (Rocket) Richard, the team's career goal-scoring leader with 544. An icon in Quebec, Richard's suspension for striking a linesman, touched off a riot by fans at the Forum on March 17, 1955.

The string of Stanley Cups started the following the year as Jean Beliveau, Dickie Moore, Boom Boom Geoffrion, Doug Harvey, Jacques Plante and Maurice's kid brother Henri led a star-studded cast coached by Toe Blake, who would win eight Cups in 13 seasons behind the bench.

With Scotty Bowman at the helm, and such performers as Jacques Lemaire, Guy Lafleur, Larry Robinson and Ken Dryden, the Canadiens added four straight Stanley Cups between 1975-76 and 1978-79.

NEW JERSEY DEVILS

New Jersey coach Jacques Lemaire stepped down after five years in charge as the Devils ran out of goals in the playoff.

The Jacques Lemaire era in charge of the Devils ended after five years, three 100-point seasons, two conference finals and a Stanley Cup championship. The New Jersey Devils' coach did not go out on top as he would have preferred — with another Stanley Cup triumph — but instead resigned after being on the wrong side of the first playoff series win in the modern era of the Ottawa Senators.

Magic Martin

The Devils were an absolute terror during the regular season, getting more than adequate scoring and relying heavily on the team's much-vaunted neutral zone trap — a system implemented by Jacques Lemaire to great effect that basically clogs the area between the two blue lines and stifles the offensive threat of opposing teams — and the sheer brilliance of goaltender Martin Brodeur, who won his second straight Jennings Trophy for leading his team to the league's lowest goals-against average.

When it came to the playoff series against the upstart

Franchise Defenseman: Scott Stevens anchors a rock-solid defense in New Jersey.

Senators, however, the scoring dried up. The Devils managed just 12 goals in six games. Star center Doug Gilmour, keeping Father Time at bay, had five of those goals, while no one else had more than one. But New Jersey must now look elsewhere for goals, as free agent Gilmour signed for Chicago in the offseason.

Great Scott

Former checking line regulars Bobby Holik and Randy McKay broke through with 29 and 24 goals respectively. Defenseman Scott Niedermayer was able to be more aggressive offensively and tied for second among NHL defenseman with 57 points. He quarterbacked the second-best power play in the league, which operated at 18.9 percent efficiency.

Scott Stevens and Lyle Odelein were forceful at keeping other teams top lines in check. The team got a good look at someone they hope will be the Devils next scoring star — Brendan Morris, a Hobey Baker Award winner (college hockey's equivalent to the Heisman), recorded five goals and nine points in 11 games for New Jersey.

From funnies to champs

Few remember that the New Jersey Devils were once the Kansas City Scouts, and only vaguely that they were the Colorado Rockies, a club that John McMullen and his group purchased in 1982 and moved to the New Jersey Meadowlands.

Some may recall that the Devils were almost as dreadful as the Scouts and Rockies in their early years in New Jersey. In fact, after a 1983 game in which Edmonton routed New Jersey 11-4, Oilers superstar Wayne Gretzky likened the Devils to Mickey Mouse.

Until 1988, the Rockies-Scouts-Devils had qualified for a playoff berth only once in 13 seasons, and had one playoff-game victory—by Colorado in 1977-78.

But the first taste of post-season play as the Devils was memorable as they reached the Wales Conference championship before losing to Boston in seven games. The Devils did not make the conference final again until 1994. That ended in heartbreak, when Stephane Matteau's seventh-game overtime goal sent the New York Rangers, not New Jersey, to the Stanley Cup final.

But under Lemaire, part of eight Stanley Cup championships as a player with Montreal, the Devils embarked on a 1994-95 playoff run in which it lost only four of 20 games, culminating in a four-game sweep of the favored Detroit Red Wings for the first Stanley Cup in the history of the franchise.

The Devils' goaltender Martin Brodeur was in outstanding form last season winning his second straight Jennings trophy for lowest goals-against average.

⭐ ROLL OF HONOR ⭐

Conference/Division	**Eastern/Atlantic**
First season	**1972-73**
Honor roll	**Four straight Stanley Cups, 1979-80 to 1982-83**
Home rink/Capacity	**Nassau Veterans Memorial Coliseum/16,297**
Stanley Cups	**4 (1980, 1981, 1982, 1983)**

Playing Record

	W	L	T	Pts
Regular Season	928	839	291	2147
Playoffs	128	90		

With a new ownership in place, the Isles had high expectations in 1997-98, but things went wrong.

The New York Islanders know what it's like to have four straight seasons end the same way. In the early 1980s, the franchise put together a string of four consecutive Stanley Cups. In the late 1990s, the team has a streak of four straight seasons missing the playoffs.

The Isles seemed to be a team of promise heading into the 1997-98 campaign, but some key players underachieved and the team had a reputation for lacking the commitment needed to win. GM Mike Milbury didn't sit idly by. He made trades to get character veteran players such as Trevor Linden, Joe Sacco, J.J Daignealt, Gino Odjick and Jason Dawe. Milbury also replaced his coach, Rick Bowness, with himself.

Of the 13 teams in the Eastern Conference, the Isles ranked 10th in goals against. Eric Fichaud, once considered the team's future at the position, was shipped to Edmonton before the summer trade deadline for the expansion draft. That means the goalie of the present is Tommy Salo, whom Milbury has been critical of in the past. The organization is very high on the potential of Roberto Luongo, the team's top pick in 1997.

Roaring Forties
The two best players for the Isles in 1997-98 were forward Ziggy Palffy and defenseman Kenny Jonsson. Palffy scored 41 goals, one of just five players in the league to hit the 40 mark each of the past three seasons. Jonsson added an offensive dimension to his game by recording 14 goals and 40 points, and he was a workhorse. Milbury was critical of his omission from the Swedish Olympic team.

Forward Robert Reichel went to the Olympics in early 1998 and became a legend in his native Czech Republic when he scored the shootout goal that beat Canada and won the gold medal for his country. But he struggled down the stretch for the Isles, as did American Olympian Bryan Berard. The 1997 Calder Trophy winner recorded just two goals and 21 points and was minus-32 in his last 42 games.

New ownership was in place after the embarrassment of the previous season, when John Spanos bought the team on a stack of false financial reports and was eventually caught by the long arm of the law

The Islanders' plight in recent years is a reminder of the franchise's humble beginnings, after joining the Atlanta Flames as a new league member in the 1972-73 season.

Torrey magic
The Islanders managed only 12 victories and 30 points in their fledgling season but they improved dramatically from then on, as astute general manager Bill Torrey, who'd been an executive with the

Defenseman Bryan Berard failed to reproduce the form that earned him the Calder Trophy in 1997.

expansion California Seals, started weaving his magic. Torrey hired Al Arbour as head coach following the 1972-73 season. One week later, he drafted Denis Potvin, a gifted young junior defenseman. At the draft table the following year, Torrey grabbed a bruising forward named Clark Gillies, and a shifty center named Bryan Trottier.

The combative Billy Smith, a little-known goaltender Torrey had selected in the 1972 expansion draft, suddenly became a key component in the building process. In the 1977 draft, Torrey plucked a wiry, high-scoring forward named Mike Bossy from the Quebec Major Junior League and the last building block was virtually in place.

By the 1979-80 season, these five players led an Islanders charge that displaced the Montreal Canadiens as the dominant NHL force. The Canadiens were seeking a fifth straight Cup when the upstart Islanders breezed through four series, including a six-game victory over Philadelphia in the final, for the first of four consecutive Stanley Cup championships.

The Islanders narrowly missed matching the Canadiens' record five straight Cups. They reached the final in 1983-84, only to lose to the Edmonton Oilers.

Scoring Whiz: In Zigmund Palffy, the Islanders have a bona fide NHL sniper.

Despite the brilliance of Wayne Gretzky, the Rangers suffered throughout the season and lost a coach as well.

The New York Rangers were proof in 1997-98 that money can't buy happiness — or success in the NHL. Despite a massive $44 million payroll, the Rangers still couldn't get into the playoffs. Coach Colin Campbell shouldered most of the blame of this failure and paid the ultimate price, getting fired in favor of former Edmonton and Buffalo coach John Muckler.

The team's lack of success was in no way a reflection on the play of its biggest star, Wayne Gretzky. The living legend added to his already awesome reputation by tying for the league assist title, the 16th time he has either won or shared that particular crown. His play was especially strong after the Olympics in Nagano, Japan, at which Team Sweden coach Kent Forsberg (father of Colorado Avalanche star, Peter) suggested it was time for the 37 year-old Gretzky to hang up his skates and retire. It seemed that Forsberg's remark — whether intended to or not — acted as a form of motivation for the great Gretzky.

Missing Messier

Gretzky's longtime buddy, Mark Messier, who scored a club-leading 36 goals in the 1996-97 season, was sorely missed on the ice this season and especially in the locker room. The player who inherited his captaincy, two-time Norris Trophy winner Brian Leetch, had a subpar season, never hitting top form for any prolonged period. He never came close to matching his 1996-97 performance when he collected 78 points, including 20 goals. Another fellow superstar, goaltender Mike Richter, also did not enjoy his usual success.

When assessing his team after the season, Muckler gave forward Niklas Sunstrum high marks for his strong two-way play, and said he felt enigmatic winger Alexei Kovalev, who endured a disappointing 1996-97 season after shattering his knee, showed he was not only fully-recovered, but was ready to make the next step after scoring 23 goals.

The team's lack of scoring was dealt a blow when creative center Pat LaFonatine's season was cut short by more concussion problems. After missing most of the 1996-97 season because of concussions, his hockey future was in doubt as of press time.

From Cup to Cup

Success in the playoffs hasn't been a Rangers hallmark. No NHL team has won a Stanley Cup one year after joining the league, as the Rangers did in 1928, but no team has gone without a Stanley Cup for 54 years, as the Rangers did before making up for lost time and striking paydirt in 1993-94.

In the early years, Madison Square Garden echoed with exhortations for scoring star Frank Boucher, brothers Bill and Bun Cook and Lester Patrick, the club's first coach and general manager. In the second game of the 1928 Stanley Cup finals, the

Little Mess: Rugged and skilful, Adam Graves has learned his NHL lessons well from his mentor, Messier.

Goaltender Mike Richter was one of the many Rangers' superstars who never hit top form in the 1997-98 season.

44-year-old Patrick was pressed into service as the team's goaltender. He allowed only one goal, the Rangers won in overtime, and Patrick was forever etched in the club's history as a Rangers' hero.

Another brother combination — Mac and Alex Shibicky — joined with future Hall of Famer Neil Colville to lead the Rangers to their 1940 Cup triumph.

While the Rangers' Cup drought continued, the club made the playoffs nine straight years, starting in 1966-67.

The Rangers, who lost to Montreal in the 1978 final, wouldn't get another chance for nearly 20 years until 1994 in the final against Vancouver.

The Cup-clinching goal in Game 7 of the final came from Messier, a five-time Cup winner with Edmonton and one of several acquisitions made by Rangers general manager Neil Smith in building his championship squad.

The Ottawa Senators won the Stanley Cup in 1927, the first year the NHL assumed control of the Cup. Since the team re-entered the league as an expansion team in 1992, the Cup has been a far-fetched dream. That is, until the mid-1990s. On the next-to-last day of the 1996-97 regular-season schedule, they clinched their first-ever Stanley Cup playoff berth, and in 1997-98 they repeated their feat. And a little bit more as well. Perhaps that crazy dream will soon become reality for the dedicated Sens supporters.

The Senators not only finished above .500 for the first time and made the playoffs for the second straight year, they actually won their first series, a 4 games to 2 upset of Eastern Conference No. 1 seed New Jersey. Goaltender Damian Rhodes dyed his hair blonde and the change of color seemed to inspire not only him, but his teammates as well. Rhodes engineered the biggest success in the modern Senators' history with his outstanding play. After the disappointment of last season when Rhodes was sidelined in February with a leg injury, it was particularly satisfying for the goalie. The Devils were limited to just 12 goals in the six games.

Awesome Alexei

The man who led the way in 1997-98 was center Alexei Yashin, who was not only brilliant on the ice but generous off it. The bitter contractual disputes of a couple of years ago were swept away as Yashin carried on from where he had left off in 1996-97.

He was tied for 18th in the league with 72 points, including 16 in the last 17 games when the Sens were battling for a playoff spot. He also picked up a silver medal at the Nagano Olympics in February as a member of Team Russia and pledged $1 million to the National Arts Centre.

Daniel Alfredsson continued to shine for the Sens, even though he was limited by injury. The skilled Swede had 45 points in just 55 games. He also led the team with nine points in 11 playoff games. Offense was a problem with the Sens. Only two teams in the league had fewer goals.

Coach Jacques Martin had his team play a very disciplined style to make up for not being overstocked with an abundance of talent. The Sens took the fewest penalty minutes of any team in the league and the players played in an aggressive trap — dropping back when the other team had clear possession, but attacking when it sensed a turnover. It was a smart team that didn't beat itself.

Walking the plank

While last season was a huge ray of sunshine for the Senators, there continue to be plenty of stormy moments in their brief history. Mel Bridgman, the club's first general manager was fired immediately after the Senators' maiden season of 24 points—second-lowest in NHL history for a minimum 70-game schedule. The first-year Senators also tied an NHL record with only one road victory.

The abysmal record gave Ottawa the first draft choice in 1993, and the Senators grabbed Quebec Junior League scoring whiz Alexandre Daigle. Signed to a whopping five-year, $12 million contract, Daigle struggled his first two seasons, before notching 26 goals in 1996-97, second-highest on the club.

Yashin, meanwhile, missed three months in 1995-96 before a settlement was reached in his contract dispute. In the interim, the popular Rick Bowness—Ottawa's head coach from Day One—was fired, and key administrative personnel left the organization in frustration.

Sexton, too, eventually walked the plank, replaced by Pierre Gauthier, a rising executive with the San Jose Sharks, whose first move was to sign Yashin to a five-year deal. He then dumped interim coach Dave Allison and brought in the seasoned Martin, before Gauthier himself quit in late June, 1998.

Swedish Sharpshooter: Daniel Alfredsson's multi-talented game helps give Ottawa fans hope for a promising future.

Big Shoulders: The Ottawa Senators are hoping talented center Alexei Yashin can carry their franchise to the playoffs again.

⭐ ROLL OF HONOR ⭐

Conference/Division	**Eastern/Northeast**
First season	**1992-93**
Honor roll	**First Stanley Cup playoff berth, 1996-97**
Home rink/Capacity	**The Palladium/18,500**
Stanley Cups	**0**

Playing Record

	W	L	T	Pts
Regular Season	116	293	53	285
Playoffs	8	10		

★ ROLL OF HONOR ★

Conference/Division	Eastern/Atlantic
First season	1967-68
Honor roll	Consecutive Stanley Cups, 1974-75
Home rink/Capacity	CoreStates Center/19,500
Stanley Cups	2 (1974, 1975)

Playing Record

	W	L	T	Pts
Regular Season	1216	847	377	2809
Playoffs	145	129		

After reaching the Stanley Cup Finals in 1997, the Flyers flew south in 1998. Philly finished 12 points out of first place in the Atlantic Division during the regular season, then were upset in the first round of the playoffs by the Buffalo Sabres in five games.

But the real drama and turmoil for the Flyers occured behind the bench. Coach Terry Murray was fired after the 1997 Finals and replaced by Wayne Cashman. But Cashman fared no better and didn't even last the season, taking a demotion to assistant coach to make room for the oft-traveled Roger Neilson.

Captain Eric Lindros, who was sidelined for the first 23 games of last season, was the target of some criticism about his leadership, although not by his teammates. Matters weren't helped when Lindros was once again hit by the injury bug, playing in just 63 games. In what will probably be a season Lindros will try to forget, he experienced more disappointment as the captain of Team Canada at the Japan Winter Olympics in the side that finished out of the medals.

Goaltending was once again a sore subject in Philly. GM Bob Clarke made deals attempting to shore up the team's shortcomings in net. In the summer, he signed Florida's ace free agent John Vanbiesbrouck to replace midseason signing Sean Burke, who had not proved to be the savior anticipated. Clarke also continued his quest to be the biggest team in the league. The other newcomers included defensemen Luke Richardson (6-4, 210 lbs) and Dan McGillis (6-2, 225 lbs), and forward Chris Gratton (6-3, 212 lbs).

But in the playoffs, the smaller Buffalo Sabres regularly out-quicked the Flyers to the puck. There was a crackdown on obstruction after the Olympics, which held through the playoffs as well. That change in officiating did not favor the bruising Flyers' style of play.

John LeClair continued his offensive output, finishing one goal off the league lead with 51. He was named the Flyers' MVP for a second straight season. The native of Vermont became the first American in NHL history to record three consecutive 50-goal seasons.

Intimidating force

There's always been something special about the Flyers, one of the six expansion teams to join the NHL for the 1967-68 season. Six years later, they became the first expansion team to win the Stanley Cup, an exploit repeated in 1974-75. The Flyers of that era were tough and talented, attributes exemplified by acknowledged on-ice leader Bobby Clarke, who today is the Flyers' president and general manager.

Enforcers Dave (The Hammer) Schultz, Bob (Hound Dog) Kelly and Don Saleski did plenty of body-thumping. The Flyers' bruising defense corps of Andre (Moose) Dupont, the Watson brothers—Joe and Jim—and Ed Van Impe dished out more bitter medicine.

Once again captain Eric Lindros was hit by the injury bug playing in just 63 games last season.

But the Flyers, under coach Fred Shero, were much more than brawn. They had a 50-goal man in Rick MacLeish, another in Reggie Leach, who in 1975-76 notched 61 goals, only the second NHLer to reach that mark. And they had Bill Barber, whose 420 goals in 903 games as a Flyer remain the career best on the club.

In goal, Bernie Parent, traded to Toronto in 1971 and re-acquired two years later, won the Conn Smythe Trophy as the most valuable performer in the Stanley Cup playoffs in both 1974 and 1975, the first player to accomplish the feat.

Amid the triumphs, there was also tragedy. Barry Ashbee, one of the Flyers' best defensemen, had his career ended in 1974 after being struck in the eye by a puck, and Vezina Trophy winner Pelle Lindberg was killed in an automobile accident at the height of his goaltending career in 1985.

Rod Brind'Amour is hoping that the Flyers will have a better season than the one they've just experienced.

PHOENIX COYOTES

Despite a season that nearly ended in a playoff win, much of the Coyotes 1997-98 was mediocre.

For the Phoenix Coyotes, the second season in the desert was pretty much a mediocre experience all round. Under first-year coach Jim Schoenfeld, the team finished at exactly .500 — 35-35-13. The Coyotes also ranked in the middle of the NHL pack in such categories as team penalties (15th out of 26) and power play efficiency (14th).

In the playoffs, however, the mediocrity very nearly turned to excellence. In a first-round matchup against the defending Stanley Cup champion Detroit Red Wings, the Coyotes jumped to a 2-1 series lead. Unfortunately for Phoenix fans, the Wings stormed back to win three straight and send the Coyotes packing. Twice in the series Phoenix lost games in which it had the lead (Games 4 and 6), indeed the Coytotes lost a grand total of 20 such games this season — the most in the NHL.

Coyote Keith Tkachuk was the main man in the Phoenix side's offense last season.

Keith Tkachuk was once again the main offensive cog. On the heels of back-to-back 50-goal seasons, he scored 40 in just 69 games. He endured some criticism for not having a big playoffs (three goals), and he left for the summer intent on renegotiating his contract. One of his closest friends, playmaking center Craig Janney, was shipped to Tampa Bay after the season.

Rocket Tocchet

The top scorers in the playoffs were Rich Tocchet (six goals) and Jeremy Roenick (five). Tocchet was his usual hard-nosed self, while Roenick seemed intent on proving that the *Hockey News* had it wrong when it slapped him on the cover with the emblazoned caption: "Why Isn't Jeremy Roenick Still a Top Goal-Scorer?" After the trials and tribulations of the 1996-97 season when Roenick's season was prematurely ended by a nasty knee injury in Game 6 of the playoffs, the five goals he scored would have boosted Roenick's confidence as headed into a summer break before the start of the 1998-99 season.

Nikolai Khabibulin logged his usual heavy load in net (70 games), although his stats weren't quite up to their usual standards. After his superb 1996-97 season, when he posted seven shutouts and a 2.83 goals against average, it was always going to be hard for Khabibulin to reproduce that sort of form. His 2.74 goals-against average and .900 save percentage were below the league averages of 2.51 and .903.

Shaping influence

The Coyotes' NHL roots are in Winnipeg, where the Jets entered the league in 1979. While not very proficient in the NHL, the club was instrumental in the evolution of European players and, so, had much to do with shaping the style and substance of the game.

While Swedish stars Ulf and Kent Nilsson, and Anders Hedberg from Winnipeg's WHA years didn't accompany the Jets to the NHL, European stars such as Willy Lindstrom and Lars-Erik Sjoberg carried the torch successfully. The Jets also had NHL scoring great Bobby Hull for 18 games that first season, before trading him to Hartford.

As the 1980s unfolded, two players emerged to become the cornerstones of the Jets franchise. Dale Hawerchuk, a rangy center who was the No. 1 overall pick in the 1981 NHL draft, was the team's leading scorer for the next nine years, a remarkable stretch of form that catapulted him to the team's all-time leader in goals (379) and points (929).

Thomas Steen, of Sweden, wasn't a prolific scorer. But he combined toughness, speed and grace for 14 seasons with the Jets, making him the club's longest-serving player. There wasn't a dry eye in the Winnipeg Arena when the Jets retired Steen's No. 25 in a ceremony following the 1995 season.

The Coyotes' Jeremy Roenick (right) showed great determination to come back from a bad knee injury.

☆ ROLL OF HONOR ☆

Conference/Division	**Western/Pacific**
First season	**1979 (Winnipeg);**
	1996 (Phoenix)
Honor roll	**Club record 43 wins and 96**
	points in 1984-85
Home rink/Capacity	**America West Arena/17,500**
Stanley Cups	**0**

Playing Record

	W	L	T	Pts
Regular Season	579	732	191	1349
Playoffs	24	51		

It was inevitable that the post–Lemieux era of the Penguins would be full of drama and upheaval. And so it proved.

The post-Mario Lemieux era began with mixed results. On the one hand, the Pittsburgh Penguins finished first in the Northeast Division in their first season without their retired superstar center. On the other hand, the Penguins were bumped out of the playoffs in the first round, falling to the Montreal Canadiens in six games. Plus, Lemieux was out of sight but not out of mind — or the newspaper headlines — when it emerged that compensation he was owed by the Penguins hadn't been paid.

Penguins Co-owner Roger Marino admitted to feeling disappointed about the outcome of the playoffs, but nonetheless expressed his satisfaction with the season. "We had a season that was far above expectations and, winning another division championship, the fifth one of this decade, is something to be proud of."

The post-Lemieux Penguins had a decidedly different approach — a defensive approach. Kevin Constantine got his players to buy into his defense-first philosophy. The result was a comeback season for goaltender Tom Barrasso and the fourth-lowest team goals-against average in the league.

The comeback kid

Barrasso wasn't the only player to experience a rebirth. Right winger Rob Brown, once a 49-goal scorer on Lemieux's wing, returned to the NHL after a five-year absence. He reinvented himself as a reliable defensive forward with an occasional scoring touch (15 goals). And Stu Barnes thrived on the top line with Jaromir Jagr and Ron Francis, netting goals.

Francis captured the Lady Byng Memorial Trophy for the second time in his career which is awarded each season to "the player adjudged to have exhibited the best type of sportsmanship and gentlemanly conduct combined with a high standard of playing ability". Francis accumulated just 20 penalty minutes during the 1997-98 season, while compiling 87 points in 81 games (25 goals and 62 assists). The Penguins will miss Francis in 1998-99, as the free agent center signed with the Carolina Hurricanes.

Offensively, Jagr may have missed Lemieux, but he dominated. Jagr won his second Art Ross Trophy as the NHL's points leader (his first was in the strike-shortened 1994-95 season tallying 70 points in 48 games), becoming the only player to top the century mark in points at 102 (35 goals and 67 assists). In addition, Jagr was named to the First All-Star Team for the third time in his career. One of the few players left who won two Cups with Jagr in the early 1990s, goaltender Ken Wregget, was sent to the Calgary Flames shortly before the 1998 expansion draft.

Despite the loss of Wregget, the Penguins have been bolstered by the acquisition of some new players. Centers German Titov and Todd Hlushko were acquired from the Flames in exchange for Wregget, while right winger Boris Protsenko from the Ukraine and Czech defenseman Michael Rozsival both arrived from the Western Hockey League.

Goaltender Tom Barrasso thrived in the Penguins' defense-first philosophy as he relaunched his NHL career.

Bolstering a center

The history of the Penguins did not start on June 9, 1984, the day they selected Lemieux as the top pick in the NHL entry draft — but the fortunes of the franchise improved dramatically as of that date. Gradually, general manager Patrick assembled strong support for Lemieux. Jagr, a gifted Czechoslovakian, was grabbed in the 1990 entry draft, two-way center Francis was obtained in a trade with Hartford, and rangy Larry Murphy was added to the defense corps to clear the goal crease for netminder Tom Barrasso.

Two great hockey minds joined the Penguins for the 1990-91 season — (Badger) Bob Johnson as coach and Scotty Bowman as director of player development. Together, the former Stanley Cup-winning duo made the Penguins, out of the playoffs in seven of the previous eight seasons, into sudden Stanley Cup champions.

Bowman made it two straight Cups in 1992 when he relieved Johnson as coach at the start of that season. Johnson died of cancer several weeks later and fans honored his memory in a candlelight ceremony at the Civic Arena.

Simply the Best: Sublime is the most appropriate word to describe Mario Lemieux's extraordinary talent—now lost to the Penguins.

⭐ **ROLL OF HONOR** ⭐

Conference/Division	**Eastern/Atlantic**
First season	**1967-68**
Honor roll	**five division titles, two Stanley Cups in last eight years.**
Home rink/Capacity	**Civic Arena/17,181**
Stanley Cups	**2 (1991, 1992)**

Playing Record

	W	L	T	Pts
Regular Season	1004	1106	330	2338
Playoffs	88	78		

★ ROLL OF HONOR ★

Conference/Division	**Western/Pacific**
First season	**1991-92**
Honor roll	**Reached conference semifinal 1993-94, 1994-95**
Home rink/Capacity	**San Jose Arena/17,190**
Stanley Cups	**0**

Playing Record

	W	L	T	Pts
Regular Season	161	329	52	374
Playoffs	13	18		

After their disastrous 1996-97 season, the Sharks regained some pride with a much improved display.

The Sharks got some bite back in 1997-98 with a display that said much about their strength of character, both individually and collectively. A year after finishing one point away from the worst total in the NHL, San Jose got back into the playoffs — albeit as an eighth seed — and put the smile back on the faces of their fans.

The 17-point improvement in the standings was not the only measure of the team's improvement since the previous season. No-nonsense coach first-year Darryl Sutter instilled the same work ethic that he and his famous brothers regularly displayed during their own hockey careers into the current set of Sharks' players. With the arrival during the summer of Bob Berry at San Jose in the role of assistant coach to Sutter, the Sharks have another experienced head on board. Berry ranks 12th on the all-time list of games coached in the NHL and knows the Sutter way of thinking, having served as assistant coach to Brian, Darryl's brother, while at St. Louis.

GM Dean Lombardi added other veteran players such as Mike Ricci, John MacLean, Bryan Marchment and Joe Murphy, boosting the roster without sacrificing the team's long-term goals. After December 2, the team was four games over .500.

Young guns

Although the veterans were a big influence, the young guys all made their mark too. Three rookies made the roster coming out of the preseason. Forwards Patrick Marleau and Marco Sturm finished fourth and fifth respectively in the rookie scoring race and have vast potential.

Jeff Friesen, who seems older than his 21 years because he has played four years in the league, tied the franchise record with 31 goals. A pair of other young veterans, defensemen Marcus Ragnarsson and Mike Rathje, also had excellent years.

Although there was some controversy in the Dallas Stars's six-game win over San Jose in the playoff's first round — Jamie Langenbrunner was clearly in the San Jose crease on the winning goal in Game 5, but the referee didn't consult the video judge — the Sharks came away from the season with a positive feeling and optimism for the coming season.

New faces

There were several new acquisitions over the summer break, including defenseman Brad Stuart from the Regina Pats of the Western Hockey League — the Sharks' first selection (third overall) in the 1998 NHL Entry Draft. Also new are goaltending prospect Terry Friesen, Steve Shields, and right wing Matt Bradley, drafted by the Sharks in the fourth round in the 1996 Draft. Last season, as a member of the Kingston Frontenacs of the OHL, Bradley netted 83 points and finished among the top 20 scorers in the OHL.

Owen Nolan continues to shine for the Sharks after arriving three seasons ago from the Colorado Avalanche.

Still only 21 years old, Jeff Friesen tied the franchise record for the Sharks with 31 goals in the 1997-98 season.

Killer sharks

San Jose joined the NHL for the 1991-92 season, 17 months after the league granted permission to George and Gordon Gund to sell the Minnesota North Stars in return for the rights to an expansion team in San Jose.

A first order of business was to come up with a suitable nickname for the new club that would appeal to the fans. A competition was held and the Sharks emerged as the favorite.

The nickname is fitting for a franchise that has frequently struck without warning and shattered the Stanley Cup aspirations of the old guard. Ask the Detroit Red Wings, a strong Cup contender in 1993-94 who were ripped apart by the Sharks in the first round, losing in an emotion-charged seventh game. San Jose was in only its third season at the time, and had managed only 11 victories in an 84-game schedule the previous year.

The Sharks, whose team colors of Pacific teal, gray, black and white were an instant merchandising hit with the fans, pulled another major surprise in 1994-95, eliminating the second-seeded Calgary Flames in seven games in the opening round of the Western Conference playoffs.

ST. LOUIS BLUES

Buoyed by their awesome defense, the Blues had a superb season that almost brought them the Stanley Cup.

The St. Louis Blues of 1997-98 were good, very good. But, ultimately, they were just not good enough to get their hands on the Stanley Cup. They tied for the fourth-most points (98) in the league during the regular season, and were the only team to record a sweep (of the Los Angeles Kings) in the first round of the playoffs. However, when the Blues met their playoff Nemesis, the Detroit Red Wings, they once again went home without the cup.

Joel Quenneville did an excellent job in his first full year behind the bench. He had plenty of proven veterans in his arsenal — Brett Hull, Al MacInnis, Pierre Turgeon, Geoff Courtnall, Steve Duchesne and Grant Fuhr. Of those, Hull, Turgeon, Courtnall, Pavol Demitra and Jim Campbell all had at least 20 goals for the highest-scoring team in the league.

Young captain Chris Pronger was one of the Blues' star players in the 1997-98 season as he thrived in defense.

Brilliant blueliner

While the offensive stars were impressive, perhaps the team's best two players were on defense — MacInnis and young captain Chris Pronger. MacInnis was his usual hard-shooting self, while Pronger matured into a Norris Trophy finalist. The big, physical blueliner was a factor all over the ice.

Another bright spot was the emergence of Jamie McLennan as a backup to Fuhr. After beating disease and long odds to even make it to the NHL, McLennan posted an impressive 16-8-2 record with a low 2.17 goals-against average.

MacInnis was one of the cadre of star players for the Blues who was eligible for free agency after the season. His value was such that he was the first of that group management got to sign after the season. His new contract means that MacInnis will likely retire as a Blue. However, St. Louis did lose two of its key men when Duchesne went to the Los Angeles Kings and — after 10 glorious seasons — Hull signed for the Dallas Stars.

Sentimental favorites

In their early years, the Blues, a product of the NHL's 1967 expansion, provided every hockey fan with a trip down memory lane, drafting or signing many of the heroes of their youth—Glenn Hall and Jacques Plante in goal, Doug Harvey, Al Arbour and Jean-Guy Talbot on defense, center Phil Goyette and diminutive forward Camille Henry. The first year, the Blues even managed to coax the former Montreal Canadiens great Dickie Moore and his aching knees out of retirement.

Teaming up with young snipers such as Red Berenson, Gary Sabourin and Frank St. Marseille, the old-timers were sprightly enough to get the Blues into the Stanley Cup final in each of the club's first three seasons, winning the West Division regular-season title in two. They were sentimental favorites in each of the Stanley Cup finals but, despite a gritty effort, they were swept two straight years by Montreal and by Boston in 1969-70. Scotty Bowman, launching a Hall-of-Fame coaching career, was behind the Blues' bench for the latter two seasons.

The Blues haven't returned to the Stanley Cup final since those halcyon days, despite a number of talented performers passing through their ranks. Brett Hull, acquired in a 1988 trade, emerged from virtual obscurity to become the Blues' career goal-scoring leader, including 86 goals in 1990-91, a single-season output topped only by the great Wayne Gretzky.

The latter became Hull's teammate for the last few weeks of the 1995-96 season, after the Blues obtained his services in an unsuccessful bid to reach the Stanley Cup final.

Pierre Turgeon was once again in superlative form for the Blues scoring 20-plus goals for the highest-scoring team in the league.

★ ROLL OF HONOR ★

Conference/Division	**Western/Central**
First season	**1967-68**
Honor roll	**Made Stanley Cup final first three years in NHL**
Home rink/Capacity	**Kiel Center/19,260**
Stanley Cups	**0**

Playing Record

	W	L	T	Pts
Regular Season	1034	1040	366	2434
Playoffs	111	135		

⭐ ROLL OF HONOR ⭐

Conference/Division	**Eastern/Southeast**
First season	**1992-93**
Honor roll	**NHL single-game attendance record: 27,227 (1993)**
Home rink/Capacity	**Ice Palace/19,500**
Stanley Cups	**0**

Playing Record

	W	L	T	Pts
Regular Season	157	252	53	367
Playoffs	2	4		

It was a dark season for the Lightning with off-ice problems allied to poor on-ice performances.

Seemingly everything that could have gone wrong for the Tampa Bay Lightning in 1997-98 did go wrong. The ownership situation was a mess much of the year and the product on the ice was just as bad. The Lightning finished with the worst record in the league at 17-55-10 for 44 points, 19 worse than the Florida Panthers, who had the second-worst total.

New ownership was finally found after the season ended, and GM Phil Esposito was busy trying to fix what went wrong on the ice. Before the expansion draft he made trades to acquire goalie Bill Ranford, a former playoff MVP, and crafty center Craig Janney.

The Lightning scored the fewest goals in the league, 41 fewer than Chicago, which was the second-lowest and gave an indication of just how hard the Lightning found it to come by goals in the season. Their 151 goals made them the fourth-lowest scoring team of the modern era since 1949-50. Tampa also became the first team since 1955-56 to not have a 20-goal scorer. The leader in points, Paul Ysebaert (40 points), did so with the lowest total for a team leader since 1955-56. Not only didn't Tampa score, it was the second worst in the league in goals allowed. Daren Puppa was able to play just 26 games because of a back problem. On top of everything else, cancer struck a trio of the Lightning family. Forward John Cullen missed the season and is now attempting a comeback from non-Hodgkins lymphoma. Coach Jacques Demers' wife Debbie and scout Peter Mahovolich were also diagnosed with cancer. With all that went wrong in 1997-98 for the Lightning, there is reason to believe that things can only get better.

Big box office

While the Lightning's six seasons have produced ups and downs in the standings, the team was a record-setter at the box office. Because it moved in its second season into the ThunderDome, with the largest seating capacity in the league, the team drew more than 23,000 fans several times, including an NHL record 27,227 for its 1993-94 home opener against state-rival Florida Panthers.

The Lightning left the Dome after the 1995-96 season, and now frequently play in front of a capacity crowd at the 19,500-seat Ice Palace in downtown Tampa. But after the trauma of last season, the Lightning were forced to slash their season ticket prices at the start of the 1997-98 season in a bid to ensure the fans don't desert.

One player who didn't move to the new building was goaltender Manon Rheaume. But she remains a part of the club's early history, as the first woman to play one of the four professional major sports in North America. Rheaume made one appearance in an exhibition game, making seven saves in a 20-minute period before joining a Tampa Bay minor league affiliate.

Tampa's Paul Ysebaert notched up 40 points in the 1997-98 season — the lowest total for a team leader since 1955-56.

Lightning goaltender Mark Fitzpatrick is one of many Tampa players who will be hoping for better things in 1998-99.

Esposito hasn't been idle as an executive. He grabbed Gratton and defensemen Roman Hamrlik and Mike McBain in the entry draft, signed left-winger Rob Zamuner as a free agent and acquired serviceable veterans Jeff Norton, Jamie Huscroft and goaltender Rick Tabaracci to bolster the team's defense.

Lecavalier comes to Lightning

Morale in the Lightning camp was boosted over the summer months with the arrival of several new faces at the Ice Palace. Center Vincent Lecavalier was made the top overall pick in the NHL draft at Buffalo and arrives with a big reputation. The 18-year-old has drawn comparisons with Mario Lemieux and, according to the National Hockey League's Central Scouting Bureau, was the top-rated skater available. Lecavalier was Rookie of the Year in major junior hockey in 1997 collecting 103 points.

Coach Mike Murphy paid the price for a poor season as the Maple Leafs missed the postseason for the second year in a row.

The Leafs finished closer to last place in the Western Conference in 1997-98 than they did to the eighth playoff seed. Toronto's 69 points was just five better than the Western Conference cellar-dwelling Vancouver Canucks, and nine points out of the last playoff spot occupied by the San Jose Sharks.

Coach Mike Murphy paid the price for that. Eventually. Murphy was finally relieved of his coaching duties two months after the Leafs completed their disappointing season. Although Toronto did improve by one point in the first year under the direction of president/GM and Hall of Fame goaltender Ken Dryden, the Leafs missed the postseason for the second year in a row with Murphy as coach. It wasn't what the fans wanted, and it wasn't what Dryden wanted either. As a player he was on six Stanley Cup winners with Montreal and Dryden's mandate when he stepped into the president's hotseat was to "bring a Stanley Cup to Toronto".

Of course, in his defence, Murphy wasn't exactly provided with a roster loaded with superstars. With 194 goals, third-fewest in the league, this was the first Leafs team in 34 years to score fewer than 200 goals.

In with the new

Captain Mats Sundin, for so long the linchpin of the Leafs line-up, had 74 points, tied for 14th in the league, to become the first Leaf since Darryl Sittler to lead the club in scoring in four consecutive years. He was helped in the offense department by rookie Mike Johnson, who was never drafted by an NHL team, but tied for the NHL rookie lead with 47 points (15 goals and 32 assists). The only 20-goals scorer besides Sundin was Derek King.

Murphy's replacement behind the bench is his mentor, former Canucks GM and sometimes coach Pat Quinn. Quinn will guide the Leafs into two new homes in 1998-99: the Eastern Conference and the Air Canada Centre. Toronto gets its wish to move to the Eastern Conference, which will restore its natural rivalry with the Montreal Canadiens and its regional rivalry with the Ottawa Senators and Buffalo Sabres. Those teams and the Boston Bruins will form the revamped Northeast Division.

As for the Air Canada Centre, the Leaf's new arena is scheduled to open in February, meaning the last of the great old barns — Maple Leaf Gardens — will be vacated. Doubtless, the Leafs will be hoping their ills of the past few years will be left behind, too.

Colorful heroes

The Leafs, who have won 13 Stanley Cups—second to the 24 hoisted by Montreal—are steeped in history, with colorful personnel such as (Happy) Day; (King) Clancy; (Turk) Broda;

Mike Johnson (left) tied for the NHL rookie lead with 47 points and was a great support in offense to captain Mats Sundin.

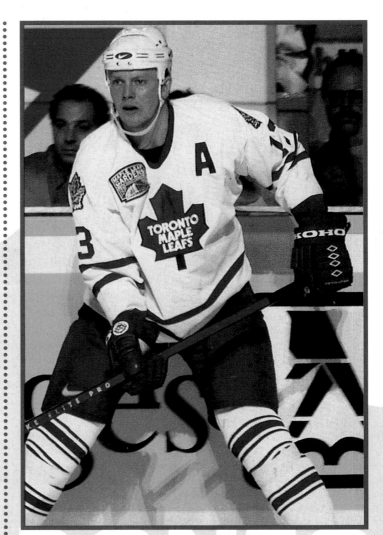

Luxury Swede: Mats Sundin's size, speed and scoring prowess have made him a prized commodity in the NHL.

(Busher) Jackson; (Teeder) Kennedy; (Punch) Imlach; and 'The Big M' among those who proudly wore the Maple Leaf, emblematic of the franchise that joined the NHL in 1927.

The Leafs' most satisfying Cup was the one in 1942, when they became the only NHL club to overcome a 3-0 deficit in games in a Stanley Cup final, against Detroit. They were the first team to win three straight Cups, between 1947-49, and again won three consecutive times 1962-64; but the 1967 Cup triumph was their last.

The Cup-less interval has had great performers, notably Darryl Sittler, defenseman Borje Salming, and forward Wendel Clark.

It was Sittler who on February 7, 1976, scored six goals and added four assists in Toronto's 11-4 rout of Boston. Sittler's ten points are still a single-game NHL record.

VANCOUVER CANUCKS

Mark Messier has been considered the best leader in hockey, but his highly touted arrival in 1997-98 couldn't lead the Vancouver Canucks to respectability. Messier did not play to his usual high standards, but very few Vancouver players did as the team finished with the worst record in the Western Conference, collecting a paltry 64 points in the process.

Among the high-profile Canucks suffering from a downturn in form were goaltender Kirk McLean, center Trevor Linden and winger Alexander Mogilny. Of that trio, only Mogilny was not dealt during a turbulent season that saw second-year coach Tom Renney axed in favour of Mike Keenan.

Even one player who did have an outstanding season, Pavel Bure, who rediscovered his scoring touch with a run of good health, requested a trade. Bure's 51 goals were tied for third-most in the league (one less than Peter Bondra and Teemu Selanne and even with John LeClair), and he also paced the goal-scoring rate in the Olympics, netting a tournament-high nine goals for Russia in earning a silver medal.

Missed playoffs

There were no medals being handed out in Vancouver, however, as they missed the playoffs for the second straight year. The Canucks' 25-43-14 record included franchise records for home losses (22), consecutive losses (10), and 224 was their fewest full-season goal total since the 1970s. Vancouver also was last in team defense.

One of the most pressing needs during the off-season was to get a No.1 goalie. The team has entrusted such personnel issues to its new head of hockey operations, Brian Burke, who returns to team management after overseeing the NHL's hockey operations. One luxury Burke has is one of the best young defensemen in the NHL in Mattias Ohlund. The native of Sweden was runner-up for the Calder Trophy as the league's top rookie.

Burly original

One of the men who would have felt the pangs of frustration more than most was franchise torch-bearer Pat Quinn — an original Canuck, a burly defenseman selected in the 1970 expansion draft, when Vancouver, a new entry that year along with Buffalo, started to stock its franchise. As a player, Quinn left after two seasons, but he returned as general manager in 1987 and later added coaching duties. Once Quinn returned behind the bench he became the most successful skipper in team history, fashioning a .554 winning percentage from to 1992 to '95. But he has now left the team and is head coach in Toronto.

After winning a division title in 1992-93, Vancouver advanced to the Stanley Cup final for only the second time in its history the following year. The Canucks spent many of their early years in the shadow of the Sabres, their expansion cousin who, on the spin of a wheel, got the first choice in the NHL entry, and selected center Gilbert Perreault. That left Vancouver with defenseman

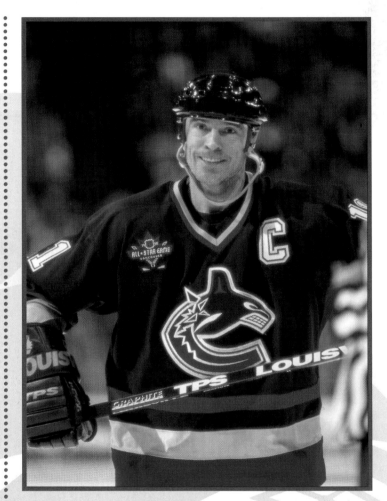

Mark Messier arrived in Vancouver carrying the
burden of expectation, but he failed to live up to his
normally sky high standards.

Dale Tallon, who was not quite the impact player Perreault was. But Vancouver, with Andre Boudrias leading the team in scoring for the second straight year, won its first Smythe Division title in 1974-75, the same year Buffalo was first in the Adams Division.

The signature phrase of Frank Griffiths, the patriarch of the family who formed the Canucks and were its long-time owners, was "2 points", the number awarded to a team for each victory. The two points were easier to come by once Quinn arrived as GM in 1987.

He engineered an aggressive rebuilding plan, starting with the selection of Linden in the 1988 entry draft and adding another cornerstone—the Soviet League star Bure—in the 1989 draft.

Defenseman Matthias Ohlund won a host of admirers last season as he finished runner-up for the Calder Trophy.

★ ROLL OF HONOR ★

Conference/Division	**Western/Northwest**
First season	**1970-71**
Honor roll	**Reached Stanley Cup final, 1981, 1994**
Home rink/Capacity	**General Motors Place/18,422**
Stanley Cups	**0**

Playing Record

	W	L	T	Pts
Regular Season	805	1086	323	1933
Playoffs	54	70		

WASHINGTON CAPITALS

So close to winning their first Stanley Cup, the Caps can be proud of their form in the 1997-98 season.

There was only one way the 1997-98 season could have been better for the Washington Capitals, and that's if the team could have found a way to win four more games. The Caps had their most successful season yet, advancing to the Stanley Cup Finals for the first time in their history. Unfortunately, Finals-savvy Detroit swept Washington away in four straight.

Many Cap fans will be playing the "what if" game for a long time to come, as in what if playoff-tested forward Esa Tikkanen hadn't missed a wide open net that would have given Washington a two-goal lead with time running out in game 2 of the Finals. The Caps might have won that game rather than losing it to the Red Wings in overtime, and the tenor of the series might have changed.

Godzilla

That is just conjecture. What is indisputable is the emergence of Olaf Kolzig, who took full advantage of an injury to Bill Ranford to move from career backup to the No. 1 goalie post. The big netminder entered into the elite classification for netminders and set several team records, including save percentage (.920). 'Godzilla' came out on the winning end of a duel with Sabres superstar Dominik Hasek in the conference finals, backstopping three overtime winners.

While Kolzig was a pleasant surprise, Peter Bondra kept up his usual pace on the wing. The sniper fired in a league-high 52 goals (tied with Teemu Selanne). Bondra has led the league in goals twice in the last four years. Also impressive was the Caps' team discipline and penalty killing. Washington took the third-fewest penalty minutes per game and led the league in penalty killing at nearly 90 percent efficiency.

This was a veteran team of thirtysomethings that peaked in the playoffs. Joe Juneau was especially impressive, netting a team-high seven postseason goals. He tied playmaking center Adam Oates with a team-high 16 playoff points in an excellent season's display.

Right from the start of its NHL existence, the only way was up for the Capitals. It could not have gotten any lower for a team that joined the NHL as an expansion franchise in 1974-75 and proceeded to set all kinds of modern-day league records for futility. Most of the records are still in the book, more than two decades later.

But that first year? "It was demoralizing and depressing, but you tried not to have a defeatist attitude," remembers Doug Mohns, an NHL veteran. The 1974-75 Capitals established a record for the fewest points—21- in a 70-game season. Their .131 winning percentage remains the lowest in NHL history. They managed only one victory on the road. In one stretch they lost 17 games in a row, still a record. They went through three coaches, allowed an all-time record 446 goals and one of its goaltenders—Michel Belhumeur (which translated from French means good humor) appeared in 35 games and was the winning goaltender in none.

The emergence of Olaf Kolzig as the No. 1 netminder was a big plus for the Washington Capitals last season.

Out of the pit

But climb the Capitals did—incrementally at first as Guy Charron arrived as a bonafide scorer and, finally, beyond the .500 mark and into the playoffs for the first time in 1982-83. That coincided with the arrival of the inspirational David Poile. Under Poile the Capitals had only two seasons under .500, and captured one Patrick Division title, in 1988-89.

Key draft picks such as sparkplugs Mike Gartner, Bobby Carpenter and Ryan Walter joined with defensemen Scott Stevens, Larry Murphy and Rod Langway—the latter pair coming after big trades with Los Angeles and Montreal—to continue Washington's rise from rags to respectability in the competitive cauldron of the NHL.

Peter Bondra was in typically dynamic form in 1997-98 firing in a league-high 52 goals.

★ ROLL OF HONOR ★

Conference/Division	**Eastern/Southeast**
First season	**1974-75**
Honor roll	**Lost out to Detroit Red Wings in the 1998 Stanley Cup Final.**
Home rink/Capacity	**MCI Arena/20,500**
Stanley Cups	**0**

Playing Record

	W	L	T	Pts
Regular Season	797	859	246	1840
Playoffs	64	73		

NHL EXPANSION

Nashville is best known as the country music capital. But starting this season, it will be known for pucks as well.

The Nashville Predators start play this season in the Volunteer state, far from the hockey mainstream of Canada and the northern USA. The Predators are the first of four new expansion teams to enter the league by the 2000-01 season. Next season, the Atlanta Thrashers join the fray. The year after that the NHL welcomes the Columbus (Ohio) Blue Jackets and the Minnesota Wild.

Predators GM David Poile and his staff had the task of building most of a team from scratch over a 48-hour period in late June. That's when the NHL held an Expansion Draft to help stock the new franchise. Nashville selected a player from each of the 26 existing clubs, which got to protect a certain number of their players. A day later was the NHL Entry draft of 18-year-old prospects. That two-day period went a long way to determining the Predators' future.

First up for Dunham

The cornerstone of any team is goaltending, and the Predators gave Mike Dunham the first shot at being the No.1 goalie. Dunham was the only player on hand for the expansion draft. "I'm excited to get this opportunity," said Dunham. "I've just been waiting for this opportunity. I look at this as another step."

Another step for the Predators was taken the next day at the Entry Draft, when the team traded up a spot to take speedy forward David Legwand at No.2 overall. Legwand is a potential superstar down the road, and for this new market it doesn't hurt that he's American. A Detroit-area native, Legwand will likely get every chance to make the team as an 18-year-old.

A former Detroit Red Wing, Doug Brown was among the highest-profile players selected in the expansion draft. It appeared after the Expansion Draft that the Predators had every intention of keeping the veteran forward who scored two goals in the Wings' clinching Game 4 win in the Stanley Cup Finals but, as things turned out, he was traded back to Detroit in July.

Free agents

The same could not be said of goalie Mike Richter and defenseman Uwe Krupp, both unrestricted free agents whom Nashville didn't intend to sign. Instead, the team selected the players because it will receive future compensatory draft picks when other teams sign them up. "This Expansion Draft has provided us with 26 opportunities to help shape our franchise," said Poile. "We've selected a number of players who will be important parts of the 1998-99 inaugural Predators' team, while other selections will enable us to acquire additional draft picks or players."

Besides Brown, other players from the Expansion Draft include center Greg Johnson (Chicago) and defenseman John Slaney (Phoenix) and J.J. Daigneault (New York Islanders).

Right wing Marian Cisar was the first player to be acquired by the Predators when he arrived from Los Angeles Kings.

ATLANTA	MINNEAPOLIS	COLUMBUS
Owned by the Turner Broadcasting Company, Atlanta have a new 20,000 seat arena scheduled to open in fall 1999. Nicknamed the Thrashers, Atlanta has a population of 4.3 million and their first season will be 1999-2000. The NHL expansion Flames played in Atlanta from 1972 to 1980.	In charge of Minneapolis/St. Paul is Robert O. Naegele, Jnr. Their new arena is due to open in 2000, and will play as the Minneapolis Wild. Joining a year after the Atlanta Thrashers, Minneapolis has a population of 3.8 million. The Expansion North Stars operated from 1967 to 1994.	John H. McConnell owns Columbus, who have a new 18, 500 seat arena scheduled to open in 2000. Nicknamed the Columbus (Ohio) Blue Jackets, they have the smallest population of the four new expansion franchises with just 1.9 million. Their first season will be 2000-01.

HOCKEY HEROES

I t's a truism in professional team sports that collective play wins championships. It's no less true that fans come out to watch the stars of the game, to marvel at their virtuosity, as much as to root for a winner.

Across its 79-year history the National Hockey League has produced and continues to produce as richly varied a cast of sporting legends as any professional league in the world.

Each generation of fans, it turns out, has its Golden Age; each new wave of player talent leaves behind indelible memories of sporting brilliance that resonate forever in the collective imagination.

Some of the memories are passed down, like the legend of One-Eyed Frank McGee, who once scored 14 goals—eight of them consecutively—in a Stanley Cup game, a 23-2 drubbing of Dawson City by the Ottawa Silver Seven. McGee's nickname was no joke—he lost an eye when he was struck there by the butt end of a hockey stick.

Keen hockey fans, even the young ones, know of Frank Nighbor, who perfected the poke check, of Fred (Cyclone) Taylor, said to have scored a key Stanley Cup goal while skating full speed backwards, of Joe Malone, who once scored 44 goals in a 20-game season.

They certainly know the story of Lester Patrick, the coach of the New York Rangers, who in a 1928 Stanley Cup game, shed his jacket, shirt and tie and put on the goalie pads, and replaced the injured Lorne Chabot. The Rangers won the game and, later, the Cup.

Patrick was surely one of many stars of his era. The NHL of the 1920s and 1930s boasted names like Syl Apps, Ace Bailey, King Clancy, Clint Benedict, the first goalie to wear a mask, and Howie Morenz, known as the Stratford Streak, and the most electrifying player of his time.

What's my line?

The 1930s, 1940s and 1950s were famous for the marvelous forward lines that made hockey magic. The Toronto Maple Leafs had the Kid Line, with Gentleman Joe Primeau flanked by Harvey (Busher) Jackson and Charlie Conacher. The Boston Bruins featured the Kraut Line—Milt Schmidt, Bobby Bauer and Woody Dumart.

Ice Hard: It is hard to find a weakness in the Colorado Avalanche lineup, which combines speed, skill, size and toughness right through the lineup.

The Montreal Canadiens delivered the Punch Line, with 'Elegant' Elmer Lach centering for Maurice (Rocket) Richard and Hector (Toe) Blake, The Old Lamplighter. Richard was the first to score 50 goals in 50 games, the first to reach 500 goals.

And Detroit, the automobile center of America, assembled the Production Line, with Sid Abel centering for Gordie Howe and Terrible Ted Lindsay, as tough and mean a player as he was skilled.

Stars like Rocket Richard, Henri (Pocket Rocket) Richard, Jean Beliveau, Jacques Plante, Doug Harvey, Dickie Moore and Bernard (Boom Boom) Geoffrion took the Montreal Canadiens to the Stanley Cup finals for ten straight years in the 1950s. They won six Cups, including a record five in a row.

In the early 1960s, goaltender Glenn Hall, defenseman Pierre Pilotte, and fowards Stan Mikita and Bobby Hull, The Golden Jet, made the Chicago Blackhawks a feared opponent.

Stars on ice

The Toronto Maple Leafs, blending the talents of aging stars such as Bob Baun, Tim Horton and Johnny Bower with the emerging brilliance of Frank (The Big M) Mahovlich and Davey Keon, won three straight Stanley Cups.

Sublime individual feats remained a constant as the NHL expanded, first from six to 12 teams in 1968, then to 14 and 18, on up to its current — with the arrival of the Nashville Predators for the 1998-99 season — 27-team membership.

Guy Lafleur's six straight 50-goal, 100-point seasons with the Montreal Canadiens in the 1970s; Mike Bossy saying he would match Richard's 50 goals in 50 games, then going out and doing it in 1981; Denis Potvin breaking the legendary Bobby Orr's goal-scoring and points records. The stars, indeed, keep on coming.

In the 1980s, sprightly Wayne Gretzky kept coming and coming, like a bad dream, his opponents thought. Here was Gretzky, scoring 92 goals, bagging 212 points, both records in 1982, winning the scoring championship by 65-point margin. There was Greztky, winning seven straight scoring titles, breaking the all-time scoring marks of Gordie Howe, leading the Edmonton Oilers to four Stanley Cups in five years.

And suddenly, The Great One had a rival — Mario Lemieux, The Magnificent One, who scored 85 goals and added 114 assists for 199 points in 1989.

As the NHL entered the 1990s, the league's galaxy of stars had become truly international, with names like Jaromir Jagr, Sergei Fedorov, Pavel Bure, Alexander Mogilny, Peter Forsberg and Teemu Selanne taking their place in the pantheon. As spectacular as the NHL's stars have been for 80 years, the best, it seems reasonable to suggest, is yet to come.

Jaunty Jaromir: Since the retirement of the incomparable Mario Lemieux, the Pittsburgh Penguins' Jaromir Jagr has shouldered a larger burden.

RAY BOURqUE

Bobby Orr was the ultimate Bruin of the late 1960s and 70s, and Ray Bourque has been Mr. Bruin in the 1980s and 90s. Like Orr, Bourque is a defenseman with sublime offensive skills, capable of changing the tempo of a game on his own. Like Orr, Bourque arrived in the NHL as an élite player who made an immediate impact.

ICE TALK

"THERE'S NO WAY I'LL LET PEOPLE DOWN BY NOT GIVING EVERYTHING I'VE GOT OR NOT SHOWING UP AND PLAYING HARD. I FEEL EVERYONE SHOULD FEEL THAT WAY. THAT'S JUST MY MAKEUP."

RAY BOURQUE

Bourque bounced back from the Bruins bad run in 1996-97 to get them back on track last season.

In 1995-96, on a Bruins team bothered by injuries to stars like Cam Neely and others, and struggling under a rookie coach, Bourque found himself speaking up in the dressing room more than he normally wants to. Fearful of hurting his teammates' feelings, he had to force himself to prod the Bruins to perform better.

"It's not something that was easy for me to do," he says. "I had to grow into that role off the ice. On the ice, it's (leading by example) always been easy."

The prodding obviously helped. In danger of missing the playoffs, the Bruins lost just six of their final 19 games to qualify for the Stanley Cup tournament for the 29th straight season.

Tough times

Bourque and the Bruins had a rougher go in 1996-97, though. After leading all defensemen in 1995-96 with 80 points, Bourque slipped to 50 points and the Bruins failed to make the playoffs for the first time in 30 seasons.

It was a rare absence from the Stanley Cup tournament for the classy defenseman, yet he was back in the groove in 1997-98 as the Bruins made amends for their bitterly disappointing showing the season before. They went from the worst record in the league to fifth seed in the Eastern Conference playoff. It's no coincidence that when Bourque is on fire, the Bruins are pretty hot, too.

In his rookie season, Bourque scored 17 goals and added 48 assists for 65 points, an NHL record (since broken) for points by a rookie defenseman. Not surprisingly, Bourque was named rookie-of-the-year in the NHL and was named a first-team NHL all-star, establishing a nearly annual NHL tradition. He has been the best defenseman of his era, winning the James Norris Trophy five times in his career.

Boston centerpiece

In an era of unprecedented player movement—Wayne Gretzky has played for four NHL teams—Bourque has been a fixture in Boston, where he has been the centerpiece player for 19 seasons. He's also been a workhorse on talent-thin Bruins teams that win through the brilliance of Bourque and a handful of others, and the relentless hard work of the supporting cast. None works harder than Bourque, though. He routinely plays 25-30 minutes a game.

Bourque has scored more than 20 goals in a season nine times, including a 31-goal performance in 1983-84, when he totaled 96 points, the most in his career. He also posted a plus-minus record that season of plus 51. That means Bourque was on the ice for 51 more goals by his own team at even strength than the Bruins' opponents scored, a barometer of his effectiveness at both ends of the ice.

A quiet leader who prefers to let his on-ice performance speak for itself, Bourque was named co-captain (with Rick Middleton) of the Bruins at the beginning of the 1985-86 season. He has been the lone captain there since 1988.

CAREER RECORD

Personal				
Birthplace/Date	**Montreal, Quebec/12-28-60**			
Height/Weight	**5-11-215**			

Awards				
Calder Memorial Trophy	**1980**			
First All-Star Team	**1980, 1982, 1984-85, 1987-88, 1990-94, 1995-96**			
James Norris Memorial Trophy	**1987-88, 1990-91, 1994**			
King Clancy Memorial Trophy	**1992**			

NHL Career   **19 seasons Boston Bruins**

Playing Record

	Games	Goals	Assists	Points	PIM
Regular Season	1372	375	1036	1411	1033
Playoffs	168	35	116	151	137

Brodeur picked up the William Jennings Trophy for the lowest goals-against average.

Fate helped goaltender Martin Brodeur get a skate in the door as the No. 1 goaltender with the New Jersey Devils, but his stellar play and nothing but has kept him there.

It was two on the trot for the 26-year-old Brodeur when he scooped his second Jennings Trophy at the end of 1997-98.

The year before Brodeur emerged as one of the best young goalies in the National Hockey League, the Devils' goaltending combination consisted of Chris Terreri and Craig Billington, both solid veteran goaltenders.

But Billington was shipped to Ottawa in a trade that brought Peter Sidorkiewicz to New Jersey. Sidorkiewicz, it turned out, had not recovered from a severe shoulder separation and was not ready for the 1993-94 training camp. Enter Brodeur, a promising minor-league goalie at the time.

Brodeur's play was so good as a rookie that he eased Terreri out of the No. 1 job. Brodeur played in 47 games, posted a won-lost-tied record of 27-11-8 and a regular-season goals-against average of 2.40.

As impressive as his regular-season performance chart was, Brodeur was even more brilliant in the playoffs. He posted an 8-9 won-lost mark in the Stanley Cup tournament, with a sparkling goals-against average of 1.95 as he backstopped the Devils to the Eastern Conference Finals.

Devils' Cup

By this time, Brodeur had not only supplanted Terreri as the top goalie in the Devils organization, he had staked a claim as the best goaltender in the NHL—period.

Brodeur played 40 of the 48 games for New Jersey in the lockout-shortened 1994-95 season, going 19-11-6 with a 2.45 goals-against average in regular-season play.

His playoff performance was spookily brilliant. He played in all 20 of the Devils' playoff games, winning 16, three of them by shutout. All three shutouts came in the Devils' first-round victory over the Boston Bruins, and produced this unlikely linescore for Brodeur: a 4-1 won-lost record; an 0.97 GAA and a .962 save percentage.

The wonder is that the Bruins won a game at all, facing goaltending that stingy. Brodeur's brilliance carried the Devils' to their first-ever Stanley Cup victory, but it was winger Claude Lemieux who won the Conn Smythe Trophy as the top playoff performer, as he scored 13 goals in New Jersey's playoff run.

Rink rat

There was a certain resonance about Brodeur playing so well and winning a Stanley Cup on a team coached by Jacques Lemaire, a brilliant center with the great Montreal Canadiens teams of the 1960s and 70s. Lots of Canadian kids are rink rats, but Brodeur grew up hanging around the Montreal Forum, where his father, Denis, was the team photographer for the Canadiens. Brodeur had been just 14 when Devils teammates Stephane Richer and Claude Lemieux had helped the Canadiens win the Stanley Cup in 1986.

With 10 shutouts in the 1997-98 season, not to mention a goals against average of 1.89 (compared with 1.88 the previous year!), Brodeur collected the William Jennings Trophy for the second consecutive season. This time, though, Brodeur claimed the trophy outright as backup Mike Dunham had not made the required number of appearances. At this rate, the Quebec-born goaltender will have to have the trophy prised from his grasp.

CAREER RECORD

Personal

Birthplace/Date	Montreal, Quebec/ 5-6-72
Height/Weight	6-1/205

Awards

NHL All-Rookie Team	1994
Calder Memorial Trophy	1994
Jennings Trophy	1997, 1998
NHL Career	**5 seasons New Jersey Devils**

Playing Record

	Games	Wins	Losses	Ties	GAG
Regular Season	305	162	84	47	2.16
Playoffs	54	31	23	0	1.84

PAVEL BURE

The 'Russian Rocket' exploded into awesome life last season as he hit the ice running. Unfortunately his teammates couldn't keep up.

After Pavel Bure's first game with the Vancouver Canucks, the media nicknamed him the 'Russian Rocket' and his brilliant rookie season touched off Pavelmania among the long-suffering Canucks fans.

In Bure, the Canucks finally had landed a superstar to build a true contender around.

The 5-foot-10, 187-pound right winger certainly arrived in Vancouver with pedigree. He first dazzled North American hockey people at the World Junior Championships in Anchorage, Alaska in 1989-90. Playing on a line with Sergei Fedorov and Alexander Mogilny, Bure scored eight goals and added six assists for 14 points to help the USSR win the gold medal in that tournament. He was named the tournament's top forward.

The following year, he helped the Soviets win gold at the World Hockey Championships. He starred for both the junior and senior men's teams in 1990-91 also, helping the juniors win a silver medal and the senior men win the bronze.

Bure frenzy

The Canucks had drafted Bure in the sixth round of the 1989 entry draft, only to have then-NHL president John Ziegler rule him ineligible. The decision was reversed more than a year later, clearing the way for Bure to join the Canucks.

Three years after Bure was named rookie-of-the-year in the Soviet National League, he scored 34 goals for the Canucks and won the Calder Trophy as the top freshman in the NHL—and

CAREER RECORD

Personal

Birthplace/Date	Moscow, USSR/3-31-71
Height/Weight	5-10/187

Awards

Calder Memorial Trophy	1992
First All-Star Team	1994

NHL Career   7 seasons Vancouver Canucks

Playing Record

	Games	Goals	Assists	Points	PIM
Regular Season	428	254	226	478	328
Playoffs	60	34	32	66	72

created a frenzy among Vancouver hockey supporters.

In 1992-93, Bure scored 60 goals and added 50 assists for 110 points, becoming the first Canuck ever to score as many as 50 goals and reach 100 points in a season.

Bure snapped off another 60-goal season in 1993-94, slipping to 47 assists and 107 points. He then led all playoff goalscorers with 16, leading the Canucks to the Stanley Cup final, which they lost in a seven-game thriller to the New York Rangers.

Bure negotiated a rich new contract in the midst of the playoff run, which pushed some noses out of joint. Bure obviously had learned that leverage matters in the free enterprise system, another indicator that he was a quick study in adapting to North American life and the NHL.

Some thought the swift, creative Bure too slight to withstand the inevitable physical pounding NHL forwards are subjected to. Owing to his total commitment to his sport, Bure spent his first summers in North America adhering to a severe fitness regimen overseen by his father, Vladimir, a former swimmer and three-time Olympian for the Soviet Union.

Bure meets Boris

In the 1995-96 and 1996-97 seasons, Bure was affected by injuries that hampered his performances. After suffering a torn anterior cruciate ligament in his right knee three years ago, injuries forced him out of 19 games in 1996-97, when he scored 23 goals and added 32 assists for 55 points.

But Bure gritted his teeth at the start of the 1997-98 season determined to prove wrong those people who said he was past his best. His total of 90 points, including 51 goals, was his best return for the Canucks in four years. Bure also carried his goal-scoring touch to the 1998 Olympics where he netted a tournament-high nine goals as Russia picked up the silver medal.

To cap it all for Bure, President Boris Yeltsin presented him with the prestigious Order of Honor during a ceremony at The Kremlin shortly after the Olympics—an illustration of just how highly the Canucks' sharpshooter is regarded in his homeland.

Bure's 51 goals during the 1997-98 season were tied for third-most in the league, proof that he was back in gear.

Not everything went smoothly for the Russian in 1997-98, but he still emerged as a winner.

SERGEI FEDOROV

ICE TALK

"FEDOROV IS AS GOOD AS ANYBODY IN ANY ERA SKILLWISE. FEDOROV IS ONE OF A KIND."

AN NHL SCOUT

When Sergei Fedorov arrived in Detroit, the Red Wings already had a No. 1 center— veteran Steve Yzerman. So Fedorov, brilliantly talented offensively, was asked to handle a big part of the defensive load. That would seem a waste. Except Fedorov applied himself to the task and, in his second season in the NHL, he was named runner-up to Guy Carbonneau for the Frank J. Selke Trophy as the league's best defensive forward.

Two years later, in 1994, he won the trophy.

He also won the Hart Trophy that year as the league's most valuable player, was named to the first all-star team and won the Lester B. Pearson Award, voted on by his peers and awarded to the league's outstanding player.

It wouldn't be a stretch to suggest that not only is Fedorov the best all-around player in hockey, but everyone in hockey knows it.

Russian might

He came to the league with impeccable credentials. As a junior in Russia, he centered a line with wingers Pavel Bure and Alexander Mogilny—one of the most electrifying trios ever assembled.

Fedorov played four years with Central Red Army, and helped the Soviet National team win gold medals at the World Championships in 1989 and 1990.

With his speed, improvisational moves executed at full speed, and all-around game, Fedorov made an immediate impact on the NHL, leading all rookies in goals (31), assists (48) and points (79) in 1990-91. He finished runner-up to Ed Belfour in the voting for the Calder Trophy.

As exciting as his skills are, Fedorov always has understood that even star players perform best as part of an ensemble.

Luckily, his Detroit coach, Scotty Bowman, understands this also. It was Bowman who acquired veteran Russian Igor Larionov and assembled a five-man unit with Fedorov, Vyacheslav Kozlov, Vlyacheslav Fetisov and Vladimir Konstantinov.

The unit, used selectively by Bowman, a master strategist, performed brilliantly for the Red Wings in 1995-96. Fedorov, ever the team man, moved to right wing on the unit, ceding the center

Opponents rarely contain Detroit Red Wings star Sergei Fedorov, whom many consider the best all-around player in the NHL.

position on the line to Larionov, who centered the famous KLM (Vladimir Krutov, Larionov and Sergei Makarov) for the Soviet National team in the 1980s.

Like the five-man units in the Russian national teams, Detroit's unit stressed puck control and patience, preferring to circle back in the neutral zone, and to hold on to the puck in the offensive zone rather than try a low percentage play.

Russian light

Fedorov's spectacular play, sly sense of humor and good looks convinced Nike to make him their poster boy for their hockey equipment. He showcased Nike's new line of skates and is considered very worthy of attention by the newspapers.

The 1997-98 season threw up highs and lows for Fedorov. A free agent following Detroit's 1997 Stanley Cup victory, he sat out the first half of the year over terms and played his first hockey of the season for Russia at the Olympic Games in Nagano. Just after Fedorov had returned, with a silver medal, Carolina made a huge offer, which Detroit matched, so he returned to the Red Wings.

Fedorov made a slow start in his return to NHL action, but he re-discovered his touch during the Stanley Cup Finals, especially in Game 3, when Detroit downed the Washington Capitals 2-1.

CAREER RECORD

Personal

Birthplace/Date	Pskov, USSR/ 12-13-69
Height/Weight	6-1/200

Awards

All-Rookie Team	1991
First All-Star Team	1994
Frank J. SelkeTrophy	1994, 1996
Lester B. Pearson Award	1994
Hart Trophy	1994

NHL Career — 8 seasons Detroit Red Wings

Playing Record

	Games	Goals	Assists	Points	PIM
Regular season	527	248	361	609	371
Playoffs	110	37	80	117	81

Fleury has proved to the Flames that small is not only beautiful, but powerful too.

In the hyper-macho world of the NHL, size is said to matter above all. Theoren Fleury's entire career has been a refutation of that cliché. Not outlandishly larger than the average thoroughbred jockey, Fleury—swift, skilled, creative and combative—has been a star at every level of hockey. He has forced hockey people, who don't let go of their stereotypes easily, to see past his stature and recognize the dazzling things he can do with the gifts he possesses, to forget about the things he cannot do.

As a junior star with the Moose Jaw Warriors, Fleury was an offensive machine, racking up 472 points in four seasons. In his final year as a junior, he produced 160 points, including 68 goals—and 235 minutes in penalties in the rough and tumble Western Hockey League.

He was a member of Canada's National Junior Team in 1987 and 1988, when the team won a gold medal.

Rarely has a junior player achieved more than Fleury did. Yet he was taken 166th in the NHL Entry Draft in 1987, his low selection an obvious function of his size.

Playing big

He began his pro career in the minors playing for Calgary's Salt Lake City farm club, but by season's end that year—1988-89—he was playing for the NHL Flames in Calgary, helping them win their first Stanley Cup championship by beating the fabled Montreal Canadiens, and in the legendary Forum, to boot.

In his first full season with the Flames, he scored 31 goals, 30 being a benchmark of excellence.

The following season—1990-91—he bagged 51 goals, establishing himself as a star. He has delivered big scoring numbers every season he has played in the NHL. And playing on a team that has featured bigger, stronger players like Gary

Roberts, Brett Hull and Doug Gilmour, Fleury has led the Flames in scoring five of the last seven years.

Dream on

Fleury continues to shine on the international stage, as well, as he did while a junior. Twice (1990 and 1991) Fleury has played for Canada at the World Hockey Championship, helping them win a silver medal in 1991, and he was also a member of the 1998 Olympic "Dream Team" who competed in Nagano, Japan, in February. Unfortunately, on that occasion, things didn't go to plan and Canada failed to win even a bronze medal as they went down first to the eventual winners, the Czech Republic, and then Finland in the bronze medal game.

Nevertheless, for a guy considered too small early in his career, Fleury certainly has scaled impressive heights in hockey.

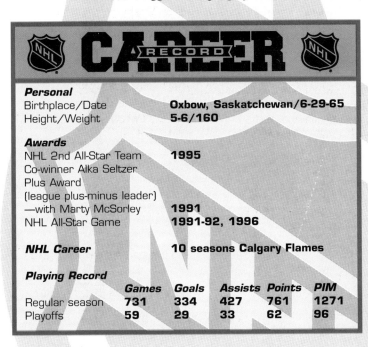

CAREER RECORD

Personal

Birthplace/Date	Oxbow, Saskatchewan/6-29-65
Height/Weight	5-6/160

Awards

NHL 2nd All-Star Team	1995
Co-winner Alka Seltzer Plus Award (league plus-minus leader) —with Marty McSorley	1991
NHL All-Star Game	1991-92, 1996

NHL Career — 10 seasons Calgary Flames

Playing Record

	Games	Goals	Assists	Points	PIM
Regular season	731	334	427	761	1271
Playoffs	59	29	33	62	96

Fleury played like a man possessed in the 1997-98 season racking up 78 points and sending out a message to one and all: "I'm back to my best".

PETER FORSBERG

Colorado Avalanche's fiery Peter Forsberg breaks the mould of the traditionally timid European player

The stereotype of the European player has been that of a player with great skill but no grit and determination. Colorado Avalanche center Peter Forsberg lays waste to that notion. He's got the skilled part — few players in the league can match him in that department — but he's also got a mean streak that seems hewn right out of the Canadian plains.

Forsberg is that rare combination of athlete — he is very creatively offensively, but he also has a defensive conscience. He skates back hard and is not afraid of blocking a shot. He's also an intelligent player, but he also likes to get in people's faces and stir up a bit of trouble.

No retreat

"I'll tell you what sticks out in my mind isn't so much his talent level, but his toughness," says Craig Billington, whose role as Colorado's backup goalie has given him the best seat in the house on many nights to watch the gifted Swede. "He's tough," continues Billington. "When you watch him play, he's gritty and tough and he doesn't back down; and he gives it back. You get a lot of people who are skilled in this game, but who perhaps don't have the grittiness."

New Jersey Devils goaltender Martin Brodeur, perennial winner of the Jennings Trophy for lowest goals-against average, has written of Forsberg: "To me, Forsberg is the most complete hockey player in the game today. There are so many ways he can hurt you — a clutch pass, a precise slap shot or wrist shot upstairs, he does it all!"

He may come from over the Atlantic Ocean, but only a madman would tell Forsberg he didn't have the necessary grit to survive in the cauldron of the NHL.

Peer respect

Many hockey people agree with Brodeur's assessment. In a Toronto Sun poll of hockey experts last year, Forsberg was deemed top performer in hockey. Said an ESPN analyst, one of the panelists for the poll: "Forsberg can do so many things. But what impresses me most is the way his peers talk about him. They just shake their heads in awe at Forsberg's play, game in and game out."

Forsberg is not only a great player, he is a winner — and passionate about it. He hates losing, he can't stand it. In 1994, he scored the gold medal-winning goal for Sweden in the Olympic final versus Canada. It was in a shootout, and the unorthodox deke he used has been immortalized on a Swedish Postage stamp. Two years later, he helped lead the former Quebec Nordiques to the Stanley Cup in their first season as the Colorado Avalanche.

As for individual honors, Forsberg was the Calder Trophy winner as rookie of the year in 1995 and this past season he was named as the First All-Star center. He combines with fellow center Joe Sakic to give the Avs an unbeatable one-two combination in the middle.

Forsberg's GM, Pierre Lacroix, has said: "He could win the scoring championship and at the same time win the Selke award (as best defensive forward)." Don't be surprised if the Swede one day pulls off that feat.

CAREER RECORD

Personal

Birthplace/Date	Ornskoldsvik, Sweden/7-20-73
Height/Weight	6-0/190

Awards

Calder Trophy	1995
All-Rookie Team	1995
First All-Star team	1998

NHL Career

1 season Quebec Nordiques
3 seasons Colorado Avalanche

Playing Record

	Games	Goals	Assists	Points	PIM
Regular season	266	98	245	343	230
Playoffs	49	23	32	55	44

He just keeps on going
WAYNE GRETZKY

The Great One once again gave his all despite playing for a Rangers' side struggling to find some form.

Perhaps it was inevitable that Wayne Gretzky would wind up, somehow, in New York City. The question a lot of observers had was, how much of his incomparable act remained intact. Plenty, it turned out, to the surprise of more than a few.

After all, Gretzky's quarter-season stay in St. Louis at the end of 1995-96 had been nothing but the Blues. The supporting cast was paper thin and the specter of Gretzky and Brett Hull combining to lead the Blues on a lengthy playoff run didn't materialize.

Joining the New York Rangers, rejoining old Edmonton Oilers teammate Mark Messier, turned out to be a far better fit. As young players, Gretzky and Messier had been the linchpins of the Oilers' Stanley Cup dynasty in the 1980s.

With a stronger ensemble cast around him in New York, Gretzky was able to go about his business.

Throughout his career, Gretzky has managed to be at once brilliant and unobtrusive, a rare combination.

Studied foresight

A deceptively swift skater, preternaturally able to anticipate the game's patterns, Gretzky rarely absorbs punishing body checks. And phenomenal energy enables him to play at a high level even in a game's late stages.

He shares with Bobby Orr the gift of redefining the game, making it his own. One skill he brought to the NHL involved setting up behind the opposition's net, where he could see the entire pattern of play in the attacking zone and feed passes to onrushing teammates. His Oilers teammates called this space Gretzky's 'launching pad.'

He led them to four Stanley Cups in five years. The talent-rich Oilers sandwiched a pair of Cups around a surprise cup victory by the Montreal Canadiens in 1986.

"Nine out of ten people think what I do is instinct," Gretzky once said. "It isn't. Nobody would ever say a doctor had learned his profession by instinct; yet in my own way I've spent almost as much time studying hockey as a med student puts in studying medicine."

Gretzky became a hockey demigod in Edmonton. When Oilers owner Peter Pocklington, viewing him merely as a depreciating asset, traded Gretzky to the Los Angeles Kings in 1989, an entire country felt betrayed.

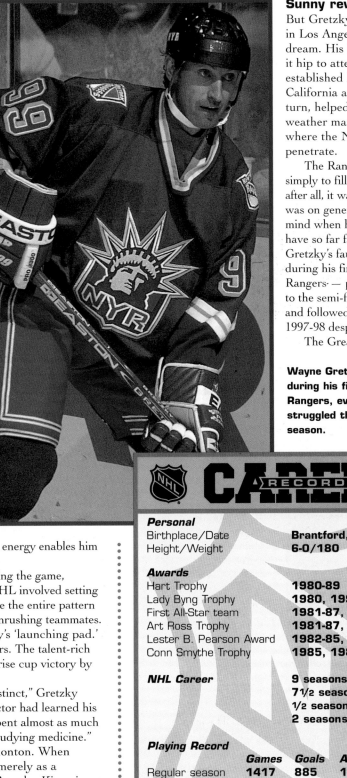

Sunny revival

But Gretzky became something greater in Los Angeles. He was a marketer's dream. His high-profile presence made it hip to attend Kings games and re-established hockey in Southern California as a trendy pastime. That, in turn, helped sell the game to warm-weather markets such as South Florida, where the NHL had long yearned to penetrate.

The Rangers didn't sign Gretzky simply to fill Madison Square Garden — after all, it was already full. A Stanley Cup was on general manager Neil Smith's mind when he signed Gretzky. That they have so far fallen short certainly isn't Gretzky's fault. He racked up 97 points during his first regular season with the Rangers — plus 10 goals as he led them to the semi-final of the Stanley Cup — and followed that up with 90 more in 1997-98 despite his teammates' poor form.

The Great One is a great one still.

Wayne Gretzky has been in great form during his first two seasons with the Rangers, even though the side struggled throughout the 1997-98 season.

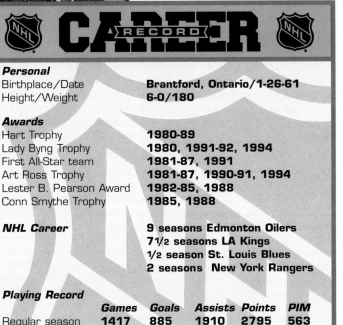

CAREER RECORD

Personal

Birthplace/Date	Brantford, Ontario/1-26-61
Height/Weight	6-0/180

Awards

Hart Trophy	1980-89
Lady Byng Trophy	1980, 1991-92, 1994
First All-Star team	1981-87, 1991
Art Ross Trophy	1981-87, 1990-91, 1994
Lester B. Pearson Award	1982-85, 1988
Conn Smythe Trophy	1985, 1988

NHL Career

9 seasons Edmonton Oilers
7½ seasons LA Kings
½ season St. Louis Blues
2 seasons New York Rangers

Playing Record

	Games	Goals	Assists	Points	PIM
Regular season	1417	885	1910	2795	563
Playoffs	208	122	260	392	66

Czech superstar Hasek is probably the best player around at the moment.

DoMINIK HASEK

Wayne Gretzky, recognized as the best player of all time in a comprehensive poll of hockey experts by *The Hockey News,* says this about Buffalo Sabres goaltender Dominik Hasek: "I think right now, he is the best player in the game. He's just at a level that nobody else is at right now. He's simply sensational."

Hasek joined a select band in 1998 when he won his second straight Hart Trophy as league MVP. Don't bet against a third!

That's a pretty ringing endorsement, considering the source. Hasek has earned such an accolade, and the awards are stacking up as proof. In 1997, he became the first goalie in 35 years to win the Hart Trophy as league MVP. He repeated his 'Hart' trick in 1998, joining immortals Wayne Gretzky, Guy Lafleur, Bobby Clarke, Bobby Orr, Stan Mikita, Bobby Hull, Gordie Howe, Eddie Shore and Howie Morenz as the only players to win consecutive Hart trophies. He is the only netminder to win the award more than once

Vezina monopoly

As for the award designed for goaltenders, the Vezina Trophy, Hasek has won that four of the last five years. In 1997-98, Hasek endured early boos from the home crowd to post an historic season. Popular Sabres coach Ted Nolan was not brought back for the season after winning the 1997 Jack Adams Award as

coach of the year. It was no secret that Hasek was not a Nolan supporter, and fans in Buffalo made Hasek into one of the villians at the start of the year. He heard boos in Marine Midland Arena and that admittedly affected his play.

Hasek was not the 'Dominator' until December, when he recorded six shutouts and got himself back on track. He eventually went on to lead the league in save percentage (.932) for the fifth straight season and his 13 shutouts were the most since Tony Esposito's 15 in 1970. Along the way Hasek took the time to lead his underdog Czech Republic to a gold medal in the 1998 Winter Olympics in Nagano, Japan, in dramatic fashion. He stoned Canada in a shootout in the semi-finals, stopping all five attempts by Canadian players in the shootout while the Czechs scored once, then shut out Russia in the gold-medal game to win 1-0.

The acrobat

In the 1998 NHL playoffs, Hasek led the Sabres further than they'd been in a long time. Buffalo advanced to the conference final for the first time since 1980. Hasek's strong play erased the unpleasant lingering images of the 1997 postseason, when he got injured and then, amid a barrage of unwanted publicity, got involved in a physical confrontation with a Buffalo sportswriter that did no one much good.

When it comes to style, there is none like Hasek. He flops, he does splits, he makes sprawling saves that no one expects. One of his most famous moves is to drop his stick and grab the puck with his blocker hand — unorthodox to say the least.

One NHL scout says: "He has one of the most unorthodox styles I think I've ever seen in a goalie, but he gets the job done. Just when you think you've beaten him, he comes up with an amazing save. I have seen him stop shots with his blocker, glove, mask and legs, among other parts of his body. He does it standing up, sitting down, laying down on his back and stomach. The man is amazing. I've never seen anyone like him in goal."

NHL CAREER RECORD

Personal	
Birthplace/Date	**Pardubice, Czech/1-29-65**
Height/Weight	**5-11/168**

Awards	
NHL First All-Star Team	**1994, 95, 97, 98**
Vezina Trophy	**1994, 95, 97, 98**
Hart Trophy	**1997, 98**
Jennings Trophy	**1994**
NHL Career	**2 seasons Chicago Blackhawks**
	2 seasons Buffalo Sabres

Playing Record

	Games	Wins	Losses	Ties	GAG
Regular Season	350	165	121	48	2.34
Playoffs	37	16	16	0	2.22

The son of a star has made his
own goal-scoring way to
the top in St. Louis.

The Blues' High-scorer
BRETT HULL

When Bobby Hull was on the ice, all eyes were on him. Brett Hull plays a different game from his dad. A labored skater, the younger Hull moves quietly around the ice, particularly in the offensive zone, circling into spaces others have left, positioning himself to accept a setup pass. He tries to draw as little attention to himself as possible, laying in the weeds, as the hockey players say. Until, that is, he unleashes The Shot.

By the time the defenders realize it is Hull who is shooting, it often is too late. Possessed of one of the fastest, hardest slap shots in hockey, Hull is a prolific but mostly unflashy scorer. He has been called the NHL's Stealth Bomber.

Quietly to the top

Similarly, Hull insinuated himself into the NHL élite quietly. Because of his name, the NHL saw Hull coming up through the junior and college ranks, but he was not regarded as a rising star.

The Calgary Flames selected Hull in the sixth round of the 1984 entry draft, an unheralded 117th overall out of the University of Minnesota-Duluth.

In his full first NHL season—1987-88—Hull scored 26 goals in 52 games for the Flames, who traded him before season's end to St. Louis.

With the Blues, Hull was paired with Adam Oates, one of the league's

CAREER RECORD

Personal	
Birthplace/Date	Belleville, Ontario/8-9-64
Height/Weight	5-10/200

Awards	
NHL First All-Star Team	1990-92
Lady Byng Trophy	1990
Hart Memorial Trophy	1991
Lester B. Pearson Award	1991

NHL Career	
	1 season Calgary Flames
	10 seasons St. Louis Blues

Playing record

	Games	Goals	Assists	Points	PIM
Regular season	801	554	433	987	298
Playoffs	108	71	51	120	51

top playmakers. Hull and Oates quickly became a hit.

Hull scored 41 goals and added 43 assists for 84 points in his first full season with the Blues, but that was merely the warm-up.

In 1989-90, Hull scored 72 goals to lead the NHL in goal-scoring for the first of three straight seasons. The following year his quick-release shot found the net 86 times and another 70 times in 1991-92.

Along with the goal-scoring blitz came official recognition. Hull was a first-team all-star three straight times, won the Lady Byng as the league's most sportsmanlike player and the Hart Trophy as the most valuable player.

Ups and downs

He was named captain of the Blues, but he had made himself something more important to St. Louis—its franchise player.

The Blues traded Oates, the set-up man, to the Bruins in February 1992, but replaced him with Craig Janney, another able playmaker. Still, some of his fans were disappointed when Hull 'slumped' to 54 goals in 1992-93 and managed 'only' 57 goals in 1993-94. In the lockout-shortened 1994-95 season, Hull delivered 29 goals in 48 games, which pro-rates to 49 goals over an 82-game schedule. Strictly routine for the Golden Brett, some would say.

Head coach Mike Keenan stripped Hull of the captaincy in 1995-96. Nothing personal, he assured people. "The heck it's not personal," Hull said. "It's a complete slap in the face."

Gone, too, was the playmaking Janney, who had been traded to San Jose during the 1994-95 season. In March 1996, Keenan traded for Wayne Gretzky, the ultimate playmaker, but the Hull-Gretzky duo was shortlived. Gretzky left for New York as a free agent at season's end. Partway through the 1996-97 season, yet another playmaking center was brought in—Pierre Turgeon.

Then, in the summer of 1998, it was the Golden Brett himself who was involved in a move. Hull had St. Louis hockey fans singing the blues as signed as a free agent for the Dallas Stars.

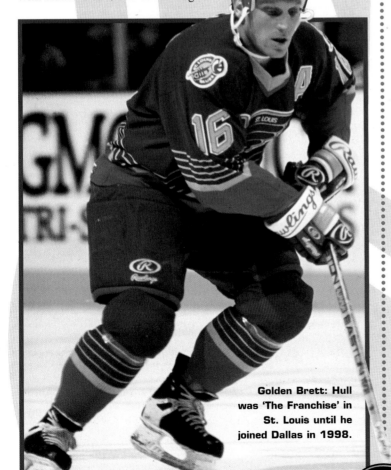

Golden Brett: Hull was 'The Franchise' in St. Louis until he joined Dallas in 1998.

JAROMIR JAGR

He's young, he's an artist, he scores goals like no one else—and he picks up the odd trophy now and again

Jaromir Jagr is the closest thing the NHL has to a rock star. He's young (26), good-looking, and has long, unruly hair, much too long for his helmet to contain. Jagr loves to laugh, too, and who can blame him? There seems little the 6-foot-2, 208-pound forward cannot do.

"He's still young," says former teammate Rick Tocchet. "He's going to be a force in this league for a long time."

He's already a force, has been since his rookie season in 1990-91. He made the all-rookie team that year, scoring 27 goals and adding 30 assists. He added 13 points in the Pittsburgh Cup-winning playoff run.

He is a fixture as one of the top offensive players in the league. Indeed, in 1994-95, Jagr won the scoring title with 70 points, including 32 goals in the lockout-shortened, 48-game regular season.

More important, he arrived as a mature player, having to step up and shoulder the burden of being the go-to guy for the Penguins. Teammate Mario Lemieux took the season off to recover from his bout with Hodgkin's Disease and chronic back problems.

Record breaker

Playing the star comes effortlessly for Jagr, who has a long, fluid, deceptively swift skating stride, and he's equally fluid handling the puck. He truly creates art on ice.

"He is a master of deception," said New York Rangers goaltender Mike Richter. "If you try to anticipate with him, you'll often guess wrong. And if you just try to react, he's too fast and you get beat."

In 1995-96, Jagr lifted his artistry to new heights. He and Lemieux became the first pair of teammates in NHL history to score more than 60 goals each in a single season.

On March 28, Jagr displaced Peter Stastny from the record books when he recorded his 140th point of the season, which was also his 60th goal.

Many experts consider Jaromir Jagr the best one-on-one player in the NHL.

In 1995-96, Jagr and Lemieux separated from the scoring pack early in the season, putting on their own personal scoring race.

But the two were friendly, complementary talents, not rivals. Jagr says he never has felt overlooked, never worried that he was playing Lemieux's shadow.

"No, I never looked at it that way when we were winning the Stanley Cup," said Jagr. "As long as we were winning, nothing else mattered. It's still the same now. I don't need a lot of attention."

Center Stage

With Lemieux retired, and classy center Ron Francis a recent departure to the Carolina Hurricanes, Jagr figures to receive more special attention than ever before.

He potted 47 goals and added 48 assists for 95 points in 1996-97, but improved on that last season by becoming the only man to top the century mark (102 points — 35 goals and 67 assists). The subsequent Art Ross Trophy was the second of his career and rounded off a spectacular season for Jagr that also brought him his Third First All-Star appearance and a chunk of gold that was pretty unexpected.

In February 1998, Jagr was a member of the Czech Republic squad which won the gold medal at the Winter Olympics in Nagano, Japan, beating Russia 1-0 in the final. Let's hope next season is just as rewarding.

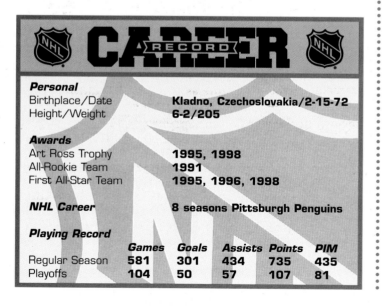

CAREER RECORD

Personal

Birthplace/Date	Kladno, Czechoslovakia/2-15-72
Height/Weight	6-2/205

Awards

Art Ross Trophy	1995, 1998
All-Rookie Team	1991
First All-Star Team	1995, 1996, 1998

NHL Career — 8 seasons Pittsburgh Penguins

Playing Record

	Games	Goals	Assists	Points	PIM
Regular Season	581	301	434	735	435
Playoffs	104	50	57	107	81

Anaheim's Paul Kariya is rated as one of the fastest men on the ice in the NHL

When he gets his motor running, there's nobody more dangerous in the NHL than Mighty Ducks of Anaheim left wing Paul Kariya. At top speed, Kariya is a blur rushing down the ice, with enough moves in his arsenal to reduce even the best defensemen in the league into pilons.

Kariya sets the excitement meter on atomic and, teamed with linemate Teemu Selanne, he proves just how entertaining the game of hockey can be to watch. Heading into the 1997-98 season, Kariya was rated as the league's best player by *The Hockey News*. The magazine pointed to his breathtaking skating, his speed and quickness, his puck skills, his ability to raise his own play and that of his teammates and his work ethic. It also praised his hockey smarts, which is no surprise coming from a former dean's list student at the University of Maine.

Small is beautiful

Just about the only thing Kariya doesn't have going for him is size. He stands 5-11 and weighs a scant 175 pounds. Too small? Scotty Bowman, the NHL's all-time winningest coach, says of Kariya: "They said the same thing about Wayne Gretzky. Kariya is so good because he can carry the puck at top speed."

Kariya hasn't been able to showcase that speed as much as he would have liked the past few seasons. He missed parts of those seasons and the last two big international competitions — the 1996 World Cup of Hockey and the 1998 Olympics in Japan (from where his father's side of the family descends) — because of a succession of injuries. A concussion kept him out of the Olympics and sidelined him for the last couple of months of the 1997-98 regular season too, but he underwent acupuncture therapy and, over the summer, said that had him feeling great and looking forward to playing this season.

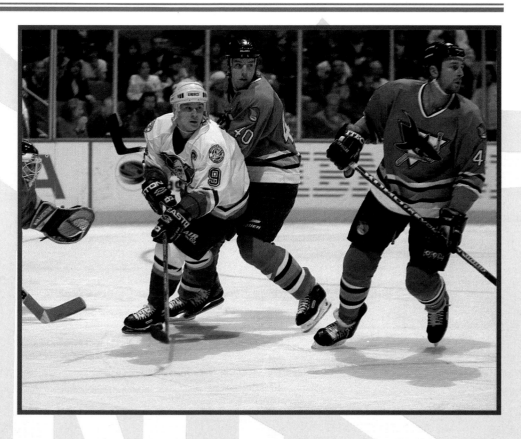

Mighty Ducks' Kariya has demonstrated that if a player has the right amount of self-belief he can live with the big boys of the NHL.

ICE TALK

"KARIYA IS SO GOOD BECAUSE HE CAN CARRY THE PUCK AT TOP SPEED"

SCOTTY BOWMAN

CAREER RECORD

Personal

Birthplace/Date	Vancouver, Canada/ 10-16-74
Height/Weight	5-11/175

Awards

All-Rookie Team	1995
First All-Star Team	1996, 1997
Lady Byng Trophy	1996, 1997

NHL Career — 4 seasons Mighty Ducks of Anaheim

Playing record

	Games	Goals	Assists	Points	PIM
Regular Season	220	129	148	277	53
Playoffs	11	7	6	13	4

JoHN LeCLAIr

Hungry for hockey and tough on ice, this rock-loving powerhouse excels at golf, works for good causes, and is a superb role model.

In his days with the Montreal Canadiens, strapping left winger John LeClair had the nickname of Marmaduke, after the playful but uncoordinated comic-strip canine. "John used to fall down a lot," recalled defenseman Kevin Haller, a teammate of LeClair's both in Montreal and in Philadelphia.

"He didn't have real good balance and he wasn't strong on his skates. Now, he's totally the opposite."

Indeed, LeClair, who was a member of the Flyers' Legion of Doom line with Eric Lindros and Mikael Renberg until the latter was traded, is solid as a rock in every facet of the game. He sends opposing players scattering like bowling pins with his 6-foot-3, 225-pound frame. He has developed into one of the NHL's finest two-way forwards, while at the same time being one of its top sharpshooters, following up on a 51-goal season in 1995-96 with a 50-goal performance the following season and then, in 1997-98, he became the first American in NHL history to record three straight 50-goal seasons as he netted 51 goals.

"He is a great two-way player," admitted former teammate Renberg. "He's strong in our zone, and along the boards. He's also a great role model for our younger players."

Rockin' and scorin'

LeClair, the only player from the U.S. state of Vermont to make the NHL, emerged from obscurity with the Canadiens in the 1992-93 playoffs, in which Montreal surprisingly won the Stanley Cup. LeClair scored an overtime goal in both the third and fourth games of the series, which Montreal won in five games. He became the first player to score consecutive overtime game-winners in the Stanley Cup finals since Don Raleigh of the Rangers in 1950.

But LeClair could do no better than a 19-goal output the following season—matching his total of the previous year. Early in the 1994-95 season, with both LeClair and the Canadiens struggling, he was dealt to the Flyers, along with defenseman Eric Desjardins and forward Gilbert Dionne, for the high-scoring Mark Recchi.

The change in scenery had an immediate effect on LeClair. "It was a situation where I wasn't expected to score in Montreal," said LeClair, attempting to account for the transformation. "Here, they put me with Eric and Mikael right away, and it was an entirely different philosophy."

LeClair started to rock, which is an appropriate term for someone who is a huge fan of U2 and 1980s rock music, with more than 500 CDs in his collection. A tireless worker, LeClair improved his skating, refined his already booming shot, and used his imposing frame to create havoc around the net.

"My shot is hard, but a lot of times it's not how hard you shoot it, it's how quick you get it away," explained LeClair. "I think that's one of the things I've really worked on."

Hungry Flyer

Even as a youngster, growing up in St. Albans, Vermont, which is only a one-hour drive from Montreal, LeClair would spend hour after hour whacking a tennis ball against a shed. That's when he wasn't racing to be the first person in the bathroom each morning, since there were seven in the family.

Whether it is golf, a sport at which he also excels—according to Lindros, LeClair has Babe Ruthian drives off a golf tee—or the many charitable causes in which he is involved, LeClair has a hunger to succeed.

That passion is evident even at Flyers practices. "John is the hungriest guy on the ice, even in practice," says Flyers goaltender Ron Hextall.

The Wonder from Vermont made it three 50-plus seasons on the trot when he notched up 51 goals in the 1997-98 season.

CAREER RECORD

Personal

Birthplace/Date	St. Albans, Vermont/4-7-69
Height/Weight	6-3/226

Awards:

NHL First All-Star Team	1995, 1998
NHL Second All-Star Team	1996
Played in All-Star Game	1996

NHL Career	3½ seasons Montreal Canadiens
	3½ seasons Philadelphia Flyers

Playing record

	Games	Goals	Assists	Points	PIM
Regular Season	507	226	222	448	265
Playoffs	88	28	33	61	54

In this era of transition hockey, the Smythe-decorated Texan keeps the Rangers' on top.

BRIAN LEETCH

A compact package combining quick acceleration and excellent straightahead speed, playmaking brilliance, a hard accurate shot and sound defensive ability, Brian Leetch is a Renaissance player—a defenseman who can do it all.

It was Leetch, lifting his game to new heights of virtuosity, who led the New York Rangers to a Stanley Cup championship in 1994, the club's first in 54 years. He led all playoff scorers with 34 points, including 11 goals. He scored five times in the seven-game final series against the Vancouver Canucks and fully earned the Conn Smythe Trophy as the most valuable performer in the post-season.

Texas hockey

He was the first American-born player—born in Texas, but raised in Connecticut—to capture the Conn Smythe.

He joined the Rangers in 1988-89, after a year with the U.S. National team, and an Olympic appearance as captain of the U.S. team. The international experience, coupled with one year with the Boston College Eagles had fine-tuned his explosive raw talent—Leetch was named rookie-of-the-year in his first NHL season.

His numbers dropped off next season, scoring 11 times and adding 45 assists, before being knocked out of action by a fractured left ankle, the first of many disruptive injuries.

But in 1990-91, Leetch re-asserted his claim to being a franchise defenseman by scoring 16 goals and adding 72 assists for 88 points, breaking Hall of Famer Brad Park's team record for most points (82) in a season by a defenseman.

In 1991-92, Leetch totaled 102 points, including 22 goals and won the James Norris Memorial Trophy as the best defenseman in the league. He won the award again in 1996-97.

Some of Leetch's best work in 1996, though, came before the NHL regular season. He was brilliant for Team USA as the

On the Move: Leetch's acceleration launches him on rinklength dashes that often result in goals—by the speedy defenseman or one of his teammates.

Americans upset Canada to win the inaugural World Cup of Hockey.

Undeterred by injury

Injuries hit Leetch in 1992-93, when he missed 34 games with a neck and shoulder injury. Then he slipped on some ice on a Manhattan street, fracturing his right ankle, and missed the final 13 games that season. The injury was ominous for a player whose game is based on speed, but Leetch achieved a superb regular-season (23 goals, 56 assists) and sublime playoff performance.

He was also strong in the 1994-95 playoffs, generating 14 points (6 goals) in 10 games as the Rangers failed to advance beyond the second round. Since the 1993-94 season, Leetch has not missed a game, an Ironman string of 296 straight regular-season games. His reliability permitted the Rangers to trade the talented but superfluous Sergei Zubov, and gain Ulf Samuelsson in 1995. Leetch was also one of the main reasons that Wayne Gretzky signed with the Rangers as a free agent in 1996.

"As much as I've done offensively, I know that to win championships, you need defense," Gretzky said. "The Rangers have great defense. Playing with Brian Leetch was obviously part of the attraction. He reminds me of Paul Coffey."

Leetch's claim to greatness could not possibly be stamped with more authenticity than that.

ICE TALK

"I WOULD BEG ANYONE TO ARGUE THAT BRIAN'S NOT THE BEST TWO-WAY DEFENSEMAN IN THE NHL TODAY."

RANGERS TEAMMATE ADAM GRAVES

CAREER RECORD

Personal

Birthplace/Date	Corpus Christi, Texas, USA/3-3-68
Height/Weight	5-11/195

Awards

All-Rookie Team	1989
Calder Memorial Trophy	1989
James Norris Memorial Trophy	1992, 1997
First All-Star Team	1992
Conn Smythe Trophy	1994

NHL Career 10 seasons New York Rangers

Playing record

	Games	Goals	Assists	Points	PIM
Regular Season	725	164	536	700	357
Playoffs	82	28	61	89	30

He combines the finesse of Gretzky, the size of Lemieux and the presence of Messier. Lindros' future is a no-brainer.

An astonishing blend of fearsome physical strength, speed, skill, rink savvy and unquenchable competitive desire, 6-foot-4, 229-pound center Eric Lindros moved with ridiculous ease up the hockey ladder—junior to international competition to the NHL.

ICE TALK

"HIS SOLE FOCUS IS GETTING HIS TEAM TO THE STANLEY CUP."

FORMER TEAMMATE CRAIG MACTAVISH

While still junior age, Lindros helped Canada win the gold medal at the Canada Cup. During that tournament, Lindros knocked rugged Ulf Samuelsson out of action with a devastating body check that was routinely easy for him.

Before he had played an NHL game he had served notice that he was going to be a force. He has lived up to his advance billing.

The Legion of Doom

Injuries reduced his effectiveness in his first two seasons—yet he still scored 85 goals and chipped in 87 assists in 126 games. Much of that production came while playing on a line with Mark Recchi and Brent Fedyk, both since traded. The line, called the Crazy Eights, was an instant hit in Philadelphia, where fans quickly warmed to Lindros. But he really hit his NHL stride in 1995 when Flyers coach Terry Murray grouped him with 6-foot-2, 220-pound left winger John LeClair and 6-foot-1, 218-pound right winger Mikael Renberg. As talented as any trio in the league and certainly the best combination of skill and sheer physical power, the line was christened The Legion of Doom.

Lindros totaled 70 points, including 29 goals, in 46 games in 1994-95, tying Pittsburgh's Jaromir Jagr for the points lead, but losing the scoring title, on the final day of the shortened season, because Jagr scored three more goals.

Lindros and the Legion led the Flyers to the club's first division title since 1987 and first playoff berth since 1989. The Flyers lost in the conference final to the New Jersey Devils, the eventual Stanley Cup champions. The strong performance by Lindros earned him the Hart Trophy as the most valuable player in the NHL, a mantle he assumed with a degree of unease.

"The more people you have carry the game, the better the game's going to be," Lindros said. "When everybody carries it together, it makes it stronger… We've got some great people to carry this game."

Quebec's loss

Few appear to have a greater upside potential than Lindros, whose leadership abilities were quickly recognized in Philadelphia, where he was named captain of the Flyers at 21.

In 1995-96, both Lindros and LeClair took serious runs at 50-goal seasons—Lindros finished with 47, LeClair with 51. The Flyers challenged the Penguins and the New York Rangers for first place overall in the Eastern Conference all season long.

At 25, Lindros has grown comfortable with the dominant role foreseen for him when the Quebec Nordiques drafted him first overall in 1991. He refused to report to the Nordiques, forcing a trade to the Flyers, who drained their organizational depth chart to land Lindros, sending eight players and $15 million to the Nordiques.

The 1997-98 season was not the best one that Lindros has experienced. He suffered a concussion which kept him out of action for a while, but which was especially poignant for Lindros, because his younger brother's career was curtailed by such an injury. Lindros also suffered criticism of his captaincy style at the Flyers, and some also tried to pin Canada's poor showing in the Olympics on captain Lindros. It prompted him to say as the season drew to a close. "That's not something I ever intend to go through again."

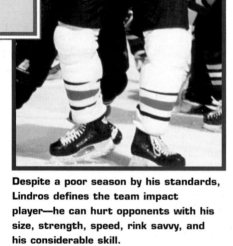

Despite a poor season by his standards, Lindros defines the team impact player—he can hurt opponents with his size, strength, speed, rink savvy, and his considerable skill.

CAREER RECORD

Personal

Birthplace/Date	London, Ontario/2-28-73
Height/Weight	6-4/229

Awards

All-Rookie Team	1993
First All-Star Team	1995
Lester B. Pearson Award	1995
Hart Trophy	1995

NHL Career 6 seasons Philadelphia Flyers

Playing record

	Games	Goals	Assists	Points	PIM
Regular Season	360	223	284	507	743
Playoffs	48	23	33	56	118

**The former Rangers'
star needs to rally
the Canucks.**

Speed defines some hockey players, strength others, still others personify skill. Mark Messier displays ample amounts of all three qualities, but to understand his essence, you start with the glare.

When Messier gets that look, his teammates get into formation behind him and opponents blanch just a little. The glare could translate into a game-breaking goal, a skilful passing play, a bone-rattling body check or even a well-timed, lethal elbow to an opponent's jaw.

Messier is the ultimate hockey player: big, fast, strong, skillful and junkyard-dog mean.

The former captain of the New York Rangers is above all an incomparable on-ice leader, the capstone player on any team he has played for. He was a central player on five Edmonton Oilers teams that won the Stanley Cup, a leader on three Canadian teams that won the Canada Cup and indisputably the central force that carried the Rangers to the Stanley Cup in 1994, their first championship in 54 years.

Some consider him the fiercest, most inspirational leader in all of North American pro sports. He certainly has the portfolio.

Trail of a giant

He has won two Hart Trophies as the league's most valuable player, one Conn Smythe Trophy as the best individual performer in the playoffs and two Lester B. Pearson Awards as the most outstanding player in the league, as voted on by his peers.

His individual performance chart reveals impressive statistics:

	NHL CAREER RECORD				
Personal					
Birthplace/Date	Edmonton, Alberta/1-18-61				
Height/Weight	6-1/205				
Awards					
First All-Star Team	1982-83, 1990, 1992				
Conn Smythe Trophy	1984				
Hart Trophy	1990, 1992				
Lester B. Pearson Award	1990, 1992				
NHL Career	12 seasons Edmonton Oilers				
	6 seasons New York Rangers				
	1 season Vancouver Canucks				
Playing record					
	Games	**Goals**	**Assists**	**Points**	**PIM**
Regular Season	1354	597	1015	1612	1654
Playoffs	236	109	186	295	244

one 50-goal season; six seasons of 100 points or more; more than 100 playoff goals and almost 300 post-season points; a record 13 playoff shorthanded goals.

But the true measure of Messier seems to be how teams he plays for perform. In 1990-91, Edmonton was 29-20-4 (won-lost-tied) with Messier in the lineup, just 8-17-2 without him.

In the 1991 Canada Cup, Team Canada coach Mike Keenan extended an eligibility deadline to make room on the team for Messier. Canada won the tournament that year.

In 1984, even with the Wayne Gretzky Oilers, it was Messier who won the Conn Smythe Trophy as the most valuable player in the Stanley Cup playoffs as Edmonton won its first Cup in franchise history.

No rash promise

The most celebrated illustration of Messier's leadership abilities came before Game 6 of the 1994 Stanley Cup semifinals against the New Jersey Devils.

The Devils held a 3-2 series lead, but Messier told a TV audience he guaranteed a victory by the Rangers in Game 6. He backed it up by scoring the hat trick as the Rangers won the game 4-2, sending the series to a seventh game in Madison Square which the Rangers won in double overtime, the third of three games decided in a second overtime period.

Not since New York Jets quarterback Joe Namath guaranteed a Super Bowl victory over the Baltimore Colts in 1969 had a New York sporting hero been so brash, then backed up his boast. Messier's guarantee had profound resonance for New York hockey fans.

Since those heady days, Messier has taken up a new challenge in Vancouver with the Canucks and experienced the other side of the NHL. The Canucks finished with the worst record in the Western Conference in 1997-98, and even Messier was off his game. With much to prove in the new season, expect fireworks from him.

For much of his career, Messier's exploits have brought smiles to all his NHL fans. But there wasn't much to grin about in Vancouver during 1997-98 as the Canucks under-achieved.

MIKE MODANO

Handsome, swift and feared as a pinpoint sharp shooter, this lad from Michigan has blossomed with the Dallas Stars.

As a kid growing up in Livonia, Michigan, Mike Modano would spend plenty of hours in the family basement honing his hockey skills. Often, he would beg his mother to serve as a goaltender and hold up the top part of a garbage can, which Mike used as a target to develop pinpoint precision in his shooting.

The hours certainly weren't wasted. Modano went on to a brilliant junior career with the Prince Albert Raiders of the Western Junior League—232 points in only 106 games in his final two seasons—before the then-Minnesota North Stars made the 6-foot-3, 200-pound center the No. 1 pick overall in the 1988 draft.

Excluding the 1994-95 strike season and an injury-hit 1997-98 campaign, Modano has led the team—which moved to Dallas prior to the 1993 season and became the Stars—in every season since 1991-92—his third year in the NHL—when he collected 77 points.

His biggest goal-scoring season, however, came in 1993-94 when he became the first center in the history of the Minnesota/Dallas franchise to score 50 goals.

"I started to improve on my ability to go to the net that season," recalled Modano. "That obviously wasn't a part of my game the first few years, but the more you do it, the more you get used to it."

Matinee idol

Modano was under a great deal of pressure to produce in the early years. The North Stars had missed the playoffs for two straight seasons prior to drafting Modano, who at the time was only the third American-born player to be selected No. 1. One year after that draft, Modano was a bonafide member of the North Stars, amassing 75 points as a rookie, including 20 points in the Stanley Cup playoffs, as the upstart North Stars went all the way to the final.

Still, Modano was a long ways from refinement. The concern for Bob Gainey, who at the time had the dual role of coach and general manager, was Modano's play in the offensive zone when he didn't have the puck. Gradually, Modano learned to let other players work the puck to him, rather than vacate a good offensive position because of his own impatience and frustration.

Modano's star continued to rise when the North Stars

Michigan Mike won't be short of dollars for the next few years after getting a great deal with the Dallas Stars.

relocated in Dallas. More than a hockey star, he became a matinée idol, especially when his handsome features found their way into some of the top women's magazines, and Giorgio Armani used him as a runway model. He also became a familar sight on the golf course, taking advantage of the Dallas climate to work assiduously at reducing his handicap, which is getting close to 0.

Sharpshooting leader

On the ice, Modano has blossomed into one of the NHL's swiftest skaters and most feared sharpshooters, to the extent that one team scout remarked, "If Dallas beats you, two things probably happened: they got strong goaltending, and Mike Modano was one of the three stars."

After suffering a succession of injuries for much of 1997-98 — he scored just 21 goals in limited ice time — Modano ended the campaign strongly. He played well in the Western Conference finals, and then announced a new six-year contract with the Stars worth $43.5million.

"I feel like my career is getting started now," he said shortly after the deal. "I'm turning the corner."

CAREER RECORD

Personal

Birthplace/Date	Livonia, Michigan/7-10-70
Height/Weight	6-3/200

Awards:

NHL All-Rookie Team	1980
Played in NHL All-Star Game	1993

NHL Career

4 seasons Minnesota North Stars
5 seasons Dallas Stars

Playing record

	Games	Goals	Assists	Points	PIM
Regular Season	633	277	377	654	456
Playoffs	72	27	29	56	60

ZIGMUND PALFFY

Flair and imagination, and a formidable score count, have made Ziggy an Islanders' star.

Zigmund (Ziggy) Palffy is that much sought-after commodity in hockey—a pure goal scorer, a sniper, a right winger who not only scores in abundance but does it with flair. He's a drawing card on a franchise that is reloading and aiming to recreate the magic that carried the New York Islanders to four straight Stanley Cups from 1980 to 1983.

Palffy attracted plenty of attention at the 1991 World Junior Hockey Championship in Saskatoon, Saskatchewan, while playing with future NHL winger Martin Rucinsky and against such luminaries as Eric Lindros, Pavel Bure and Doug Weight.

Only Bure, with 12 goals and Rucinsky, with nine, scored more than Palffy's six goals at that tournament.

Palffy has lived up to the promise he showed playing on that bronze medal-winning club with the Islanders.

"When Ziggy has the puck, there's a little mystery to the game," says Islanders coach and GM Mike Milbury. "His greatest asset is his imagination—you just don't know what he's going to do."

Czech overture

Palffy did not join the Islanders organization full time until the 1993-94 season, preferring to play in the Czech Elite League for two seasons, where he whet the Islanders' appetite by scoring 79 goals in 88 games over those two years.

He then spent the better part of two seasons in the Islanders' farm system before joining the NHL club for good part-way through the 1994-95 season.

In his first full season with the Islanders—1995-96—Palffy led the team in goals (43) and points (87). In 1996-97 he went out and did it again, scoring 48 goals and registering 90 points. Then, in an awesome display of scoring consistency, he scored 41 goals in the 1997-98 season to cement his reputation as one of deadliest sharpshooters in the NHL.

When Palffy scores, he often scores in bunches, too. Over one seven-game span — from February 29 to March 12, 1996 — Palffy scored 11 goals, including back-to-back three-goal hat tricks.

No pushover

Palffy is no power forward, he's not the big, strong forward like Jaromir Jagr who can dazzle with finesse or simply bull his way past opponents.

At 5-foot-10, Palffy is small by NHL standards, but he's hardly passive. Palffy shows a feisty side if opponents start getting rough. "He's got an edge to him," says Milbury. "He'll respond to a physical challenge from the other team."

Palffy should take the attention—however distasteful—as something of a compliment. Other teams know they have to stop Palffy when they play the Islanders.

The Islanders' Zippy Slovakian Ziggy Palffy is one of just five NHL players to score more than 40 goals in each of the past three seasons.

CAREER RECORD

Personal

Birthplace/Date: **Skalica, Czech Republik/5-5-72**
Height/Weight: **5-10/183**

NHL Career: **4 seasons New York Islanders**

Playing record

	Games	Goals	Assists	Points	PIM
Regular season	281	146	135	281	139
Playoffs	0	0	0	0	0

MIKE RICHTER

An instrumental force in his team's ambitions, this goalie's goaltender keeps his cool and always gives his best.

Take it from one of his goaltending brethren: New York Rangers netminder Mike Richter is one of the best around when it comes to winning a big game or series. "There are not many goalies who can win games by themselves, but Mike is capable of doing it," remarked Martin Brodeur, the New Jersey Devils No. 1 backstop. "He did it in the World Cup, and he did it against us."

In the first instance, Brodeur was referring to Richter's stellar play in the fall of 1996, which spearheaded the United States squad to a 2-1 triumph over Canada in the best-of-three series at the first-ever World Cup hockey tournament. The second allusion was to Richter's performance against the Devils in the 1997 Eastern Conference semifinal, in which Richter stopped 178 of 182 shots, recorded two shutouts and led the Rangers to a five-game upset of the Devils in the best-of-seven series.

Richter wasn't able to lead an injury-decimated Rangers lineup past the Philadelphia Flyers in the Eastern Conference final, but that didn't detract from the accomplishments of the nimble netminder who grew up a Flyers' fan in Flourtown, Pennsylvania. The Rangers would likely not have got as far as they did without a vintage Richter, who compiled a 2.68 regular-season goals-against average.

Notorious success

Before the elimination by the Flyers, Richter revived memories of 1994, when he was an instrumental force in the Rangers ending a 54-year Stanley Cup drought. Richter started all 23 of the Rangers playoff games that year, leading the NHL with 16 wins, posting a 2.07 goals-against average and recording four shutouts, which tied a league record for shutouts in post-season play.

Perhaps Richter's finest moment in that year's playoffs was his 31-save effort in the Rangers' seventh-game double-overtime triumph over New Jersey to win the Eastern Conference finals.

Richter's notoriety earned him guest spots—along with teammates Mark Messier and Brian Leetch—on the David Letterman Show following the Stanley Cup win. Articulate and comfortable as a communicator, Richter, a past winner of the Rangers 'Good Guy Award' for cooperation with the media, was in his element on the popular U.S. late-night television program.

Two years later, Richter was in the spotlight again, when he won the Most Valuable Player Award at the World Cup. With the U.S. team trailing Canada 1-0 in the best-of-three series, Richter made 35 saves in Game 2 as the Americans tied the series and, in Game 3, he kept the U.S. in the game—the team was outshot 22-9 through two periods—enabling it to go on to a 5-2 win in the decisive third game.

Cool courage

When he's not throwing his body in front of pucks, Richter is deeply involved in social causes. He has won awards for 'Excellence and Humanitarian Concern', and an 'Award of Courage' for his work with hospitals. He has also served as honorary hockey chairman of the Children's Health Fund.

Placid and cool under the constant pressures of trying to stifle some of the game's finest sharpshooters, Richter is equally collected in his approach to his craft. "You have to realize you are probably as good or as bad as the team in front of you," he once explained. "But one of the attractions of being a goaltender is that you are the guy on the spot. There's pressure on everybody, but that's a lot easier to bear than not having the opportunity to deliver under pressure."

Mike Richter didn't enjoy his best season in 1997-98, either with the Rangers or Team USA in the Olympics.

CAREER RECORD

Personal

Birthplace/Date	Abington, Pennsylvania/9-22-66
Height/Weight	5-11/187

Awards

MVP NHL All-Star Game	1994
NHL All-Star Team	1992
World Cup MVP	1996

NHL Career — 9 seasons New York Rangers

Playing record

	Games	Wins	Losses	Ties	GAG
Regular season	424	203	144	49	2.89
Playoffs	76	41	33	0	2.68

PATRICK ROY

Eccentric, miraculous and flawless, Montreal's ex-star has proven his worth in Colorado.

Patrick Roy, a demigod in Montreal, was traded to Colorado after delivering an ultimatum to the Canadiens President in December 1995. Since then he has performed wonders for the Avalanche.

During games, the rookie goaltender talked to his goalposts, and before each game started, he skated 40 feet in front of his net, turned and stared intently at his workplace, skated hard right at the crease, veered away at the last second, then settled into his work station for another night of brilliance.

Even among goaltenders, who are known for their eccentricity, Patrick Roy was a classic from his first NHL season in 1986.

Roy was magnificent during the playoffs as the Canadiens, with a rookie-laden club, won the Stanley Cup, surprising the hockey world.

Roy won the Conn Smythe Trophy, winning 15 and losing just five playoff games and posting a goals-against average of 1.92. He had staked his claim to the title of the best goalie in the NHL.

The next three seasons, he won the William Jennings Trophy, for the goalie whose team allows the fewest goals against. Three times (1989-90, 1992) Roy also won the Vezina Trophy, awarded to the league's best goalie, as voted on by the general managers.

Roy refined his goaltending technique the hard way. As a junior goalie, playing for the sad sack Granby Bisons of the Quebec Major Junior Hockey League, it was not uncommon for Roy to face 60- or 70-shot barrages.

Stellar start

When he arrived in the NHL as a regular, Roy was only 20, and had played one single, solitary game in minor pro hockey, but he was seasoned, which he quickly proved.

Roy has been at his best in pressure situations. His stellar play led the Canadiens to three Stanley Cup finals (1986, 1989, 1993), and two Cup championships.

Both those years, he won the Conn Smythe Trophy as the most valuable player in the playoffs. His performance in the 1993 Stanley Cup playoffs, when the Canadiens won ten of 11 overtime games,

was just this side of miraculous. It's not for nothing the Forum came to be known as St. Patrick's Cathedral during his glory years there.

In 1994, Roy was stricken with appendicitis after two games of the opening-round series against the Boston Bruins and had to be hospitalized. Antibiotics forestalled the need for surgery and Roy rose from his hospital bed to record two straight victories over the Bruins, one a 2-1 overtime thriller at the old Boston Garden in which he made 60 saves.

At his best, Roy is technically flawless, using a butterfly style in which he goes to his knees and splays his leg pads to cover the lower portion of the net, protecting the upper portion with his body and his cat-quick left hand.

Superstar shock

Roy was Montreal's franchise player so it was stunning on December 2, 1995 when the goaltender, embarrassed by an 11-1 pounding he had absorbed from the Detroit Red Wings, told club president Ronald Corey—on national TV—that he had played his last game with the Montreal Canadiens. Three days later, Roy was traded to Colorado. Never mind. Roy would make his new home his shrine. In his first season with the Avalanche, he backstopped Colorado to the Stanley Cup. In 1996-97, he was brilliant again, but the Avalanche were eliminated in the semifinals to eventual Stanley Cup champion Detroit Red Wings.

Last season he was in awesome form, representing Canada in the Olympics — shutting out Belarus — and he set an NHL record with his 8th 30 win season with the defeat of the Mighty Ducks of Anaheim in March.

CAREER RECORD

Personal	
Birthplace/Date	**Quebec City/10-5-65**
Height/Weight	**6-1/192**

Awards	
Conn Smythe Trophy	**1986, 1993**
William Jennings Trophy	**1987-89, 1992**
Vezina Trophy	**1989-90, 1992**
First All-Star team	**1989-90, 1992**

NHL career	
	10½ seasons Montreal Canadiens
	2½ seasons Colorado Avalanche

Playing record	Games	Wins	Losses	Ties	GAG
Regular Season	717	380	224	87	2.69
Playoffs	160	99	59	0	2.38

Sakic missed nearly a quarter of the 1997-98 season through injury. And he also missed an Olympic medal.

He's not big, in fact, he's almost small by National Hockey League standards, but Joe Sakic is water-bug elusive, a slick, clever passer, an accurate shooter and perhaps the most unassuming superstar in hockey.

Sakic was a first-round draft pick by the then-Quebec Nordiques in 1987. He was taken 15th overall after a monster season (60 goals, 133 points) with the Swift Current Broncos of the Western Hockey League.

When he joined the once-mighty Nordiques, for the 1988-89 season, they had just finished last in the Adams Division and were about to embark on the darkest period in franchise history. They would finish last overall in the NHL the next three years in a row. Sakic's NHL apprenticeship did not come easy.

Nordique blues

Sakic was fortunate enough to have Nordiques' star center Peter Stastny around for most of his first two seasons as a role model. Sakic, it turned out, didn't need that much guidance.

He scored 23 goals and added 39 assists for 62 points in his first season, then recorded the first of four 100-plus point seasons the very next year, when he led the Nordiques with 39 goals and 63 assists.

When the Nordiques traded Stastny, their first real superstar, to the New Jersey Devils in 1990, the torch had been passed to the smallish, shifty Sakic. The Nordiques would soon surround Sakic with some of the best young talent in the game.

As the club improved, adding players like Owen Nolan, Mats Sundin, Curtis Leschyshyn, Stephane Fiset, Valeri Kamensky et al, expectations began to soar, also.

In 1992-93, the Nordiques made the playoffs for the first time in five years and drew provincial rival Montreal Canadiens as their first-round opponent. The talent-rich Nordiques won the first two games.

But Montreal goalie Patrick Roy stiffened and the Canadiens stunned the Nordiques, winning the next four games in a row. The critics howled, many of them at Sakic, but the quiet-spoken Sakic took the loss as a learning experience.

The following season, the Nordiques slumped as a team. They missed the playoffs again.

In the lockout-shortened 1994-95 season, Sakic's 19 goals and 43 assists put him fourth in league scoring and the Nordiques finished first overall in the Eastern Conference, then lost to the more experienced Rangers in the opening round of the Stanley Cup playoffs.

Colorado dawn

In Colorado's first full season in Denver, Sakic collected 120 points, finishing third in the regular-season scoring race. Then he guided the Avalanche to the Stanley Cup, winning the Conn Smythe Trophy as the most valuable player in the playoffs.

In the 1997-98 season, things didn't go so well as Sakic picked up an injury while playing for Team Canada in the Nagano Olympics. A collision with teammate Rob Blake during the quarter-final win against Kazakhstan left Sakic with a sprained knee that sidelined him for several weeks.

A one-match ban and fine for a trip during the last game of the regular season summed up Sakic's disappointing 1997-98.

Sakic didn't enjoy the best of 1997-98 seasons, but expect him to bounce back when the new season opens.

CAREER RECORD

Personal

Birthplace/Date	Burnaby, British Columbia/ 7-7-69
Height/Weight	5-11/185

Awards

All-Star Game Participant	1990, 1994
Conn Smythe Trophy	1996

NHL Career 10 seasons Quebec Nordiques/ Colorado Avalanche

Playing record

	Games	Goals	Assists	Points	PIM
Regular season	719	334	549	883	311
Playoffs	57	35	40	75	36

TEEMU SELANNE

The Hitman from Helsinki was in devastating form during the 1997-98 season scoring 52 goals.

When you blend world-class skill and offensive creativity with eye-popping speed, you really discombobulate a defense. That description fits Teemu Selanne perfectly.

Selanne, The Finnish Flash, blazed through the National Hockey League in his first season with the Winnipeg Jets, scoring 76 goals and adding 56 assists to shatter the records for most goals.

Fully-grown rookie

The 6-foot, 200-pound Finnish speedster zoomed into the NHL in 1994 at 22, two or three years older than the average rookie. To say he made the adjustment from Jokerit in the Finnish Elite League with ease is to understate the magnitude of his achievement.

Selanne recorded his first three-goal hat trick in his fifth NHL game. In late February that season, Selanne scored four goals in a victory over the Minnesota (now Dallas) Stars.

He produced a string of scoring streaks that left Jets fans dizzy: an eight-game scoring streak (nine goals and 11 assists); a five-game goal-scoring streak in which he recorded 11 goals; a nine-game goal-scoring streak in which he scored 14 goals; a 17-game points streak that produced 20 goals and 14 assists. He rocketed through the Jets' final six games, scoring 13 goals and adding two assists.

In his first NHL playoff game, against the Vancouver Canucks, he not only scored a goal, he recorded another three-goal hat trick.

His Calder Memorial Trophy award as the top rookie in the league was expected. Astonishing was his arrival as a fully formed superstar, competing with both rookies *and* the best players.

His 76 goals tied for the league lead with Alexander Mogilny and he was selected as the right winger on the first All-Star team.

Kid start

Selanne was a mature player upon arrival in North America because he had not hurried his development in his native Finland.

He grew up in the minor hockey system in Helsinki, playing for KalPa-Espoo from the age of five. By nine, he was competing against players two years his senior, and at 16 he joined Jokerit,

CAREER RECORD					
Personal					
Birthplace/date	Helsinki, Finland/7-3-70				
Height/Weight	6-0/200				
Awards					
Calder Memorial Trophy	1994				
First All-Star Team	1994, 1998				
NHL Career	3½ seasons Winnipeg Jets				
	2½ seasons Anaheim Mighty Ducks				
Playing record	Games	Goals	Assists	Points	PIM
Regular Season	410	266	271	537	155
Playoffs	17	11	5	16	6

one of the most successful of the teams in the Finnish Elite League for five seasons before he made the jump to the NHL.

"It is good to play there and get better and then come (to the NHL) later, when you are ready," he has said. "I had dreams to play in the World Championship and the Olympic Games before I came here and when I came here, I had done all that. I left with a clear conscience."

It's also clear the Mighty Ducks plan to construct a championship team around Selanne and Paul Kariya, who give Anaheim one of the most highly skilled duos in all of hockey.

Unfortunately for Mighty Duck fans, Kariya was sidelined for much of the 1997-98 season, but Selanne perservered alone and reaped his reward with 52 goals and the MVP of the All-Star game. The hat-trick he scored in that game was the first by a European in all All-Star game.

ICE TALK

"WHEN I WAS YOUNGER, THE NHL WAS JUST A DREAM BECAUSE I DID NOT KNOW HOW MUCH OF A SACRIFICE IT TOOK TO MAKE IT TO THIS LEVEL. BUT WHEN I WAS 18 OR 19, I STARTED HAVING MORE SUCCESS AND THEN MY GOAL WAS TO PLAY IN THE NHL."

TEEMU SELANNE

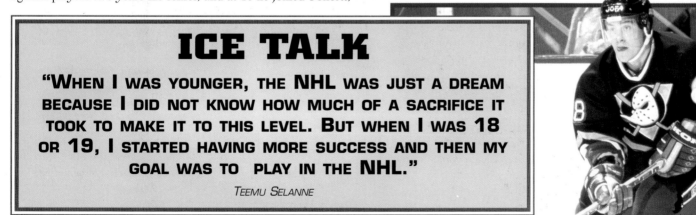

Ever since Selanne left Winnipeg he has warmed to life on the West coast and has quickly become a favorite with the fans.

This tough scorer got his second Stanley Cup.

BRENDAN SHANAHAN

The Detroit Red Wings were so eager to welcome rugged left winger Brendan Shanahan into the fold that the team delayed a morning practice so that Shanahan, who was on a flight from Hartford following his trade from the Whalers in October 1996, could join them.

There were definitely great expectations for Shanahan—and with good reason. While Detroit was the fourth stop for the quintessential power forward, Shanahan had established a reputation as one of the NHL's premier players. Selected No. 2 overall by New Jersey in the 1987 entry draft, Shanahan scored 81 goals in his last three seasons with the Devils prior to being dealt to St. Louis, where he topped 50 goals in two of his three seasons, and then it was on to Hartford, where he had 78 points in 74 games in 1995-96.

Disgruntled in Hartford, Shanahan pressed for a trade because the club wasn't a contender, and the cash-strapped franchise really couldn't afford to keep him. Enter the Red Wings, a team that had both the money and contending status, and needed a productive, strapping forward to put it over the top.

Fighting start
The October 9 trade saw Shanahan and defenseman Brian Glynn head to Detroit for Keith Primeau, a hulking forward who still hadn't blossomed offensively, veteran defenseman Paul Coffey, and a first-round pick in the 1997 entry draft. "I don't look at this as the end of something," Shanahan said when he learned of the trade. "I look at it as the beginning. The Red Wings' game is to win the Stanley Cup, and that's my game, too."

They were prophetic words indeed. Shanahan fit into the Red Wings lineup like a glove, blending strong physical play—he got into his first fight four minutes into his first game with Detroit—along with a knack around the net to score 46 goals and collect 87 points in 79 regular-season games. He also racked up 131 minutes in penalties.

Shanahan contributed nine goals and eight assists in 20 post-season games, helping the Red Wings end a 52-year Stanley Cup drought. It was mission accomplished, both for Shanahan and the Red Wings, who were still smarting from a four-game sweep by the New Jersey Devils in the Stanley Cup final two years earlier.

Missing link
Shanahan said watching the Devils, his former team, win the Cup, only increased his yearning to join a contender. "I saw friends and fans I know celebrate that Cup win, and it hit pretty close to home," said Shanahan, who had left New Jersey when St. Louis signed him as a free agent in July, 1991. The Devils were awarded defenseman Scott Stevens as compensation for signing Shanahan. "I really thought I was going to get a Cup win in St. Louis," added Shanahan. But in July, 1995, he was on the move again—to Hartford for defenseman Chris Pronger. To some, the Blues made the trade for economic reasons. Shanahan believes it was because Blues coach Mike Keenan "wanted to bring in his own guys."

In his only full season with the Whalers, Shanahan was named the team captain, a testimony to his leadership abilities. When he arrived in Detroit, he was immediately made an assistant captain to captain Steve Yzerman.

"I know that I am a missing piece of the puzzle," Shanahan said after joining the Red Wings. "But just a piece. I'm not the guy who's going to change things."

His teammates who giddily paraded around the ice after the Red Wings' second consecutive Stanley Cup victory would undoubtedly dispute Shanahan's claim.

CAREER RECORD

Personal	
Birthplace/Date	Mimico, Ontario/23-01-69
Height/Weight	6-3/215

Awards	
First All-Star Team	1994
NHL All-Star Game selection	1994, 1996, 1997

NHL Career
4 seasons New Jersey Devils
3 seasons St. Louis Blues
1 season Hartford Whalers
2 seasons Detroit Red Wings

Playing record

	Games	Goals	Assists	Points	PIM
Regular season	788	363	380	743	1626
Playoffs	91	34	37	71	193

Power forward Brendan Shanahan has added grit, drive, leadership and offense to the already powerful Detroit Red Wings.

With his effortless offensive drive, Sundin continues to be the beacon of hope for the Toronto Maple Leafs.

Mats Sundin had franchise player written all over him when he was drafted first overall in the 1989 Entry Draft. As things have unfolded, Sundin has filled that office for not one franchise, but two.

Big, strong, a swift, powerful skater with a hard, accurate shot and an impressive bag of creative offensive tricks, Sundin certainly has the requisite tools to be the key player wherever he earns his pay cheque.

For four years, Sundin was one of the building blocks around whom the Quebec Nordiques were going to surge from the ashes to contend for a Stanley Cup.

But Sundin only had one shot at Stanley Cup playoff action with Quebec (now the Colorado Avalanche). That was in 1992-93, the year Sundin scored 47 goals and totalled 114 points in all, tops on the talent-rich Nordiques, whose lineup boasted Joe Sakic and Valeri Kamensky.

Tall hustler

The Nordiques won the first two games of their only playoff series that spring against the Montreal Canadiens, but that was it. The Canadiens would ride the goaltending brilliance of Patrick Roy to the Stanley Cup championship that season, while the Nordiques would take a year to recover from the shock. The following season, they missed the playoffs altogether.

For many, a lasting image of that Stanley Cup opening-round failure is that of then-Nordiques head coach Pierre Page yelling in Sundin's ear on national TV as the seconds ticked down on the final loss of the series.

Some fans, too, can be critical of Sundin, whose sublime offensive achievements often appear too effortless.

"Sometimes it doesn't look like bigger guys hustle as much as the little guy who has to take maybe three strides while the bigger guy takes one," Sundin says. "I'm known to have been criticized sometimes, when people say that I'm kind of cruising around or pacing myself. I'm 6-foot-4 1/2, almost 6-foot-5, and I know that when I'm on the ice, I'm always working hard."

One of the few bright spots for the lowly Toronto Maple Leafs in 1997-98 was the play of Mats Sundin, their offensive leader.

Toronto hope

Sundin was traded to the Toronto Maple Leafs in a blockbuster trade that sent popular Maple Leafs winger Wendel Clark to Quebec. If there was pressure in replacing the fan idol Clark, it has not been evident. Sundin has led the Maple Leafs in scoring all four seasons he has played there — the first Leaf to achieve such a level of consistency since Darryl Sittler.

Over that span, Sundin has scored 130 goals, including 41 (and 97 points) in 1996-97, when he was the only bright light in a dismal Toronto season that saw many veterans dispatched to other teams as the Maple Leafs desperately attempted to swap aging talent for young prospects. It was a similar story in 1997-98 when his 74-point output was the lone source of comfort to the fans. And there may be worse news for the Toronto faithful … Sundin's summer was spent as the main bait in trade rumors.

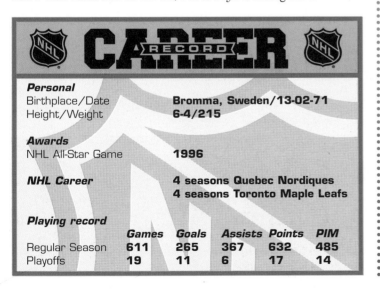

CAREER RECORD

Personal

Birthplace/Date	Bromma, Sweden/13-02-71
Height/Weight	6-4/215

Awards

NHL All-Star Game	1996

NHL Career

	4 seasons Quebec Nordiques
	4 seasons Toronto Maple Leafs

Playing record

	Games	Goals	Assists	Points	PIM
Regular Season	611	265	367	632	485
Playoffs	19	11	6	17	14

The Tough Coyote
KEITH TKACHUK

The qualities that made this U.S. high-scorer the Coyotes' youngest captain continue to bolster Phoenix.

Captain Courageous: If the Phoenix Coyotes are going to live up to their considerable potential, it will be due to the leadership and talent of players like Keith Tkachuk.

after Winnipeg matched a five-year, $17-million offer sheet he had signed with the Chicago Blackhawks after he became a restricted free agent. Tkachuk quickly became the fans' target.

Despite the pressure, Tkachuk lived up to the trust shown him when he was named captain by scoring 41 goals and adding 40 assists and staking a solid claim to being one of the best young power forwards in hockey.

But it was in 1995-96 and 1996-97 that Tkachuk really blossomed. He scored 50 goals in 1995-96 and 52 in 1996-97, the franchise's first in its new home in Phoenix as the Coyotes, not the Jets. The scoring achievement made him just the third U.S.-born player to score 50 or more goals in two different seasons (the others are Pat LaFontaine and John LeClair). Tkachuk, just 24, is poised to set a new standard for scoring excellence for American-born players.

Smile for the hitman

The 1996-97 preseason was when Tkachuk established himself on the international hockey stage by helping lead Team USA to the gold medal in the inaugural World Cup of Hockey in September.

He scored five goals in seven games and managed to find an outlet for his renowned toughness, too, breaking the nose of Claude Lemieux in a fight.

"There were a lot of toothless smiles around the league," said Phoenix winger Jim McKenzie.

Tkachuk's style always has involved blending physical toughness with offensive skill, and he managed it again during the 1997-98 season as he racked up 40 goals in 69 games. Although he endured some criticism for failing to find the net more often during the playoffs (he netted three times against the Detroit Red Wings), there's no doubt that Tkachuk will remain the main offensive weapon in the Coyotes' armory.

To long-suffering fans in hockey-crazed Winnipeg, Keith Tkachuk was nothing less than the saviour when he arrived there as a 19-year-old following the 1992 Winter Olympics in Albertville, France.

It did not take him long to demonstrate he belonged in The Show. In his first complete season — 1992-93 — Tkachuk scored 28 goals and racked up 201 minutes in penalties.

The following season, Tkachuk was named captain of the Jets at the tender age of 21, the youngest captain in franchise history. Being captain of the Jets was no trivial responsibility, and Tkachuk has the grey hair to prove it.

"Try being captain of the Winnipeg Jets at age 21 and see what it does to your hair," Tkachuk once said.

Making the grade

When he joined the Jets, they were in the middle of one of their periodic rebuilding campaigns but still underachieving, despite the likes of Teemu Selanne and Alexei Zhamnov in the lineup. To make matters worse, the club was in rocky financial shape. Tkachuk, through no fault of his own, put them deeper in a hole

CAREER RECORD

Personal				
Birthplace/Date	Melrose, Massachusett/2-28-72			
Height/Weight	5-2/210			

Awards				
Second All-Star Team	1995			

NHL Career				
	6 1/2 seasons			
	Winnipeg Jets/Phoenix Coyotes			

Playing record	Games	Goals	Assists	Points	PIM
Regular season	458	236	205	441	1167
Playoffs	32	17	5	22	83

ALEXEI YASHIN

This steady, strong offensive power scorer has carved himself a center place in the Senators' strengthening line-up.

When the Ottawa Senators drafted Alexei Yashin second overall in the NHL Entry Draft in 1992, his name hardly resonated with that city's hockey fans. For starters, the Senators were expected to select Roman Hamrlik, a feisty, skilled defenseman from the Czech Republic.

A lot of Russians were well known to North American hockey fans before they crossed the Atlantic. Not Yashin.

Unlike, for example, Pavel Bure or Alexander Mogilny, Yashin had not made a name for himself as a junior virtuoso. To a lot of Ottawa fans, Yashin was simply the first of a slew of Russians, and other Europeans, claimed in the first round of that draft.

"The greatest thing that ever happened to this franchise was losing a coin flip," John Ferguson, the Senators' director of player personnel at the time, boasted. "Last February I said Yashin would be rookie-of-the-year."

Yashin would not win the Calder Trophy, but he took a run at it, in his own creative, if somewhat methodical fashion.

He certainly isn't the typical Russian player. Compared to speed merchants like Bure, Mogilny and Sergei Fedorov, Yashin's a plodder, strong on his skates, clever with the puck, but no end-to-end flash.

Interludes in Russia

Yashin, as it happened, was in no hurry to get to Ottawa after he was drafted. Rather than endure the inevitable growing pains of an expansion franchise's first season, Yashin played an extra year with Moscow Dynamo, and joined the Senators for the start of the 1993-94 season, along with another rookie—Alexandre Daigle, the first overall pick in the 1993 Entry Draft.

He obviously was worth the wait. In his first season, Yashin scored 30 goals and totalled 79 points, tops on the Senators that season. He also was a finalist for the Calder Trophy as the NHL's best first-year player.

He managed such a productive season despite the fact that the Senators traded winger Bob Kudelski, Yashin's linemate, who was enjoying a career season, part-way through the year.

The following season, the lockout-shortened 1994-95 campaign, Yashin put together a 44-point season in 47 games, including 21 goals.

Having established himself as Ottawa's top player, Yashin chafed knowing that the under-achieving Daigle was earning far more than he. And so he became a contract holdout in 1995-96. He began that year playing for CSKA in Moscow, and sitting out almost half the season before signing and rejoining the Senators.

It took the big, strong Russian most of the rest of that season to regain the form he had shown as a rookie, yet he still managed 39 points in 46 games for Ottawa.

Growing strong

In 1996-97, the Senators fortunes improved dramatically. Under general manager Pierre Gauthier and head coach Jacques Martin, both of whom had been hired by the Senators part-way through the 1995-96 season, the club took a run at making the playoffs for the first time in the club's young history.

Not surprisingly, Yashin helped lead the charge, scoring 35 goals and adding 45 assists to lead the Senators in scoring. The Senators set franchise records for victories (31) and points (77), and received strong performances from Daigle (26 goals, 51 points) and sophomore winger Daniel Alfredsson (24 goals, 71 points).

Making their first playoff appearance, the Senators pushed the Buffalo Sabres to seven games before losing

The Senators made the playoffs again in 1997-98 and, once more, it was largely due to the 72 points from Yashin. As well as enjoying success with his franchise, the Russian also picked up a silver medal during the 1998 Olympic Games.

CAREER RECORD

Personal

Birthplace/Date	Sverdolsk, Russia/5-11-73
Height/Weight	6-3/215

Awards

NHL All-Star Game	1994

NHL Career   5 seasons Ottawa Senators

Playing record

	Games	Goals	Assists	Points	PIM
Regular season	340	134	175	309	138
Playoffs	18	6	8	14	10

Alexei Yashin's strong offensive contribution is a key reason the Ottawa Senators have emerged as a strong force.

THE STANLEY CUP
THE ULTIMATE GOAL

It's known as the National Hockey League's second season and it may well be the most exciting post-season tournament in professional sports. The Stanley Cup playoffs stretch from mid-April to mid-June as 16 of the NHL's 26 teams compete for the Stanley Cup, one of the most cherished pieces of sporting silverware in the world. The champion must win four best-of-seven series—16 games out of a possible 28 in total, all played after the 82-game regular season concludes in mid-April.

This annual North American Rite of Spring has unfolded, in various formats, since 1893, one year after Lord Stanley, the Earl of Preston and Governor-General of Canada, donated the challenge cup to symbolize the hockey championship of Canada.

Lord Stanley returned to England without ever seeing a championship game or personally presenting the trophy that bears his name. He wasn't around when the Montreal Amateur Athletic Association hockey club became the first winner of the trophy. He certainly could not have foreseen that his trophy would become the property of the National Hockey League, which did not exist until 1917 and did not assume control of the Stanley Cup competition until the 1926-27 season.

Still, the rich and colorful history attached to the silver cup that Lord Stanley purchased for 10 guineas ($48.67 Cdn) more than lives up to the spirit of the annual hockey competition he envisioned more than 100 years ago.

The institution of the trophy kicked off a parade of legendary performances. In 1904, One-Eyed Frank McGee scored a record five goals in an 11-2 victory for the Ottawa Silver Seven over the Toronto Marlboros. The following year, McGee scored 14 goals for the Silver Seven, who demolished the Dawson City Nuggets 23-2. The Nuggets had journeyed to Ottawa via dogsled, boat and train to challenge for Lord Stanley's Cup.

A special time

The quality of competition has tightened considerably since those early days, and transportation is decidedly less rustic, also. But the mystique of the best four-out-of-seven game final series still holds powerful appeal for hockey fans.

The Stanley Cup final can pit speed and finesse against size and toughness, slick offense versus stingy defense, age against youth and, sometimes, brother against brother. The first time that happened was March 16, 1923 when the Denneny brothers, Cy and Corb, and the Boucher siblings, George and Frank, faced off against each other. Cy and George were members of the Ottawa Senators, Corb and Frank played for the Vancouver Maroons. Ottawa won that game 1-0 and went on to capture the Stanley Cup.

In a playoff game between the Montreal Canadiens and the

Cup of Honor: Lanny McDonald (left), the Calgary Flames' bearded veteran, capped off a 16-year NHL career with a Stanley Cup triumph in 1989.

Quebec Nordiques in the 1980s, Montreal's Mark Hunter missed a golden opportunity to pot an overtime winner at one end, then watched, crestfallen as older brother Dale put the game away for the Nordiques (now the Colorado Avalanche) at the other end.

The Stanley Cup tournament is a special event, when there's no time for injuries to heal, so the great ones simply play through the pain, no matter how excruciating. Hall of Fame defenseman Jacques Laperriere once played the finals with a broken wrist, goaltender John Davidson gritted his teeth and played with a wonky knee in the 1979 finals. Montreal left winger Bob Gainey once completed a playoff series against the New York Islanders with not one but two shoulder separations. And in 1964, Toronto Maple Leafs defenseman Bob Baun scored an overtime winner with a broken ankle in Game 6, then played Game 7 without missing a shift. He then spent two months on crutches recuperating. No doubt, the Stanley Cup ring helped soothe his pain.

The Stanley Cup is about unlikely heroes, like Montreal goalie Ken Dryden being called up from the minors to backstop Montreal to a first-round upset over the heavily favored Boston Bruins in 1971, then going on to win the Conn Smythe Trophy, not to mention the Stanley Cup, both before winning the Calder Trophy as rookie-of-the-year the following season.

It's a showcase for the game's greatest stars, like Maurice (Rocket) Richard, who once scored five goals in a playoff game in 1944. Richard's record of six career playoff overtime goals has stood up for 36 years.

Alberta Magic: Few would have guessed that Wayne Gretzky's fourth Stanley Cup in Edmonton would be his last in an Oiler uniform.

A fitting showcase

In the 1990s, the first round of the playoff tournament has captivated hockey fans, providing some stunning upsets, like the expansion San Jose Sharks knocking out the Detroit Red Wings in seven games in 1994. The Sharks rolled right to the Western Conference semifinal, extending the Toronto Maple Leafs to seven games before losing.

In 1993, the New York Islanders surprised the Washington Capitals in the opening round, then stunned the two-time defending champion Pittsburgh Penguins in the division final, a series victory that helped pave the way for Montreal's surprising Stanley Cup triumph. The Canadiens had fallen behind 2-0 to the talent-rich Quebec Nordiques before winning four straight games to eliminate their provincial rivals from the tournament.

There are those who criticize the Stanley Cup playoffs as far too long, who suggest, not without justification, that hockey is simply not meant to be played in June, taxing the ice-making machinery, the fans' attention span and the players' fitness level.

Few would dare to suggest, however, that the two-month-long tournament is not a fitting showcase for professional hockey. Boring is something the Stanley Cup playoffs most certainly are not.

Lord Stanley never knew what he missed; nor had he any idea how rich a sporting tradition he initiated all those years ago.

Stanley Cup Results 1927-1998 (NHL assumed control of the Cup in 1927)

Year	W/L	Winner	Coach	Runner-up	Coach
1998	4-0	Detroit	Scott Bowman	Washington	Ron Wilson
1997	4-0	Detroit	Scott Bowman	Philadelphia	Terry Murray
1996	4-0	Colorado	Marc Crawford	Florida	Doug MacLean
1995	4-0	NJ Devils	Jacques Lemaire	Detroit	Scott Bowman
1994	4-3	NY Rangers	Mike Keenan	Vancouver	Pat Quinn
1993	4-1	Montreal	Jacques Demers	LA Kings	Barry Melrose
1992	4-0	Pittsburgh	Scott Bowman	Chicago	Mike Keenan
1991	4-2	Pittsburgh	Bob Johnson	Minnesota	Bob Gainey
1990	4-1	Edmonton	John Muckler	Boston	Mike Milbury
1989	4-2	Calgary	Terry Crisp	Montreal	Pat Burns
1988	4-0	Edmonton	Glen Sather	Boston	Terry O'Reilly
1987	4-3	Edmonton	Glen Sather	Philadelphia	Mike Keenan
1986	4-1	Montreal	Jean Perron	Calgary	Bob Johnson
1985	4-1	Edmonton	Glen Sather	Philadelphia	Mike Keenan
1984	4-1	Edmonton	Glen Sather	NY Islanders	Al Arbour
1983	4-0	NY Islanders	Al Arbour	Edmonton	Glen Sather
1982	4-0	NY Islanders	Al Arbour	Vancouver	Roger Neilson
1981	4-1	NY Islanders	Al Arbour	Minnesota	Glen Sonmor
1980	4-2	NY Islanders	Al Arbour	Philadelphia	Pat Quinn
1979	4-1	Montreal	Scott Bowman	NY Rangers	Fred Shero
1978	4-2	Montreal	Scott Bowman	Boston	Don Cherry
1977	4-0	Montreal	Scott Bowman	Boston	Don Cherry
1976	4-0	Montreal	Scott Bowman	Philadelphia	Fred Shero
1975	4-2	Philadelphia	Fred Shero	Buffalo	Floyd Smith
1974	4-2	Philadelphia	Fred Shero	Boston	Bep Guidolin
1973	4-2	Montreal	Scott Bowman	Chicago	Billy Reay
1972	4-2	Boston	Tom Johnson	NY Rangers	Emile Francis
1971	4-3	Montreal	Al McNeil	Chicago	Billy Reay
1970	4-0	Boston	Harry Sinden	St. Louis	Scott Bowman
1969	4-0	Montreal	Claude Ruel	St. Louis	Scott Bowman
1968	4-0	Montreal	Toe Blake	St. Louis	Scott Bowman
1967	4-2	Toronto	Punch Imlach	Montreal	Toe Blake
1966	4-2	Montreal	Toe Blake	Detroit	Sid Abel
1965	4-3	Montreal	Toe Blake	Chicago	Billy Reay
1964	4-3	Toronto	Punch Imlach	Detroit	Sid Abel
1963	4-1	Toronto	Punch Imlach	Detroit	Sid Abel
1962	4-2	Toronto	Punch Imlach	Chicago	Rudy Pilous
1961	4-1	Chicago	Rudy Pilous	Detroit	Sid Abel
1960	4-3	Montreal	Toe Blake	Toronto	Punch Imlach
1959	4-1	Montreal	Toe Blake	Toronto	Punch Imlach
1958	4-2	Montreal	Toe Blake	Boston	Milt Schmidt
1957	4-1	Montreal	Toe Blake	Boston	Milt Schmidt
1956	4-1	Montreal	Toe Blake	Detroit	Jimmy Skinner
1955	4-3	Detroit	Jimmy Skinner	Montreal	Dick Irvin
1954	4-3	Detroit	Tommy Ivan	Montreal	Dick Irvin
1953	4-1	Montreal	Dick Irvin	Boston	Lynn Patrick
1952	4-0	Detroit	Tommy Ivan	Montreal	Dick Irvin
1951	4-1	Toronto	Joe Primeau	Montreal	Dick Irvin
1950	4-3	Detroit	Tommy Ivan	NY Rangers	Lynn Patrick
1949	4-0	Toronto	Hap Day	Detroit	Tommy Ivan
1948	4-0	Toronto	Hap Day	Detroit	Tommy Ivan
1947	4-2	Toronto	Hap Day	Montreal	Dick Irvin
1946	4-1	Montreal	Dick Irvin	Boston	Dit Clapper
1945	4-3	Toronto	Hap Day	Detroit	Jack Adams
1944	4-0	Montreal	Dick Irvin	Chicago	Paul Thompson
1943	4-0	Detroit	Jack Adams	Boston	Art Ross
1942	4-3	Toronto	Hap Day	Detroit	Jack Adams
1941	4-0	Boston	Cooney Weiland	Detroit	Ebbie Goodfellow
1940	4-2	NY Rangers	Frank Boucher	Toronto	Dick Irvin
1939	4-1	Boston	Art Ross	Toronto	Dick Irvin
1938	3-1	Chicago	Bill Stewart	Toronto	Dick Irvin
1937	3-2	Detroit	Jack Adams	NY Rangers	Lester Patrick
1936	3-1	Detroit	Jack Adams	Toronto	Dick Irvin
1935	3-0	Mtl. Maroons	Tommy Gorman	Toronto	Dick Irvin
1934	3-1	Chicago	Tommy Gorman	Detroit	Herbie Lewis
1933	3-1	NY Rangers	Lester Patrick	Toronto	Dick Irvin
1932	3-0	Toronto	Dick Irvin	NY Rangers	Lester Patrick
1931	3-2	Montreal	Cecil Hart	Chicago	Dick Irvin
1930	2-0	Montreal	Cecil Hart	Boston	Art Ross
1929	2-0	Boston	Cy Denneny	NY Rangers	Lester Patrick
1928	3-2	NY Rangers	Lester Patrick	Mtl. Maroons	Eddie Gerard
1927	2-0-2	Ottawa	Dave Gill	Boston	Art Ross

1992 Stanley Cup Finals
VICTORY REPLAY

Mario Lemieux and the Penguins started the playoffs slowly, then rolled to eleven straight victories and their second straight Stanley Cup.

It was the second time around in the finals for Mario Lemieux and the Pittsburgh Penguins, and they were gathering momentum. Down 3-1 to the Washington Capitals in the first round of the playoffs, they reeled off three straight victories to move past their divisional rivals.

Penguins general manager Craig Patrick had tinkered with the lineup. Gone were Paul Coffey and Mark Recchi. In were defenseman Kjell Samuelsson, power forward Rick Tocchet and winger Shawn McEachern, plus veteran Ken Wregget.

Scotty Bowman, who had been the club's director of scouting, had replaced head coach Bob Johnson, who died in November 1991. Bowman had piloted the Montreal Canadiens to five Stanley Cups in the 1970s.

Tight odds

In Game 1 of the final series, the Blackhawks jumped to a 3-0 first-period lead.

Phil Bourque got one back for the Penguins late in the opening period, but Brent Sutter restored the Blackhawks three-goal lead at 11:36 of the second period. Then the Penguins showed their mettle.

Tocchet and Lemieux sliced the lead to one goal before the end of the second period. And Jaromir Jagr tied the game with his first goal of the finals in the third.

When Blackhawks defenseman Steve Smith was whistled for hooking with 18 seconds left in the game, the Penguins seized the opportunity.

Just 13 seconds before the end of regulation time, Lemieux beat Chicago goaltender Ed Belfour on the power play to win the game for Pittsburgh.

Lemieux was front and center in Game 2, as well, scoring to lift the Penguins to a 3-1 victory and a 2-0 series lead as the final shifted to Chicago Stadium.

Depth of talent

In Game 3, the Penguins showed that they were fully capable of excelling in a tight-checking playoff game by posting a 1-0 victory.

And in Game 4, they won in a 6-5 shootout as the Blackhawks failed to match goals.

The teams entered the third period tied 4-4, but goals by Larry Murphy and Ron Francis gave the Penguins the cushion they needed.

After their slow playoff start, the Penguins had won 11 straight games, including a semifinal sweep of the Boston Bruins.

Lemieux won the Conn Smythe Trophy for the second straight year, the second player to win the playoff MVP award two straight years.

Emergent Star: Jaromir Jagr arrived as an NHL star in helping Pittsburgh win a second straight Stanley Cup in 1992.

★★★★ RESULTS ★★★★

	Game	Site	Winner	Score	GWG
May 26	Game 1	Pittsburgh	Pittsburgh	5-4	Mario Lemieux
May 28	Game 2	Pittsburgh	Pittsburgh	3-1	Mario Lemieux
May 30	Game 3	Chicago	Pittsburgh	1-0	Kevin Stevens
June 1	Game 4	Chicago	Pittsburgh	6-5	Ron Francis

OVERTIME POWERPLAY

Goaltender Patrick Roy—St. Patrick to his Montreal fans—backstopped the Canadiens to ten straight overtime victories and a surprise Cup.

★★★★ RESULTS ★★★★

	Game	Site	Winner	Score	GWG
June 1	Game 1	Montreal	Los Angeles	4-1	Luc Robitaille
June 3	Game 2	Montreal	Montreal	3-2 (OT)	Eric Desjardins
June 5	Game 3	Los Angeles	Montreal	4-3 (OT)	John LeClair
June 7	Game 4	Los Angeles	Montreal	3-2 (OT)	John LeClair
June 9	Game 5	Montreal	Montreal	4-1	Kirk Muller

Captain Kirk: Montreal's surprise Stanley Cup in 1993 was due in significant part to the gritty play of Kirk Muller.

Patrick Roy's legend reached its zenith this year as his goaltending keyed ten straight overtime victories by Montreal en route to their 24th Stanley Cup victory. The Canadiens had upset favored Quebec, swept the Buffalo Sabres and beaten the New York Islanders to reach the final series.

Los Angeles, led by Wayne Gretzky, had advanced past the Calgary Flames, Vancouver Canucks and the Toronto Maple Leafs.

In Game 1 of the Stanley Cup final, Luc Robitaille's two goals powered the Kings to a 4-1 victory. In Los Angeles, this was supposed to be the year Gretzky led the Kings to a championship.

All was going well for them, Roy or no Roy, when catastrophe struck. Canadiens captain Guy Carbonneau had noticed that Kings defenseman Marty McSorley used a stick blade whose curvature exceeded the legal one inch limit.

With just 1:45 remaining in the third period and the Kings leading 2-1, referee Kerry Fraser measured the stick. As 18,000 fans and a vast TV audience watched, the blade was shown to be clearly over the limit. McSorley was banished to the penalty box for two minutes.

During the ensuing power play, Montreal defenseman Eric Desjardins beat Kings goalie Kelly Hrudey to tie the game, sending it into overtime.

Just 51 seconds later, Desjardins scored again, lifting Montreal to a 3-2 victory. The series was tied 1-1.

Confidence restored

It gave Montreal new life.

When the series moved to LA, the Canadiens twice extended the Kings to overtime.

Twice in a row, power forward John LeClair scored the gamewinner.

The Canadiens returned to the Forum leading the series 3-1. The demoralized Kings were frustrated by Roy, whose nearly flawless play infused his teammates with confidence.

In Game 5, McSorley, seeking to make amends for his stick gaffe, scored a rare goal to lift the Kings into a 1-1 tie. It wasn't enough.

Kirk Muller, with the Stanley Cup-winning goal, made it 2-1 before the second period was over and Stephan Lebeau padded Montreal's lead with a power-play goal at 11:31 of the period. Paul DiPietro's third-period goal was merely insurance.

The Canadiens clinched the Cup with an emphatic victory in which the Kings managed just 19 shots—only five in the final period— at Roy.

Roy won the Conn Smythe Trophy as the most valuable player in the playoffs, the second time he won the award.

We Won, We Won

The long-suffering Rangers silenced their many critics by winning their first Stanley Cup championship in fifty four years.

The biggest game in New York's first Stanley Cup triumph in 54 years probably came not in the exciting, final against Vancouver, but in the seven-game semifinal against New Jersey.

It was before Game 6, with the Devils holding a 3-2 series lead, that Rangers captain Mark Messier guaranteed a New York victory to push the series to a seventh game. Then he backed up his prediction with three goals as the Rangers won 4-2 to send the series to a seventh game.

Team for a win

In the final, Vancouver grabbed a 1-0 lead, winning 3-2, but the Rangers methodically rolled to a 3-1 series lead.

Rangers' general manager Neil Smith had carefully constructed a championship team, blending talented draft selections like goalie Mike Richter, Brian Leetch, Alexei Kovalev and Sergei Nemchinov with veterans acquired through trades.

Messier was the centerpiece acquisition, but the cast of players included ex-Oilers like Glenn Anderson, Jeff Beukeboom, Adam Graves, Kevin Lowe, Craig MacTavish and Esa Tikkanen, and role players such as Stephane Matteau, Brian Noonan and Jay Wells.

The Vancouver Canucks, meanwhile, had built their team around Russian speedster Pavel Bure and Trevor Linden, their on-ice leader, who would have to go head-to-head with Messier.

An end to waiting

In Game 5, the Canucks spoiled the party at Madison Square Garden by stunning the Rangers 6-3 as Geoff Courtnall and Bure each scored twice. That meant both teams—and the Cup iself—had to make another trip to Vancouver, where the Canucks tied the series, by posting a 4-1 victory.

The final score in Game 7 was 3-2 for the Rangers, but New York was in command of the game, without question.

Leetch and Graves provided a 2-0 first-period lead, and after Linden's short-handed goal sliced the lead to one goal early in the second, Messier responded with a power-play score in the 14th minute that restored the New York lead to two goals.

Linden's power-play goal at 4:50 of the third period gave the Canucks renewed hope, but the Rangers were able to hold them off to bring the Cup back to their fans for the first time since 1940. The victory touched off days of celebrations and tributes to the Rangers.

Defenseman Leetch won the Conn Smythe Trophy, becoming the first American-born player to do so. He led all playoff scorers with 34 points, including 11 goals.

Broadway Championship: Head coach Mike Keenan piloted the Rangers to the Stanley Cup in 1994, 54 years after their previous championship in 1940.

★★★★★ **RESULTS** ★★★★★

	Game	Site	Winner	Score	GWG
May 31	Game 1	New York	Vancouver	3-2 (OT)	Greg Adams
June 2	Game 2	New York	NY Rangers	3-1	Glenn Anderson
June 4	Game 3	Vancouver	NY Rangers	5-1	Glenn Anderson
June 7	Game 4	Vancouver	NY Rangers	4-2	Alexei Kovalev
June 9	Game 5	New York	Vancouver	6-3	David Babych
June 11	Game 6	Vancouver	Vancouver	4-1	Geoff Courtnall
June 14	Game 7	NY Rangers	NY Rangers	3-2	Mark Messier

DEVILS' TRAP

Once described as a "Mickey Mouse" franchise by Wayne Gretzky, the Devils received their due with a stunning upset over Detroit.

★★★★★ RESULTS ★★★★

	Game	Site	Winner	Score	GWG
June 17	Game 1	Detroit	New Jersey	2-1	Claude Lemieux
June 20	Game 2	Detroit	New Jersey	4-2	Jim Dowd
June 22	Game 3	New Jersey	New Jersey	5-2	Neal Broten
June 24	Game 4	New Jersey	New Jersey	5-2	Neal Broten

The Cup Goes to the Devils: Claude Lemieux, who helped the Montreal Canadiens win a Stanley Cup in 1986, led the Devils' scorers as New Jersey won their first Stanley Cup.

The New Jersey Devils sprung a speed trap on Detroit in 1995 and stopped the flashy Red Wings dead in their tracks in a too-brief Stanley Cup final series. The trap—known as the neutral-zone trap and designed to choke off an opponent's attack in the neutral zone and create turnovers—couldn't have been a surprise to the Red Wings. New Jersey head coach Jacques Lemaire had the Devils using the delayed forechecking system throughout the lockout-shortened 1994-95 season.

The Devils had no easy route to the final. They had withstood the Philadelphia Flyers, who had dismissed the New York Rangers.

The Red Wings, the top team in the league during the 48-game regular season, had cruised to the final, losing just two games in three series along the way.

But the Devils rode the flawless goaltending of Martin Brodeur, the crashing, banging ensemble work of their forwards and the physical play of defensemen like Scott Stevens and Ken Daneyko to the Stanley Cup. And they made it look easy.

No chance

In three of the four series games, the Devils held the potent Red Wings—the likes of Fedorov, Yzerman, Kozlov and Sheppard—to fewer than 20 shots. The Wings managed just seven scores in the four games against New Jersey.

In Game 1, Claude Lemieux scored the game-winner in the third period. It was his 12th goal of the playoffs and he would score 13 to lead all playoff snipers before the series was over.

In Game 2, the Devils broke open a 2-1 game with three straight third-period goals for a 2-0 lead.

In Game 3, the Devils raced to a 5-0 lead. Fedorov and Yzerman just managed to score power-play goals within the game's final three minutes.

Game 4 was similarly one-sided, as the Devils held the Red Wings to just 16 shots in winning 5-2 again to capture the first Stanley Cup in franchise history.

Red Wings head coach Scotty Bowman termed the defeat "humiliating."

Lemieux won the Conn Smythe Trophy for his steady playoff scoring, and longtime Devils veterans like John MacLean, Bruce Driver, and Ken Daneyko won their first Stanley Cup after years of struggling in mediocrity.

The Devils gained bragging rights in the all-important New York City media market. Long the forgotten franchise, third in the public imagination behind the Rangers and Islanders, it was the Devils' turn to bask in some Stanley Cup glory.

Avalanche on a Roll

Upstart third-year expansion team Florida Panthers were on a playoff roll to victory until Colorado Avalanche swept their hopes away.

The Colorado Avalanche and the Florida Panthers were surprise Stanley Cup finalists in the playoff year that will forever be known as the Year of the Rat. Fans at the Miami Arena brought a new ritual to Stanley Cup play—tossing toy plastic rats onto the ice after a Panthers goal. Rats rained down on the Boston Bruins, Philadelphia Flyers, and Pittsburgh Penguins as each was eliminated.

With nightly miracles by John Vanbiesbrouck in goal, a sound, aggressive defensive system, and total commitment to hard work, the Panthers got on an effective playoff roll—first-year head coach Doug MacLean had them believing they could defeat anyone.

But in the final they confronted a team with far more talent, size, speed, and skill than they could contain.

In Game 1, Tom Fitzgerald scored to give the Panthers a 1-0 first-period lead, but the Avalanche's superior firepower showed up in the second period. Scott Young, Mike Ricci and Uwe Krupp scored consecutive goals in a span of two minutes 49 seconds as momentum shifted irrevocably to Colorado.

Outgunned

The outmanned Panthers were swept aside in Game 2 as Colorado took a 2-0 series lead with a 8-1 win. Swedish forward Peter Forsberg was the scoring star with three goals.

Goaltender Patrick Roy was the key to Colorado's Game 3 victory, a 3-2 squeaker in Miami which saw the toy rats make their first series appearance. Avalanche winger Claude Lemieux, back from a two-game suspension, converted a pass from Valeri Kamensky at 2:44 of the opening period.

Then, at 9:14, Florida's Ray Sheppard prompted the first rat shower, scoring on the power play to tie the game, and Rob Niedermayer scored a 2-1 lead just over two minutes later.

But the Avalanche soon dominated, with Mike Keane scoring at 1:38 and Sakic beating Vanbiesbrouck for the game-winner on a breakaway at 3:00. A brilliant Roy held off the Panthers until game's end.

Game 4 was a festival of saves by both Roy and Vanbiesbrouck—turning away 119 shots between them over 104 minutes and 31 seconds.

Colorado defenseman Uwe Krupp ended the third-longest game in Stanley Cup history when his slap shot from the right point at 4:31 of the third overtime period handed the Avalanche their first Stanley Cup—and the only rain of rats for the opposing team at the Miami Arena.

The rats symbolized a fairy tale Stanley Cup run for the Panthers. Colorado's performance was embodied by their team captain, Joe Sakic, who led all playoff scorers with 18 goals, 16 assists and 34 points, to earn the Conn Smythe Trophy.

Rush for the Cup: Colorado's Valeri Kamensky couldn't solve Panthers' netminder John Vanbiesbrouck on this rush, but in the end it was Patrick Roy of the Avalanche who won the goalies' duel as the Avalanche swept Florida **4-0** to claim their first Stanley Cup.

★★★★ RESULTS ★★★★

	Game	Site	Winner	Score	GWG
June 4	Game 1	Denver	Colorado	3-1	Mike Ricci
June 6	Game 2	Denver	Colorado	8-1	Rene Corbet
June 8	Game 3	Miami	Colorado	3-2	Joe Sakic
June 10	Game 4	Miami	Colorado	1-0 (3OT)	Uwe Krupp

1997 **Stanley Cup Finals**
RED WINGS SOAR

A dominating total team effort swept Detroit from 42 years of disappointment to a Stanley Cup victory for Hockeytown, USA.

Detroit put 42 years of Stanley Cup disappointment behind it in June 1997 by sweeping away the overmatched Philadelphia Flyers to win their first championship since 1955. In that bygone time, the heroes were the legendary Gordie Howe, Terry Sawchuk, (Terrible) Ted Lindsay and Sid Abel.

The 1997 champions were led by Steve Yzerman, their classy captain, goaltender Mike Vernon, who won the Conn Smythe Trophy as the most valuable player in the playoffs, and Sergei Fedorov.

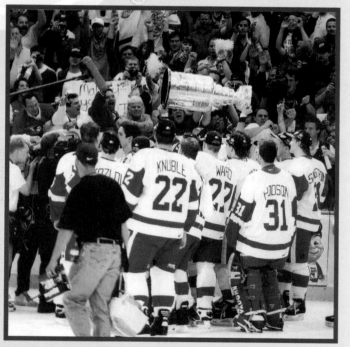

Worth the Wait: It had been 42 years since the Red Wings and their fans shared a Stanley Cup moment, so the Joe Louis Arena faithful and their heroes savored the thrill of ultimate victory in grand style.

But, just as the Red Wings had suffered an embarrassing collective collapse in 1995 when the New Jersey Devils swept them in four straight in the Stanley Cup final series, this time their dominance over the Flyers was a total team effort, as well.

As frequently happens in the Stanley Cup playoffs, unlikely heroes emerged and shone brightly for the Red Wings and their Hall of Fame head coach, Scotty Bowman.

Rising to the occasion

In Game 1, the Red Wings grabbed a 2-0 lead on a pair of Flyers defensive lapses. On the first, checking line center Kris Draper stripped Flyers captain Eric Lindros of the puck and sped away on a two-on-nothing break with Kirk Maltby during a Flyers power play. The pair of speedy Wings exchanged passes before Maltby finished off the rush by lifting a shot over a spread-eagled Ron Hextall to give the Wings an early lead.

On the second goal Philadelphia defenseman Kjell Samuelsson made an ill-conceived pass that Joey Kocur intercepted just inside the Flyers' blue line. He then danced in, with Yzerman along as a decoy. Hextall guessed that the modestly talented Kocur would pass to the future Hall of Famer Yzerman. Instead, Kocur held the puck and flicked a shot high over Hextall, and it was 2-0.

Detroit's fourth goal of the game, scored on a routine shot from just inside the blue line by Steve Yzerman, had the biggest impact on the series, though. That goal apparently convinced Philadelphia head coach Terry Murray to switch to backup goalie Garth Snow for the second game of the series.

Snow didn't last long. He, too, was victimized on a pair of long-range shots as Detroit lost Game 2.

Hextall was back in goal for Game 3, when Detroit's offensive gears meshed smoothly, and the Red Wings whacked the Flyers 6-1. The next day, Flyers coach Murray suggested his players were "choking" in an apparent attempt to motivate his overmatched team.

The Flyers, who held the lead in the series for just two minutes, certainly brought more intensity to Game 4 of the series, but to little avail.

The coup de grace was applied by unlikely scoring hero Darren McCarty, who scored the Cup-winning goal on a sublime rush on which he feinted magically past Flyers defenseman Janne Niinimaa, then swept the puck past a sliding Hextall on the backhand.

This prompted a dance of ecstasy by McCarty, a foreshadowing of a night-long party by the long-suffering Detroit fans.

Finally, the Stanley Cup had come back to stay, for a while at least, in the city that bills itself as Hockeytown, USA.

★★★★★ RESULTS ★★★★★

	Game	Site	Winner	Score	GWG
May 31	Game 1	Philadelphia	Detroit	4-2	Sergei Fedorov
June 3	Game 2	Philadelphia	Detroit	4-2	Kirk Maltby
June 5	Game 3	Detroit	Detroit	6-1	Sergei Fedorov
June 7	Game 4	Detroit	Detroit	2-1	Darren McCarty

THE WONDER WINGS

The Detroit Red Wings repeated their Cup success of 1997 and confirmed their status as one of the teams of the decade.

This time, the wait between Stanley Cups was much shorter for the Detroit Red Wings. When the team won the Cup in 1997, they ended a 42-year drought. When the Red Wings won the Cup again in 1998, they became just the second team of the decade to win back-to-back championships, joining the 1991/1992 Pittsburgh Penguins as members of the exclusive club.

The Wings were a team of destiny. Any complacency that might have settled in after their first Cup victory was wiped away six days later when star defenseman Vladimir Konstantinov and team masseur Sergei Mnatsakanov were seriously injured in a limo accident.

The Wings dedicated the season to their comrades and duly swept the Washington Capitals in the Stanley Cup Finals. It was the fourth straight Finals to end in a sweep, with Detroit having started the trend by losing to the New Jersey Devils in four games in 1995.

Brilliant Bowman
Detroit's win gave coach Scotty Bowman eight Stanley Cup rings as a coach, which tied him for the most ever with his mentor and idol Toe Blake, the great Montreal Canadiens' bench boss. Bowman got his eighth Cup thanks to a complete team effort.

The Wings boasted throughout the playoffs that they could roll four lines at any team and that held true. Evidence came in Game 1, when Grind Line winger Joe Kocur started off the scoring with his fourth goal of the playoffs. Star defenseman Nick Lidstrom added a second goal in the first period and that would be all the scoring Detroit would need in the 2-1 win at home. Wings goalie Chris Osgood faced the pressure of stepping in for the 1997 Conn Smythe Trophy winner Mike Vernon, who moved on to San Jose after the Wings' 1997 triumph. Although he let in three long goals in the first three rounds of the playoffs, he started the Finals magnificently, making 16 saves.

In Game 2, the Capitals seemed to be in control of the game in the third period. Washington led 3-1 after two periods, but even when Steve Yzerman cut the gap to 3-2 on a short-handed goal, the Caps responded 28 seconds later to stretch the lead to 4-2. Washington forward Esa Tikkanen, seemed ready to ice the game when he faked Osgood and had an open net to shoot at late in the third with the Caps ahead 4-3. But he missed the shot, and the Wings' Doug Brown scored shortly thereafter and the game headed to overtime. In the extra session, Grind Line center Kris Draper became the hero with his first goal of the playoffs.

Game 3 was played on the anniversary of the limo crash, and Detroit came out flying, outshooting the Caps 13-1 in the first period. But they only managed one goal, and Washington stayed in the game thanks to outstanding goaltending by Olaf Kolzig.

★★★★ **RESULTS** ★★★★

	Game	Site	Winner	Score	GWG
June 9	Game 1	Detroit	Detroit	2-1	Nicklas Lidstrom
June 11	Game 2	Detroit	Detroit	5-4	Kris Draper
June 13	Game 3	Washington	Detroit	2-1	Sergei Fedorov
June 16	Game 4	Washington	Detroit	4-1	Martin Lapointe

Brian Bellows tied the game in the third, but Detroit's Sergei Fedorov made a spectacular one-on-one rush to net the game-winner with five minutes to play.

Game 4 seemed more a formality than anything. Detroit got the first two goals and never looked back. Doug Brown scored twice. Konstantinov was on hand, and he made his way down to the ice in his wheelchair for the postgame celebration. The first person Yzerman handed the Stanley Cup to was an easy choice – Konstantinov. Destiny had become reality.

Detroit Red Wings Captain Steve Yzerman drinks from the Stanley Cup of success as he celebrates a second straight Cup victory for his team, this time a four-game sweep of the Washington Capitals.

THE ALL-STAR GAME

It's ironic that the NHL All-Star Game, sometimes labeled a non-contact version of hockey, came into being because of an unfortunate incident that ended a player's career. The first, unofficial All-Star game was a benefit for Ace Bailey, who had been gravely injured in a regular-season game between the Toronto Maple Leafs and the Boston Bruins on December 12, 1933.

Bruins' star Eddie Shore had been knocked down while carrying the puck up the ice. Enraged, he charged Bailey, who had not been the culprit, and upended him viciously. Bailey's head struck the ice, knocking him unconscious. Bailey never played again.

On February 14, 1934, the Maple Leafs played a team of NHL All-Stars at Maple Leaf Gardens in a benefit for Bailey. More than $23,000 Cdn. was raised for Bailey, but the format did not exactly capture the imagination of the league's governors.

Two more unofficial All-Star games were staged, both owing to personal tragedy. In November 1937, a game was organized after the death following complications from a broken leg of Montreal Canadiens star Howie Morenz.

And in 1939, a similar game was held to benefit the widow of Babe Siebert, who had drowned that summer.

It's official

The first official All-Star Game was held in 1947, with the reigning Stanley Cup champions, the Toronto Maple Leafs, playing an All-Star team. The Stars won 4-3, establishing the format that would remain for most of the next two decades.

The Dream Game notion was that the true test of just how good the Stanley Cup champions were was to pit the best players from around the league against them. There was one obvious flaw with this set-up. The All-Star team selections often were dominated, understandably, by members of the Stanley Cup champions.

In 1958-59, for example, the Montreal Canadiens placed four players on the first All-Star team and two on the second team. Inevitably, the All-Star team that faced the champions took the ice minus several of its best players.

The league experimented with a different format for two years in the early 1950s, pitting the first All-Star team against the Second Team, but otherwise did not deviate from the Stars against the Stanley Cup champions until 1969.

This was the first All-Star Game following the first major expansion in NHL history, a project that doubled the size of the league from six to 12 teams.

From 1969 through 1971, the All-Star Game pitted the stars from the so-called Original Six against the stars from the six expansion clubs. That period featured the first All-Star Game

held in an expansion city when St. Louis played host to the game in 1970.

The established stars of the East won that game 4-1, but the expansion stars surprised the Original Six when they won the 1971 game in Boston 2-1.

In 1972, the first of a series of realignments shifted the established Chicago Blackhawks into the West Division, and further expansion would continue to alter the makeup of the division.

By 1975, the league had grown to 18 teams, organized into two nine-team conferences: the Prince of Wales Conference; and the Clarence Campbell Conference, named after the longtime president of the NHL.

The Wales did All-Star battle with the Campbells until 1994, when the NHL realigned its conferences and divisions geographically, replacing the Campbell with the Western Conference, and the Wales with the Eastern. The Central and Pacific Divisions comprise the Western Conference, while the Atlantic and Northeast Divisions make up the Eastern.

New trends

The league also had new uniforms designed, in teal and violet colors, and placed new emphasis on the skills competition, a fan-friendly feature the NHL had borrowed from a highly successful skills format used in the National Basketball Association.

The game itself remains an exhibition, a non-contact shootout which showcases plenty of offensive flash but involves little or no bodychecking and little commitment to defense. The goaltenders often have to perform at their best, and just as often they are buried in an avalanche of shots.

Injuries are rare in the All-Star Game, since no one is dishing out any bodychecks. Penalties are rare, too. The 1992 and 1994 games were penalty-free, while the 1993 game involved a single infraction, a minor penalty handed out to defenseman Dave Manson.

The marketing-savvy NHL front office sees the All-Star Game as a chance to market its stars and win new fans. In 1996 the NHL signed a TV deal with Fox, and the network made a splashy, some would say gimmicky, entrée into the sport by introducing its FoxTrax puck at the All-Star Game. To TV viewers, the puck appeared with a blue aura highlighting it for greater visibility. Fired at high speed, the blue aura turned into a red rocket and the speed at which the puck was shot was displayed on the screen.

Purists in Canada howled, but the high-tech gimmick certainly drew plenty of free publicity for the league in the United States. The idea seemed harmless enough. After all, the NHL All-Star Game has never been for purists, anyway.

All-Star Game Results 1948-1998

Year	Venue	Score	Coaches
1998	Vancouver	North America 8, World 7	Scott Bowman; Ken Hitchcock
1997	San Jose	Eastern 11, Western 7	Doug MacLean; Marc Crawford
1996	Boston	Eastern 5, Western 4	Doug MacLean; Scott Bowman
1994	New York	Eastern 9, Western 8	Jacques Demers; Barry Melrose
1993	Montreal	Wales 16, Campbell 6	Scott Bowman; Mike Keenan
1992	Philadelphia	Campbell 10, Wales 6	Bob Gainey; Scott Bowman
1991	Chicago	Campbell 11, Wales 5	John Muckler; Mike Milbury
1990	Pittsburgh	Wales 12, Campbell 7	Pat Burns; Terry Crisp
1989	Edmonton	Campbell 9, Wales 5	Glen Sather; Terry O'Reilly
1988	St. Louis	Wales 6, Campbell 5(OT)	Mike Keenan; Glen Sather
1986	Hartford	Wales 4, Campbell 3(OT)	Mike Keenan; Glen Sather
1985	Calgary	Wales 6, Campbell 4	Al Arbour; Glen Sather
1984	New Jersey	Wales 7, Campbell 6	Al Arbour; Glen Sather
1983	NY Islanders	Campbell 9, Wales 3	Roger Neilson; Al Arbour
1982	Washington	Wales 4, Campbell 2	Al Arbour; Glen Sonmor
1981	Los Angeles	Campbell 4, Wales 1	Pat Quinn; Scott Bowman
1980	Detroit	Wales 6, Campbell 3	Scott Bowman; Al Arbour
1978	Buffalo	Wales 3, Campbell 2 (OT)	Scott Bowman; Fred Shero
1977	Vancouver	Wales 4, Campbell 3	Scott Bowman; Fred Shero
1976	Philadelphia	Wales 7, Campbell 5	Floyd Smith; Fred Shero
1975	Montreal	Wales 7, Campbell 1	Bep Guidolin; Fred Shero
1974	Chicago	West 6, East 4	Billy Reay; Scott Bowman
1973	New York	East 5, West 4	Tom Johnson; Billy Reay
1972	Minnesota	East 3, West 2	Al McNeill; Billy Reay
1971	Boston	West 2, East 1	Scott Bowman; Harry Sinden
1970	St. Louis	East 4, West 1	Claude Ruel; Scott Bowman
1969	Montreal	East 3, West 3	Toe Blake; Scott Bowman
1968	Toronto	Toronto 4, All-Stars 3	Punch Imlach; Toe Blake
1967	Montreal	Montreal 3, All-Stars 0	Toe Blake; Sid Abel
1965	Montreal	All-Stars 5, Montreal 2	Billy Reay; Toe Blake
1964	Toronto	All-Stars 3, Toronto 2	Sid Abel; Punch Imlach
1963	Toronto	All-Stars 3, Toronto 3	Sid Abel; Punch Imlach
1962	Toronto	Toronto 4, All-Stars 1	Punch Imlach; Rudy Pilous
1961	Chicago	All-Stars 3, Chicago 1	Sid Abel; Rudy Pilous
1960	Montreal	All-Stars 2, Montreal 1	Punch Imlach; Toe Blake
1959	Montreal	Montreal 6, All-Stars 1	Toe Blake; Punch Imlach
1958	Montreal	Montreal 6, All-Stars 3	Toe Blake; Milt Schmidt
1957	Montreal	All-Stars 5, Montreal 3	Milt Schmidt; Toe Blake
1956	Montreal	All-Stars 1, Montreal 1	Jim Skinner; Toe Blake
1955	Detroit	Detroit 3, All-Stars 1	Jim Skinner; Dick Irvin
1954	Detroit	All-Stars 2, Detroit 2	King Clancy; Jim Skinner
1953	Montreal	All-Stars 3, Montreal 1	Lynn Patrick; Dick Irvin
1952	Detroit	1st Team 1, 2nd Team 1	Tommy Ivan; Dick Irvin
1951	Toronto	1st Team 2, 2nd Team 2	Joe Primeau; Hap Day
1950	Detroit	Detroit 7, All-Stars 1	Tommy Ivan; Lynn Patrick
1949	Toronto	All-Stars 3, Toronto 1	Tommy Ivan; Hap Day
1948	Chicago	All-Stars 3, Toronto 1	Tommy Ivan; Hap Day

All-Star Hockey Mosts

Most Games Played
23   Gordie Howe, from 1948 through 1980.

Most Goals
12   Wayne Gretzky, in 15 appearances.

Most Points, One Game
6   Mario Lemieux, Wales, 1988 (3 goals, 3 assists)

Most Goals In One Game
4   Wayne Gretzky, Campbell, 1983
Mario Lemieux, Wales, 1990
Vincent Damphousse, Campbell, 1991
Mike Gartner, Wales, 1993

Most Goals, Both Teams, One Game
22   Wales 16, Campbell 6, 1993 at Montreal

Gunning for Goals in Philly

CAMPBELL 10 - WALES 6

The Golden Brett was the star of the show in 1992 in Philadelphia. He scored twice and assisted on another to lead the Campbells over the Wales. This game was not only the typical All-Star no-hitter, it was a game in which no penalties were called, an All-Star Game first. There was nothing to get in the way of five-on-five gunning for goals.

Six goaltenders faced 83 shots in all in this shootout, with Washington Capitals goalie Don Beaupre having the toughest time. He yielded six goals on 12 shots in the second period, as the Campbell Conference built an 8-3 lead. Both of Hull's goals came against Beaupre.

"I didn't have a chance to look up to see which one of their guns was coming at me," said Beaupre. "For a while it seemed like everything was going by me. There were a lot of tips and rebounds and I'm not ready to go through anything like that anytime soon."

Beaupre and the other goalies had the other players' sympathy, for whatever that might have been worth.

"It's totally unfair for goalies," said Wayne Gretzky. "I think everybody understands this game is going to be like that."

Fateful pairing

Four first-time all-stars were able to record goals in Philadelphia: Gary Roberts of the Calgary Flames; Owen Nolan of the Quebec Nordiques; Alexander Mogilny of the Buffalo Sabres; and Randy Burridge of the Washington Capitals.

"It was nice getting on the scoreboard," said Burridge. "I've got the puck in my bag and I'll always have it."

The game was notable for the pairing of Gretzky with Hull, a fantasy pairing that would actually come true years later in St. Louis.

All-Star Theoren: In 1992, Theoren Fleury and the Campbell Conference beat the Wales Conference.

As All-Star teammates, Gretzky and Hull combined for three goals and three assists.

"I've said this a million times — I've always wanted a chance to play with Wayne," said Hull. "Sitting next to Wayne and Stevie Y (Yzerman of the Detroit Red Wings) in the dressing room was unbelievable. Those guys are my idols in this game."

Campbell Blues in Montreal

WALES 16 - CAMPBELL 6

Wayne Gretzky is certainly not a stranger to All-Star games, having been selected a first-team all-star eight times and a second-team player five times. But the spotlight was on him at the All-Star Game in Montreal for an entirely different reason.

Rumors were circulating rapidly that the man many consider the best player in the history of the game was going to be traded to the Toronto Maple Leafs. Los Angeles Kings owner Bruce McNall was forced to hold a news conference to deny everything.

Big deal

Once the controversy subsided and the game began, everybody scored, or so it seemed. Even Brad Marsh, a cautious defenseman for the expansion Ottawa Senators potted one, earning a standing ovation from the Montreal Forum fans.

"Kevin Stevens made a great pass," Marsh said later. "I just put my stick on the ice and it went in off it. I've gone whole seasons without scoring a goal, so any time I do score, it's a big deal."

The goal was all the sweeter for Marsh, who had been embarrassed during the target-shooting portion of the skills competition when he failed to hit a single target in eight tries.

"I knew I was in trouble after I missed the first six," Marsh said. "My excuse is that I'm not supposed to be shooting at targets, anyway."

Mike Gartner took home the MVP award by scoring four goals and adding an assist. The Wales Conference built a 9-0 lead by early in the second period, and a 12-2 lead after 40 minutes of play, as they strafed goalies Ed Belfour and Mike Vernon for six goals each.

Things could have been much worse for the Campbell team when it's considered that Mario Lemieux missed the game.

Lemieux, who had been diagnosed with Hodgkin's Disease four weeks earlier, was undergoing treatment and unable to play. But he was introduced before the game to the fans at the Forum, who gave a five-minute standing ovation to the Montreal-born superstar.

All-Star Shootout: The teams combined for a record 22 goals in the 1993 All-Star Game, including six in the first period against goalie Ed Belfour.

NHL goes United Nations

EASTERN 9 – WESTERN 8

Beginner's Luck: Alexei Yashin, the only rookie in the game, scored two goals including the winner in 1994.

The NHL had been realigned into Eastern and Western Conferences and hip new uniforms had been designed in time for this game, which was another penalty-free contest. Despite the lopsided result, there was sparkling goaltending, and it was a good thing, considering the teams combined for a record 102 shots.

Mike Richter stopped 19 of the 21 shots the Eastern Conference unleashed at him. Only Paul Coffey and Sandis Ozolinsh beat him.

The acrobatic Richter stopped Vancouver speedster Pavel Bure five times, including twice on breakaways, as the Madison Square Garden fans roared their approval.

"I didn't want to come into this game and not be tested," said Richter. "You're playing against the best in the world. If they pepper you with a bunch of shots and you're feeling good, it's fantastic. You want more."

More was what the winning Eastern Conference team got—more money. The victory was worth $5,000 U.S. for each winning player as the NHL decided to sweeten the pot for All-Star participants in an effort to add some competitive zip to the often tepid game.

"If they're giving you $5,000, you might as well try to win it," reasoned Rangers defenseman Brian Leetch.

Still, the All-Stars do have one unwritten rule, no matter how competitive they or the league might try to intensify things: no hitting.

"We didn't do any checking but at least we got into each other's way," said Chicago defenseman Chris Chelios, with a laugh.

The game also illustrated the growing international make-up of the NHL. Among the participants there were five Russians, two Latvians, a Czechoslovakian, a Finn, eight Americans and 24 Canadians.

One of the Latvians—Sandis Ozolinsh—and one of the Russians—rookie Alexei Yashin—each scored two goals. Yashin's second was the gamewinner for the Eastern Conference.

"It was all luck," said Yashin, the only rookie in the game.

Some of his peers—notably Wayne Gretzky—didn't agree with Yashin.

"He's a tremendous talent," said Gretzky. "I see a lot of Mario (Lemieux) in him.

"He's got good puck sense and Mario's size. To be doing what he's doing on an expansion team (Ottawa) is a credit to him, along with his coming over from Russia for his first year."

For his part, Gretzky had two assists, giving him 19 points lifetime in All-Star competition, tying Gordie Howe's record for points in All-Star games. Gretzky, though, collected his 19 points in 14 games, compared to 23 appearances for Howe.

1996 All-Star Game
FoxTraxing in Boston

EASTERN 5 - WESTERN 4

The 1995 All-Star Game was one of the casualties of the lockout-shortened 1994-95 season. The 1996 All-Star was held in Boston, but not at historic Boston Garden, which had officially closed before the season began.

Literally inches away from the funky, intimate Garden, the Bruins owners had built the FleetCenter, a state-of-the-art, 17,565-seat amphitheater.

The center of attention during the game, at least for fans watching on Fox, was a high-tech puck the network had designed to enhance viewers' ability to follow the disk in the heat of the action.

The FoxTrax puck, fashioned with infrared-emitting diodes, gave off a pale blue haze as it slid about the ice in its debut.

When a player teed up a shot at 120-kilometres-an-hour or faster, the puck became a red rocket as it zoomed netward, with a comet-like tail, describing its flight path for the viewers.

The puck was a public relations smash as the NHL and Fox generated plenty of media attention.

Hockey purists in Canada sniffed at the innovation, but Fox, attempting to boost interest in the sport across the United States, was encouraged by the fancy puck.

Local hero

The game, meanwhile, provided the perfect ending for Bruins fans, and gave them a chance to salute one of the game's greatest stars, Boston captain and wheelhorse defenseman Ray Bourque, who was playing in his 14th All-Star Game.

The early thunder in the game belonged to goaltender Martin Brodeur, who pitched a shutout in the first period, stopping 12 shots from the best of the West. The Buffalo Sabres goaltender, Dominik Hasek, faced 13 shots for the Eastern team in the third period, giving up just one goal.

It was a relatively low-scoring affair, as these things go, but the final one was a masterpiece.

That one came at 19:23 of the final period, when Bourque beat Toronto Maple Leafs goalie Felix Potvin to hand the victory to the Eastern team, take the MVP award and bask in the heat of an enormous ovation from the Boston fans.

Hometown Hero: Boston Bruins defenseman Ray Bourque thrilled the Boston fans when he scored the winner in 1996.

1997 All-Star Game
Knowing the Way in San Jose

EASTERN 11 - WESTERN 7

This was the All-Star game in which the local hero called his shot before firing in the final goal in his three-goal hat-trick and still couldn't win the All-Star game most valuable player award.

It was the All-Star game in which the guy who did win the MVP also scored a hat-trick but was booed by the understandably partisan crowd at the San Jose Arena, home of the Sharks.

"They booed me and they'll probably boo me next time I come here," said Montreal Canadiens winger Mark Recchi, whose three-goal performance helped the East All-Stars outscore the West. "I thought (the media) would give it to the home-town boy. That would have been Owen Nolan, the Sharks' power forward who also scored three goals, including one at 17:57 of the third period on Buffalo Sabres goaltender Dominik Hasek.

That one was special. Nolan pointed to an opening, then promptly threaded the needle with a shot that cleanly beat The Dominator. The goal didn't win the game for the West, but the spectacle brought the house down. The media members were apparently unmoved.

For openers, Nolan scored his first two goals, which came late in the second period, just eight seconds apart—an All-Star Game record. No big deal, the media ruled, awarding the MVP to Recchi, the latest in a lengthy line of Montreal Canadiens snipers.

"There are a lot of great all-stars who have played for the Canadiens," Recchi said. "I'm told I remind some of (Hall of Famer) Yvan Cournoyer, which is quite an honor."

Due honors

The 47th All-Star game also was an occasion to pay homage to some of the greatest players ever to play in the NHL, including the Magnificent One, Mario Lemieux.

Out of respect for Lemieux, East coach Doug MacLean sent Lemieux out for the game's final shift along with Wayne Gretzky and Mark Messier, with Raymond Bourque and Paul Coffey on defense.

"That was impressive," West goaltender Andy Moog said, ignoring the fact that he was beaten for six goals in the second period. "As I watched them, I thought, Gretz has 18 years, Mark 17, Bourque 18, Coffey 18 and Mario about 13 or 14. It was a nice tribute to the elder statesmen."

As with most NHL All-Star games, this was another chance for the snipers to shine and goalies to cringe. Even Patrick Roy, who can lay a strong claim to being the best goalie in the business, was beaten for four goals on 15 shots. He handled the blitzkrieg with his customary aplomb.

"You accept the risk when you accept the invitation," Roy said. "I enjoy everything about this weekend—except the game."

But the 17,422 fans who jammed the Arena enjoyed the game just fine, thanks.

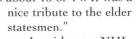

Eastern Blitz: Eric Lindros and the Eastern Conference prevailed over the Western Conference in a goal-scoring spectacular in the 1997 NHL All-Star game.

1998 All-Star Game
New Look Proves a Winner

NORTH AMERICA ALL-STARS 8 – WORLD ALL-STARS 7

I n honor of the NHL's international season, the league changed the format for the 1998 All-Star Game at Vancouver's GM Place. Rather than pit the usual Eastern Conference vs. Western Conference, the format was changed to allow a little nationalistic pride. Or, to be more accurate, continental pride.

It was the North American All-Stars vs. the World All-Stars. The World All-Stars was made up of the best players from Europe, while the North American squad featured a blend of talent from Canada and the United States. The World coach, Ken Hitchcock, added some flair when he put together national lines – the Russians, the Swedes, the Finns, the Czechs. The coach was fascinated by the way his players interacted with each other, like a mini United Nations.

Dynamic duo

But the combination that had everyone talking afterward was that of Wayne Gretzky and Mark Messier. The longtime buddies in Edmonton's glory years, who were reunited for one season with the Rangers in 1996–97, recaptured some of their old magic. Gretzky fed his old buddy for the winning goal in an 8–7 win for the North American team. Caught flatfooted on the play was another prominent figure from the Oilers' dynasty days – Jari Kurri, playing as a member of the Finland line on the World team. "People make so much of the fact that Mark and I are 37," said Gretzky, who with two assists became the career points leader in all-star competition. "But we really love to play. After Mark scored, you could see how excited we were on the ice."

"Gretzky still fools me," Kurri said, laughing. "I told him in the faceoff, 'I backcheck all those years for you (in Edmonton) and that's how you treat me? In my last all-star game? You made me look bad, awful bad.' "

The MVP of the game was Mighty Ducks of Anaheim star Teemu Selanne. He got a hat trick for the losing team, becoming the first European to record three goals in an All-Star Game. Selanne's two early goals along with one by Jaromir Jagr gave the World team a 3-0 lead just four minutes into the game, but the North American team rallied to tie the game at three by the first intermission. "I like the format," said Selanne, who won a truck as the game's MVP. "It was really nice to (play) with the other Europeans. Now North American players respect us more and more."

Slovakian Zigmund Palffy in action for the World All-Stars during their unique clash with the North American All-Stars.

THE 1998 WINTER OLYMPICS

It was Miracle on Ice, Part II. Only this time the hero goalie was not an unknown American, as when the United States shocked the world in 1980 with Jim Craig turning away nearly everything shot his way.

No, this time the goalie was recognized as the best at his position in the world, and by many as the best player in the world, period. Buffalo Sabres netminder Dominik Hasek, eight months removed from accepting the Hart Trophy as NHL MVP and Vezina Trophy as the league's top goaltender and four months away from repeating the feat, took center stage at the 1998 Olympics in Nagano, Japan.

The 'Dominator' as Hasek is known, dominated the hockey tournament and led his underdog Czech Republic team to an unlikely gold medal in the first Olympics to feature NHL stars. The league took a 17-day Winter break in February to allow more than 120 of its players to represent their countries in the Olympics. The USA, Canada and Russia were the three countries that fielded rosters exclusively made up of NHL players, and those were the three teams Hasek's Czech squad beat, in order, in its final three games. The 23-man roster for the

Action from the USA vs. Sweden game during the thrilling 1998 Olympic hockey tournament.

Czech Republic included just 10 NHLers.

The semi-final game vs. Canada was a classic, going to a shootout after regulation and 10-minute overtime left the score knotted at one. Robert Reichel scored for the Czechs during the shootout and Hasek stopped all five Canadian shooters to qualify the Czechs for the gold-medal game vs. Russia. The Czechs shut out the high-flying Russians 1–0 in the final, on a goal by defenseman Petr Svoboda. "It feels great," Hasek said. "It's probably the happiest day of my hockey career."

Czech president Vaclav Havel sent his government plane to fly the team home to Prague. Tens of thousands of fans had gathered in a city square to watch the game in the cold on giant television screens. The team got a huge reception when it arrived for a celebratory appearance.

Other countries weren't in such festive mood – foremost being the USA and Canada. The USA not only performed badly on the ice, but unnamed members of the team did $3,000 worth of damage to their living quarters. Canada, on the other hand, had to come to terms with the fact that they lost supremacy of their national sport.

★★★★★ 1998 Olympic Ice Hockey – Full Results ★★★★★

FINAL OLYMPIC MEN'S HOCKEY STANDINGS:
PRELIMINARY ROUND

Group A	GP	W	L	T	PTS	GF	GA
Kazakhstan *	3	2	0	1	5	14	11
Slovakia	3	1	1	1	3	9	9
Italy	3	1	2	0	2	11	11
Austria	3	0	1	2	2	6	9

Group B	GP	W	L	T	PTS	GF	GA
Belarus *	3	2	0	1	5	14	4
Germany	3	2	1	0	4	7	9
France	3	1	2	0	2	5	8
Japan	3	0	2	1	1	5	10

* - CLINCHED GROUP AND ADVANCED TO CHAMPIONSHIP ROUND

CHAMPIONSHIP ROUND

Group C	GP	W	L	T	PTS	GF	GA
Canada	3	3	0	0	6	12	3
Sweden	3	2	1	0	4	11	7
USA	3	1	2	0	2	8	10
Belarus	3	0	3	0	0	4	15

Group D	GP	W	L	T	PTS	GF	GA
Russia	3	3	0	0	6	15	6
Czech Republic	3	2	1	0	4	12	4
Finland	3	1	2	0	2	11	9
Kazakhstan	3	0	3	0	0	6	25

QUARTER-FINALS: Canada 4 Kazakhstan 1, Finland 2 Sweden 1
Czech R 4 USA 1, Russia 4 Belarus 1
MEDAL ROUND GAMES: Czech R 2 Canada 1 (Shootout), Russia 7 Finland 5
BRONZE MEDAL GAME: Finland 3 Canada 2

GOLD MEDAL GAME: Czech Republic 1 Russia 0

THE HOCKEY HALL OF FAME

The building that houses the state-of-the-art Hockey Hall of Fame in Toronto is a former Bank of Montreal that was built in the previous century. It's appropriate that the National Hockey League showcases its rich history in a vintage 1885 building. After all, the first recorded advertisement for a hockey game comes from the same era, having been placed in the *Montreal Gazette* in 1875.

The game that came to be known as hockey had been played for decades across Canada by that time, in a variety of forms, with a variety of names. Its 'invention' was a product of rural isolation and the need for some activity to enliven the months-long winter.

Unlike baseball, though, hockey has no Abner Doubleday, no personage who can be said, however inaccurately, to have invented the game, no bucolic equivalent of Cooperstown to cherish as the cradle of the game.

Numerous hockey historians make cases for the game originating in, variously, Kingston, Ontario, or Montreal, or a certain rural pond in Nova Scotia. Which claim is the most legitimate? Flip a coin.

But if there is no one mythology surrounding the location of the Hockey Hall of Fame it doesn't seem to matter. The ultra-modern facility is fraught with lore, rich in tradition, bursting with memories.

Golden memories

The Hall fills 51,000 square feet of space at BCE Place in downtown Toronto, a modern skyscraper that incorporates the century-old former bank building into its sprawling complex.

The displays include a surprisingly life-like re-creation of the fabled Montreal Canadiens dressing room in the old Forum, a large collection of the many strikingly artistic protective masks worn by the league's goaltenders over the years, and interactive displays that enable visitors, for example, to try their hand at play-by-play description of some of the game's golden moments.

The centerpiece of the building, which opened on 18 June 1993, is the Great Hall, a magnificent dome-ceilinged room that proudly showcases the plaques honoring the members as well as the NHL's glittering family of trophies.

The most famous trophy in the collection, of course, is the Stanley Cup, donated by Lord Stanley in 1893, the oldest trophy continuously competed for by professional athletes in North America.

Hall of Honor: The great rotunda in the imposing Hockey Hall of Fame in Toronto is a fitting setting for the array of plaques honoring all the greats of the NHL game.

The plaques honor the Hall of Fame's 304 members: 207 players; 84 builders (coaches, general managers, owners) and 13 referees and linesmen.

There also are 55 members from the media—broadcasters and print reporters—whose work helped raise awareness about, and helped foster the mythology of the game.

Honor for a league

The Hall of Fame was first established in 1943, its early members first honored in 1945. But a permanent location to house the legacy of the game wasn't found until 26 August 1961, when the collection was set up in a building on the grounds of the Canadian National Exhibition on Toronto's lakeshore.

The current location updates the museum for the 1990s and the coming century. Which is not surprising for the Hall of Fame of a league that has more than quadrupled in size in the past 30 years.

Fallen Eagleson

Alan Eagleson, once one of the most powerful men in pro hockey, became the first person to resign from the Hockey Hall of Fame. He did so in March 1998 under heavy pressure. There were strong indications that if he did not resign he would be removed from the Hall's roster after former hockey stars such as Bobby Orr, Brad Park and Ted Lindsay threatened to quit the Hall had Eagleson been allowed to stay.

Eagleson was elected to the builders' category of the Hall of Fame in 1989 for his role in the formation of the NHL Players' Association and international hockey tournaments like the 1972 Canada-Soviet Union 'Summit Series'. His misdeeds included stealing Canada Cup tournament rinkboard advertising money between 1984 and 1991. He was also found guilty of fraud involving player pensions, player career-ending disability insurance money and overcharging players as head of their union. "I do not wish the board of directors to be forced to consider a review of my status and membership in the Hall of Fame under the circumstances of threatened renunciation of membership by a number of players," the disgraced 65-year-old wrote in his resignation letter.

Inspirational Leader: Bobby Clarke overcame limited natural ability and diabetes through sheer hard work and dedication to become the key player on the Philadelhia Flyers in the 1970s.

JEAN BELIVEAU: center. A native of Victoriaville, Quebec, Beliveau became a star center with the Quebec Aces of the Quebec Senior League. Le Colisée in Quebec, where the Aces played their games, was nicknamed the House that Beliveau Built, but it wasn't his hockey home for long. In 1952, Beliveau joined the Montreal Canadiens, who held his pro rights. He remained with them for his entire 18-year NHL career, and led the Canadiens to ten Stanley Cup victories. He was the first winner of the Conn Smythe Trophy as the most valuable player in the playoffs and twice won the Hart Trophy. He retired after leading the Canadiens to the Stanley Cup in 1970-71, having played 1125 NHL games and scored 507 goals.

HECTOR (TOE) BLAKE: left winger, coach. Blake played 578 NHL games, scoring 235 goals and adding 292 assists. The left wing beside center Elmer Lach and right winger Maurice Richard on the legendary Punch Line, Blake was nicknamed the Old Lamplighter for his scoring prowess. Many regard him as the best coach in the history of the NHL. For 13 seasons he coached the Canadiens, who won eight Stanley Cups under his regime, including five straight from 1956-60. He retired after coaching his eighth Cup victory in 1968.

MIKE BOSSY: right winger. As a junior star, Bossy was considered a soft player, a one-dimensional scorer whose offensive skills would be muted in the NHL, whose defensive skills would be a liability. The Montreal Canadiens, among other teams, passed on Bossy in the Entry Draft and lived to regret it. Bossy became the best right winger in the NHL in the 1980s, scoring 573 goals in just 752 regular-season games. For nine straight years, he scored 50 or more goals. He was the sniper on the Trio Grande—a line with Bryan Trottier at center and Clark Gillies at left wing. Bossy added 85 goals in 129 playoff games as he helped the New York Islanders win four straight Stanley Cup championships from 1980-83. Chronic back trouble forced him into retirement in 1987.

JOHNNY BOWER: goaltender. Scar-faced Bower didn't make it to the NHL for good until he was 34. He played 11 seasons for the Toronto Maple Leafs, helping them win four Stanley Cups, including the fabled upset in 1967 when an aging Toronto team beat the favored Montreal Canadiens. Bower and Terry Sawchuck shared the goaltending duties that season, as well as the Vezina Trophy as the best netminding duo in the league. He retired after the 1969-70 season, the only one in which he wore a protective mask.

SCOTTY BOWMAN: coach, general manager. He apprenticed in the Montreal Canadiens system under Sam Pollock before becoming the coach of the expansion St. Louis Blues, whom he led to three straight Stanley Cup finals. Repatriated to the Canadiens as head coach in 1971, he led them to five Stanley Cup victories. He worked for the Sabres from 1979 to 1987 but didn't return to the Stanley Cup final until 1992, with the Penguins, replacing the late Bob Johnson as head coach. As head coach of the Detroit Red Wings, Bowman added the 1997 Stanley Cup to his résumé as the most successful coach in NHL history with well over 800 victories.

CLARENCE CAMPBELL: NHL president, 1947-78. Campbell was a Rhodes Scholar and won the Order of the British Empire after working as a prosecutor with the Canadian War Crimes Commission in Germany. He is remembered mostly as the man who suspended Maurice (Rocket) Richard after he slugged linesman Cliff Thompson in March 1955. Campbell's presence at the Forum on March 16, 1955 touched off a riot by outraged Montreal fans. But Campbell withstood that storm. His most notable achievement came in 1968, when he oversaw the expansion of the NHL from six to 12 teams. Before he retired in 1978, the league had grown to 18 teams.

Straight On: Al Arbour coached one of the best teams in the history of the NHL during the New York Islanders' run of four straight Stanley Cups in the 1980s.

GERRY CHEEVERS: goaltender. Starting goalie for the Boston Bruins in the Bobby Orr-Phil Esposito era. Known as a great money goaltender, Cheevers was at his best in the playoffs. He helped Boston win the Stanley Cup in 1970 and 1972.

BOBBY CLARKE: center, coach, general manager. In 1968-69, Clarke piled up 137 points with the Flin Flon Bombers of the Western Hockey League, but many teams were leery of his diabetic condition and he was taken 17th overall in the NHL entry draft. He proved the skeptics wrong, playing 15 NHL seasons for the Philadelphia Flyers, winning the Hart Trophy three times and leading the Flyers to two straight Stanley Cups in the early 1970s. He was the first player on a post-1967 expansion team to score 100 or more points in a season. His grit, determination and leadership were central to the Flyers becoming the first expansion club ever to win the Stanley Cup.

YVAN COURNOYER: right winger. Cournoyer's speed earned him the nickname 'The Roadrunner,' but he was anything but birdlike. His speed came from thickly muscled legs that teammate Ken Dryden once compared to "two enormous roasts spilling over his knees." When he joined the Montreal Canadiens in 1963-64, Cournoyer was used as a power-play specialist. He developed into one of the most explosive forwards in the game, scoring 428 goals in 16 seasons, and helping Montreal win ten Stanley Cups. He was the Canadiens captain for their four-straight Stanley Cup run in the 1970s.

MARCEL DIONNE: center. Dionne was chosen second overall behind Guy Lafleur in the 1970 entry draft and played most of his career in brilliant obscurity. After racking up 366 points in four seasons with Detroit, Dionne was traded to the Los Angeles Kings, where he quietly piled up points for years, centering the Triple Crown Line with wingers Charlie Simmer and Dave Taylor. He won a scoring championship with the Kings and ended his 18-year career with 731 goals and 1,040 assists, but no Stanley Cup victories.

KEN DRYDEN: goaltender. Dryden, 23-year-old law student and a 6-foot-4, 210-pound giant, backstopped the Montreal Canadiens to a surprise Stanley Cup victory in 1970-71 after playing just six regular-season games with the club. He was awarded the Conn Smythe Trophy as the most valuable player in the playoffs, and followed that up by winning the Calder Trophy (rookie-of-the-year) the next season. Dryden played eight seasons for the Canadiens, helping them win six Stanley Cups, while winning the Vezina Trophy five times. He retired after the 1978-79 season, after helping the Canadiens win a fourth straight Cup. On March 2, 1971, he made hockey history when he faced brother Dave Dryden of the Buffalo Sabres. The pair were the first goaltending brothers ever to face each other in goal. In 1997, Ken Dryden returned to the NHL for the first time since 1979 when he was named president of the Toronto Maple Leafs.

The Roadrunner: Montreal Canadiens sniper Yvan Cournoyer used blazing speed to zoom past opponents and score big goals.

PHIL ESPOSITO: center, coach, general manager. Esposito was a competent, but unremarkable center for the Chicago Blackhawks when he was traded, with Ken Hodge and Fred Stanfield, to the Boston Bruins in 1967 for Hubert (Pit) Martin, Jack Norris and Gilles Marotte. Esposito blossomed as a Bruin, becoming the first player to score more than 100 points in a season. He won five scoring titles in eight-and-a-half seasons in Boston, where he and Bobby Orr led the Bruins to two Stanley Cups. He won two Hart Trophies and scored 55 goals or more in five straight seasons. He played 18 seasons in all, scoring 717 goals and adding 873 assists. He retired in 1981, finishing his career as a New York Ranger.

BILL GADSBY: defenseman. Gadsby played standout defense for Chicago, New York Rangers and the Detroit Red Wings for 20 seasons over three decades, stretching from 1946-47 to 1965-66.

Gadsby was fortunate to have a career at all. When he was 12, he and his mother were returning from England when the ship they were traveling on was torpedoed and sunk. He was rescued after spending five hours in the frigid Atlantic. In 1952, he overcame a bout of polio so severe doctors told him he would never play again. He played—well enough to be named an All-Star seven times. Strangely, he never won a Stanley Cup.

BERNARD (BOOM-BOOM) GEOFFRION: left wing. Geoffrion earned his nickname by becoming the first to consistently use the slap shot as an offensive weapon in the 1950s. He won the Calder Trophy in 1952 and led the NHL in scoring in 1955. He was the second player, after teammate Maurice Richard, to score 50 goals in a season and helped Montreal win five Stanley Cups. He frequently played the point (defense) on the power play to take advantage of his booming shot. He also coached, briefly, for the New York Rangers, Atlanta Flames and Montreal Canadiens.

ED GIACOMIN: goaltender. "Ed-die, Ed-die" was the chant at Madison Square Gardens during Giacomin's decade as the No. 1 goaltender for the Rangers in the late 1960s and early 1970s. Giacomin shared the Vezina Trophy and won 226 games for the Rangers, while endearing himself to the tough Garden fans with his acrobatic style.

DOUG HARVEY: defenseman. Many consider Harvey, who played 20 NHL seasons from 1947-48 to 1968-69, the best defenseman in the history of the game. He won the Norris Trophy as the league's best defenseman seven times and helped the Montreal Canadiens win six Stanley Cups. He was the point man on the great Montreal power-play unit that included Jean Beliveau, Maurice (Rocket) Richard, Dickie Moore and Bernard (Boom-Boom) Geoffrion. The power-play unit was so effective that the NHL altered its rules so that a penalized player could leave the penalty box before his two minutes was up if the opposing team scored a goal. It was said of Harvey that he was so skilled he could control the tempo of a game, speeding its pace or slowing it down to suit the situation.

GORDIE HOWE: right winger. Howe, a physically powerful, awesomely talented but shy and humble farm boy from Floral, Saskatchewan, fully earned the nickname Mr. Hockey. Howe played 26 seasons, 34 pro seasons in all, covering five decades from 1946-47 to 1979-80. He played 1767 NHL games, scored 801 goals, added 1049 assists. At one time, he held NHL records for most games played, most goals, assists, and points in both regular season and playoffs. He became the first NHLer over the age of 50 to score a goal and the first to play on a line with his sons, Mark and Marty.

GLENN HALL: goaltender. The man who became known as Mr. Goalie didn't earn the title for nothing. Hall played 18 seasons—ten with Chicago—and was named an All-Star 11 times. He led the NHL in shutouts for six seasons, played in 115 Stanley Cup playoff games and set a league record for most consecutive games by a goalie—502, stretching from 1955 to November 7, 1962. He finished his remarkable career sharing goaltending duties with fellow Hall of Famer Jacques Plante in St. Louis, where he backstopped the Blues to three straight Stanley Cup final appearances.

BOBBY HULL: left winger. Blond-haired and dimple-cheeked handsome and built like an Adonis, Hull also had blazing speed (29.7 mph top speed) and a frighteningly hard slap shot that once was clocked at 118.3 mph. Hull quickly became known as The Golden Jet in the NHL. He scored 610 goals in a 16-year NHL career during which he became the first player ever to record more than one 50-goal season (he had five). He won the Art Ross Trophy as the league's top scorer three times, the Lady Byng Trophy once, the Hart twice. He led the Blackhawks to the Stanley Cup in 1961, the first of his 50-goal seasons. He was the first big-name superstar to jump to the World Hockey Association when he signed a $1 million Cdn. contract with the Winnipeg Jets.

GEORGE (PUNCH) IMLACH: coach, general manager, Toronto Maple Leafs, Buffalo Sabres. Imlach was a bundle of superstitions and hockey acumen who piloted the Maple Leafs to four Stanley Cups in the 1960s. In 1970-71 he gave the expansion Buffalo Sabres instant credibility when he became their first coach and general manager. Imlach was instantly recognized by his trademark lucky fedoras. His superstition prevented him from changing suits when his team was on a winning streak.

GUY LAFLEUR: right winger. Lafleur, lightning-fast, creative and possessed of a

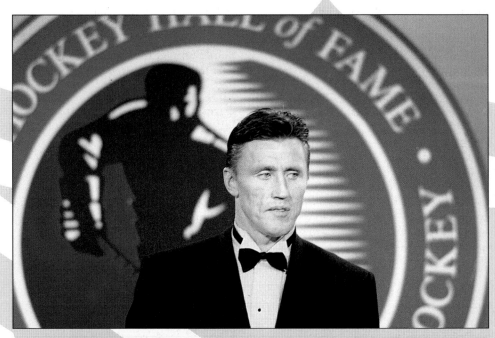

Old World Flash: Swedish defenseman Borje Salming brought an elegant skating stride and a large basket of skills to the Toronto Maple Leafs in the early 1970s. He was the first true European superstar in the NHL.

wicked slap shot was the NHL's dominant scorer of the 1970s. He was the first to score 50 goals or more in six consecutive seasons and six straight 100-point seasons. He also was the youngest player in history to score 400 goals and attain 1,000 points. He helped the Canadiens win five Stanley Cups, including four straight during his heyday from 1976-79.

TED LINDSAY: left winger. Terrible Ted Lindsay, one of the toughest players the NHL has ever seen, played on the famous Production Line with Gordie Howe and center Sid Abel. He helped the Red Wings win four Stanley Cups from 1948 to 1955. Lindsay channelled his combativeness into setting up the NHL Players' Association, which many believe led to his being traded to the Chicago Blackhawks in 1957.

FRANK MAHOVLICH: left winger. The man better known to hockey fans as The Big M possessed a booming slap shot and perhaps the smoothest, most powerful skating stride the game has ever seen. He scored 48 goals as a 23-year-old with Toronto in 1961 and helped the Maple Leafs win four Stanley Cups in the 1960s. Traded to Detroit in 1968, Mahovlich played on a line with Gordie Howe and Alex Delvecchio. Detroit traded him to Montreal in 1971 and The Big M set a playoff scoring record with 27 points and 14 goals to lead the Canadiens to the Stanley Cup. He also helped the

Canadiens win the Cup in 1973.

LANNY MCDONALD: right winger. McDonald scored 500 goals and added 506 assists in his 16-year career with Toronto, Colorado and Calgary. McDonald teamed up with Sittler as a potent one-two punch with the Maple Leafs until club owner Harold Ballard traded him to Colorado, largely out of spite. McDonald concluded a distinguished career in style, scoring a goal in Calgary's Cup-winning game against the Montreal Canadiens in 1989, the only Cup victory of his career.

STAN MIKITA: center. Born in Czechoslovakia, Mikita entered the NHL as a feisty, clever centerman, but he underwent a transformation into a gentlemanly player winning the Art Ross, Hart and Lady Byng trophies in 1967 and 1968, the first player ever to win all three in a single season. He is credited with introducing the curved stick blade to the NHL, by accident, it turns out. An angry Mikita tried to snap his stick blade by closing the door to the team bench on it. The stick bent, but did not break, and Mikita discovered it enhanced his shooting immensely.

FRANK NIGHBOR: center, defenseman. They called Nighbor the Pembroke Peach and he is credited with perfecting the poke check. He played 13 seasons in the NHL, from 1917-18 to 1929-30. He won five Stanley Cups, one with the Vancouver Millionaires in 1915, four more with the Ottawa Senators. In 1923, he became the first winner of the Hart Trophy as the NHL's most valuable player. In 1925, he was the first recipient of the Lady Byng Trophy, awarded to the league's most sportsmanlike player.

BOBBY ORR: defenseman. Played junior hockey for the Oshawa Generals and joined the Boston Bruins, at age 18, in 1966-67. Orr, one of the fastest skaters in the NHL in his time, revolutionized the defense position. With his quick acceleration, excellent straightahead speed and lateral mobility, Orr played defense like a point guard in basketball. More often than not, it was Orr who led the Bruins' offensive attacks, dishing a pass off to a teammate, or going end to end to take a shot on goal. He scored 296 goals in his 13 NHL seasons and was the first defenseman to score more than 40 goals and record more than 100 points in a season. He was the first defenseman to win the Conn Smythe Trophy. He also won the Norris Trophy eight times, the Hart three times and twice won the league scoring championship. He led the Bruins to two Stanley Cups. His career was foreshortened by a series of knee injuries.

BRAD PARK: defenseman. Contemporary of Orr and Potvin. Park played 17 years in the NHL, never for a team that missed the playoffs; but never for a team that won the Stanley Cup. He was named a first-team All-Star five times and became the second defenseman in NHL history to record 500 assists—after Orr. He scored 213 goals and added 683 assists in his career, which, like Orr's, was plagued by knee injuries. Early in his career, Park revived the seemingly lost art of the open-ice body check. Often cast in the shadow of first Orr, then Denis Potvin, Park was a superb two-way defenseman.

GILBERT PERREAULT: center. Won two Memorial Cups while a member of the Montreal Junior Canadiens. Perreault was the first draft pick of the Buffalo Sabres, for whom he played his entire 17-year career. Perreault centered the dangerous French Connection line with wingers Rene Robert and Richard Martin, amassing 1,336 points (512 goals) in his brilliant career. A virtuoso performer, Perreault was a strong, fast, slightly bow-legged skater, whose head

and shoulder fakes and quicksilver stickhandling mystified opponents. The Sabres built a credible NHL franchise in Buffalo around Perreault, who retired after the 1987-88 season.

JACQUES PLANTE: goaltender. Plante redefined his position. He was the first to roam away from the goal crease to handle loose pucks in the corners and along the end boards. After he suffered a nasty facial cut in a game in 1959, Plante donned a protective mask of his own design and, over the protests of his coach, Toe Blake, wore one from then on. Plante played 19 years in the NHL, with Montreal, New York, Toronto, St. Louis and Boston, but his years in Montreal were his finest. He won seven Vezina Trophies, six Stanley Cups and one Hart Trophy during his career.

DENIS POTVIN: defenseman. After a brilliant five-year junior career with the Ottawa 67s that Potvin began as a 14-year-old, the defenseman joined the New York Islanders as their indisputable franchise player. He led the Islanders to four straight Stanley Cups in the early 1980s. Potvin, a rugged, highly skilled player, chafed at comparisons with Orr. When his 15-year career was over, Potvin had recorded more goals (310), assists (742) and points (1,052) than any defenseman in NHL history.

Big Bird: Larry Robinson was one of the famous Big Three defenseman in Montreal, with Guy Lapointe and Serge Savard in the 1970s.

MAURICE RICHARD: right winger. The Rocket, as he was known, was a passionate presence on the ice who often saved his most brilliant performances for the most dramatic of circumstances. Among the 82 playoff goals he scored, 18 were game-winners, six of those in sudden-death overtime. He was the first player to score 50 goals in 50 games in a single season and the first to score 500 in his career. He scored 544 goals during his career, won eight Stanley Cups and won the Hart Trophy. Ironically, the man many consider the league's best-ever pure scorer, never won the Art Ross Trophy as the NHL's leading scorer.

TERRY SAWCHUCK: goaltender. Many consider Sawchuck to be the best goalie who ever played in the NHL. He posted an NHL-record 103 shutouts during his 21-year career, which saw him play for Detroit, Toronto, Boston, Los Angeles and New York Rangers. In 1952, Sawchuck carried the Red Wings to a Stanley Cup, posting four shutouts in Detroit's eight straight victories, and allowing just five goals overall. Sawchuck won the Vezina Trophy three times, including one award he shared with Johnny Bower for Toronto in 1967.

DARRYL SITTLER: center. Sittler was the heart and soul of some exciting Toronto Maple Leafs teams in the 1970s. He is remembered, as much as anything, for one brilliant night when he scored six goals and added four assists in an 11-4 Maple Leafs victory over the Boston Bruins in 1976. The same year, he scored five goals in a playoff game against the Flyers. He was the first member of the Maple Leafs to score 100 points in a season. He finished his career with 484 goals.

VLADISLAV TRETIAK: goaltender. In a perfect world, Tretiak, the brilliant goaltender for the Soviet Red Army and Soviet national teams, might have played for the Montreal Canadiens, who held his NHL rights. As a 20-year-old, Tretiak established himself as an excellent goaltender in the eight-game Canada-Soviet Summit Series in 1972. Viktor Tikhonov, the legendary Soviet coach, pulled Tretiak after the first period in the famous Miracle on Ice loss to the U.S. team at the Winter Olympics in 1980 in Lake Placid. Tikhonov would admit later this was his biggest regret as a coach.

Hockey Hall of Fame Membership Roster
(Players Only)

SID ABEL: center, Detroit Red Wings (1938-43 and 1945-52), Chicago Blackhawks (1952-54). Inducted 1969.

JACK ADAMS: forward, Toronto Arenas (1917-19), Toronto St. Pats (1922-26), Ottawa Senators (1926-27). Inducted 1959.

SYL APPS: center, Toronto Maple Leafs (1936-43 and 1945-48). Inducted 1961.

GEORGE ARMSTRONG: center, Toronto Maple Leafs (1949-71). Inducted 1975.

IRVINE (ACE) BAILEY: forward, Toronto St. Pats (1926-27), Toronto Maple Leafs (1927-34). Inducted 1975.

DAN BAIN: forward, Winnipeg Victorias (1895-1902). Inducted 1945.

HOBEY BAKER: forward, Princeton University (1910-1914). Inducted 1945.

BILL BARBER: right winger, Philadelphia Flyers (1972-84). Inducted 1990.

MARTY BARRY: forward, NY Americans (1927-28), Boston Bruins (1929-35), Detroit Red Wings (1935-39), Montreal Canadiens (1939-40). Inducted 1965.

ANDY BATHGATE: right winger, NY Rangers (1952-63), Toronto Maple Leafs (1963-65), Detroit Red Wings (1965-67), Pittsburgh Penguins (1967-68 and1970-71). Inducted 1978.

JEAN BELIVEAU: center, Montreal Canadiens (1950-51 and 1952-71). Inducted 1972.

CLINT BENEDICT: goaltender, Ottawa Senators (1912-24), Montreal Maroons (1924-30). Inducted 1965.

DOUG BENTLEY: forward, Chicago Blackhawks (1939-44 and 1945-52), NY Rangers (1953-54). Inducted 1964.

MAX BENTLEY: forward, Chicago Blackhawks (1940-43 and 1945-48), Toronto Maple Leafs (1947-53), NY Rangers (1953-54). Inducted 1966.

HECTOR (TOE) BLAKE: left winger, Montreal Maroons (1934-35), Montreal Canadiens (1935-48). Inducted 1966.

LEO BOIVIN: defenseman, Boston Bruins (1954-66), Detroit Red Wings (1965-67), Pittsburgh Penguins (1967-69), Minnesota North Stars (1968-70). Inducted 1986.

DICKIE BOON: forward, Montreal AAAs (1899-03), Montreal Wanderers (1904-06). Inducted 1952.

MIKE BOSSY: right winger, New York Islanders (1977-87). Inducted 1991.

EMILE (BUTCH) BOUCHARD: defenseman, Montreal Canadiens (1941-1956). Inducted 1966.

FRANK BOUCHER: forward, Ottawa Senators (1921-22), NY Rangers (1926-38 and 1943-44). Inducted 1958.

GEORGE BOUCHER: forward, Ottawa Senators (1915-1929), Montreal Maroons (1928-31), Chicago Blackhawks (1931-32). Inducted 1960.

JOHNNY BOWER: goaltender, NY Rangers (1953-55 and 1956-57), Toronto Maple Leafs (1958-70), Vancouver Canucks (1954-55). Inducted 1976.

RUSSELL (DUBBIE) BOWIE: forward, Montreal Victorias (1898-1908). Inducted 1945.

FRANK BRIMSEK: goaltender, Boston Bruins (1938-43 and 1945-49), Chicago Blackhawks (1949-50). Inducted 1966.

HARRY (PUNCH) BROADBENT: forward, Ottawa Senators (1912-15 and 1918-24 and 1927-28), Montreal Maroons (1924-27), NY Americans (1928-29). Inducted1962.

WALTER (TURK) BRODA: goaltender, Toronto Maple Leafs (1936-43 and 1945-52). Inducted 1967.

JOHN BUCYK: left winger, Detroit Red Wings (1955-57), Boston Bruins (1957-78). Inducted 1981.

BILLY BURCH: forward, Hamilton Tigers (1922-25), NY Americans (1925-32), Boston/Chicago (1932-33). Inducted 1974.

HARRY CAMERON: forward, Toronto Blue Shirts (1912-16), Montreal Wanderers (1916-17), Toronto Arenas (1917-19), Ottawa Senators (1918-19), Montreal Canadiens (1919-20), Toronto St. Pats (1919-23). Inducted 1962.

GERRY CHEEVERS: goaltender, Toronto Maple Leafs (1961-62), Boston Bruins (1965-72 and 1975-80). Inducted 1985.

FRANCIS (KING) CLANCY: defenseman, Ottawa Senators (1921-30), Toronto Maple Leafs (1930-37). Inducted 1958.

AUBRY (DIT) CLAPPER: defenseman, Boston Bruins (1927-47). Inducted 1947.

BOBBY CLARKE: center, Philadelphia Flyers (1969-84). Inducted 1987.

SPRAGUE CLEGHORN: forward, Montreal Wanderers (1911-17), Ottawa Senators (1918-21), Toronto St. Pats (1920-21), Montreal Canadiens (1921-25), Boston Bruins (1925-28). Inducted 1958.

NEIL COLVILLE: forward, NY Rangers (1935-42 and 1944-49). Inducted 1961.

CHARLIE CONACHER: forward, Toronto Maple Leafs (1929-38), Detroit Red Wings (1938-39), NY Americans (1939-41).

ALEX CONNELL: goaltender, Ottawa Senators (1924-31 and 1932-33), Detroit Falcons (1931-32), NY Americans (1933-34), Montreal Maroons (1934-35 and 1936-37). Inducted 1958.

BILL COOK: forward, Saskatoon Crescents (1921-26), NY Rangers (1926-37). Inducted 1952.

FRED JOSEPH (BUN) COOK: forward, Boston Bruins/New York Rangers (1926-37). Inducted 1995.

ART COULTER: defenseman, Chicago Blackhawks (1931-36), NY Rangers (1935-42). Inducted 1974.

YVAN COURNOYER: right winger, Montreal Canadiens (1963-79). Inducted 1982.

BILL COWLEY: forward, St. Louis Eagles (1934-35), Boston Bruins (1935-47). Inducted 1968.

RUSTY CRAWFORD: forward, Quebec Bulldogs (1912-17), Toronto Arenas (1917-19), Ottawa Senators (1917-18), Vancouver Maroons (1925-26). Inducted 1962.

JACK DARRAGH: forward, Ottawa Senators (1910-1924). Inducted 1962.

ALLAN (SCOTTY) DAVIDSON: forward, Toronto Blueshirts (1912-14). Inducted 1950.

CLARENCE (HAP) DAY: defenseman, Toronto St. Pats (1924-26), Toronto Maple Leafs (1926-37), NY Americans (1937-38). Inducted 1961.

ALEX DELVECCHIO: center, Detroit Red Wings (1950-74). Inducted 1977.

CY DENNENY: forward, Toronto Shamrocks (1914-15), Toronto Arenas (1915-16), Ottawa Senators (1916-28), Boston Bruins (1928-29). Inducted 1959.

MARCEL DIONNE: center, Detroit Red Wings (1971-75), LA Kings (1975-87), NY Rangers (1987-89). Inducted 1992.

GORDIE DRILLON: forward, Toronto Maple Leafs (1936-42), Montreal Canadiens (1942-43). Inducted 1975.

GRAHAM DRINKWATER: forward, Montreal AAAs (1892-93), Montreal Victorias (1893, 1895-98), McGill University (1894-95), Montreal Victorias (1899).

KEN DRYDEN: goaltender, Montreal Canadiens (1970-73 and 1974-79). Inducted 1983.

WOODY DUMART: forward, Boston Bruins (1935-42 and 1945-54). Inducted 1992.

TOMMY DUNDERDALE: forward, Winnipeg Victorias (1906-08), Toronto Shamrocks (1909-10), Quebec Bulldogs (1910-11), Victoria Aristocrats 1911-15 and 1918-23), Portland Rosebuds (1915-18), Saskatoon/Edmonton (1923-24). Inducted 1974.

BILL DURNAN: goaltender, Montreal Canadiens (1943-50). Inducted 1964.

MERVYN (RED) DUTTON: defenseman, Montreal Maroons (1926-30), NY Americans (1930-36). Inducted 1958.

CECIL (BABE) DYE: forward, Toronto St. Pats (1919-26), Hamilton Tigers (1920-21), Chicago Blackhawks (1926-28), NY Americans (1928-29), Toronto Maple Leafs (1930-31) Inducted 1970.

PHIL ESPOSITO: center, Chicago Blackhawks (1963-67), Boston Bruins (1967-76), NY Rangers (1975-81). Inducted 1984.

TONY ESPOSITO: goaltender, Montreal Canadiens (1968-69), Chicago Blackhawks (1969-84). Inducted 1988.

ARTHUR FARRELL: forward, Montreal Shamrocks (1896-1901). Inducted 1965.

FERNIE FLAMAN: defenseman, Boston Bruins (1944-51 and 1954-61), Toronto Maple Leafs (1950-54). Inducted 1965.

FRANK FOYSTON: forward, Toronto Blueshirts (1912-16), Seattle Metros (1915-24), Victoria Aristocrats (1924-26), Detroit Cougars (1926-28). Inducted 1958.

FRANK FREDERICKSON: forward, Victoria Aristocrats (1920-26), Boston Bruins (1926-29), Detroit Falcons (1926-27 and 1930-31), Pittsburgh Pirates (1928-30). Inducted 1958.

BILL GADSBY: defenseman, Chicago Blackhawks (1946-54), NY Rangers (1954-61), Detroit Red Wings (1961-66). Inducted 1970.

BOB GAINEY: left winger, Montreal Canadiens (1973-89). Inducted 1992.

CHUCK GARDINER: goaltender, Chicago Blackhawks (1927-34). Inducted 1945.

HERB GARDINER: defenseman, Montreal Canadiens (1926-29), Chicago Blackhawks (1928-29). Inducted 1958.

JIMMY GARDNER: forward, Montreal AAAs (1900-03), Montreal Wanderers (1903-11), New Westminster Royals (1911-13), Montreal Canadiens (1913-15). Inducted 1962.

BERNARD (BOOM BOOM) GEOFFRION: left winger, Montreal Canadiens (1951-64), NY Rangers (1966-68). Inducted 1972.

EDDIE GERARD: forward, Ottawa Victorias (1907-08), Ottawa Senators (1913-23). Inducted 1945.

EDDIE GIACOMIN: goaltender, NY Rangers (1965-76), Detroit Red Wings (1975-78). Inducted 1987.

ROD GILBERT: forward, NY Rangers (1960-78). Inducted 1982.

BILLY GILMOUR: forward, Ottawa Senators (1902-06 and 1908-09 and 1915-16), Montreal Victorias (1907-08). Inducted 1962.

FRANK (MOOSE) GOHEEN: defenseman, St. Paul Athletic Club (1914-28). Inducted 1952.

EBBIE GOODFELLOW: forward, Detroit Cougars (1928-30), Detroit Falcons (1930-33), Detroit Red Wings (1933-43). Inducted 1963.

MIKE GRANT: defenseman, Montreal Victorias (1893-1902). Inducted 1950.

WILF (SHORTY) GREEN: forward, Hamilton Tigers (1923-25), NY Americans (1925-27). Inducted 1962.

SI GRIFFIS: forward, Rat Portage Thistles (1902-06), Kenora Thistles (1906-07), Vancouver Millionaires (1911-19). Inducted 1950.

GEORGE HAINSWORTH: goaltender, Montreal Canadiens (1926-33 and 1936-37), Toronto Maple Leafs (1933-37). Inducted 1961.

NN HALL: goaltender, Detroit Red Wings (1952-53 and 1954-57), Chicago Blackhawks (1957-67), St. Louis Blues (1967-71). Inducted 1975.

JOE HALL: forward, Winnipeg Victorias (1903-05), Quebec Bulldogs (1905-06 and 1910-17), Brandon (1906-07), Montreal AAAs (1907-08), Montreal Shamrocks (1907-08 and 1909-10), Montreal Wanderers (1908-09), Montreal Canadiens (1917-19). Inducted 1961.

DOUG HARVEY: defenseman, Montreal Canadiens (1947-61), NY Rangers (1961-64), Detroit Red Wings (1966-67), St. Louis Blues (1967-69). Inducted 1973.

GEORGE HAY: forward, Chicago Blackhawks (1926-27), Detroit Cougars (1927-30), Detroit Falcons (1930-31), Detroit Red Wings (1932-34). Inducted 1958.

RILEY HERN: goaltender, Montreal Wanderers (1906-11). Inducted 1962.

BRYAN HEXTALL: forward, NY Rangers (1936-44 and 1945-48). Inducted 1969.

HARRY (HAP) HOLMES: goaltender, Toronto Blueshirts (1912-16), Seattle Metros (1915-17 and 1918-24), Toronto Arenas (1917-19), Victoria Aristocrats (1924-26), Detroit Cougars (1926-28).

TOM HOOPER: forward, Rat Portage Thistles (1901-05), Kenora Thistles (1906-07), Montreal Wanderers (1907-08), Montreal AAAs (1907-08). Inducted 1962.

REGINALD G. (RED) HORNER: defenseman, Toronto Maple Leafs (1928-40). Inducted 1965.

TIM HORTON: defenseman, Toronto Maple Leafs (1949-70), NY Rangers (1969-71), Pittsburgh Penguins (1971-72), Buffalo Sabres (1972-74). Inducted 1977.

GORDIE HOWE: right winger, Detroit Red Wings (1946-71), Houston Aeros (1973-77), New England Whalers (1977-79), Hartford Whalers (1979-80). Inducted 1972.

SYD HOWE: forward, Ottawa Senators (1929-30 and 1932-34), Philadelphia Quakers (1930-31), Toronto Maple Leafs (1931-32), St. Louis Eagles (1934-35), Detroit Red Wings (1934-46). Inducted 1965.

HARRY HOWELL: defenseman, NY Rangers (1952-69), Oakland Seals (1969-70), LA Kings (1970-73). Inducted 1979.

ROBERT MARVIN (BOBBY) HULL: left winger, Chicago Blackhawks (1957-72), Winnipeg Jets (1972-80), Hartford Whalers (1979-80). Inducted 1983.

BOUSE HUTTON: goaltender, Ottawa Senators (1898-1904). Inducted 1962.

HARRY HYLAND: forward, Montreal Shamrocks (1908-09), Montreal Wanderers (1909-11 and 1912-17), New Westminster Royals (1911-12), Montreal/Ottawa (1917-18). Inducted 1962.

DICK IRVIN: forward, Portland Rosebuds (1916-17), Regina Capitals (1921-25), Portland Capitals (1925-26), Chicago Blackhawks (1926-29). Inducted 1958.

HARVEY (BUSHER) JACKSON: forward, Toronto Maple Leafs (1929-39), NY Americans (1939-41), Boston Bruins (1941-44). Inducted 1971.

IVAN WILFRED (CHING) JOHNSON: defenseman, NY Rangers (1926-37), NY Americans (1937-38). Inducted 1958.

ERNIE JOHNSON: forward, Montreal Victorias (1903-05), Montreal Wanderers (1905-11), New Westminster Royals (1911-14), Portland Rosebuds (1914-18), Victoria Aristocrats (1918-22). Inducted 1952.

TOM JOHNSON: defenseman, Montreal Canadiens (1947-48 and 1949-63), Boston Bruins (1963-65). Inducted 1970.

AUREL JOLIAT: forward, Montreal Canadiens (1922-38). Inducted 1947.

GleGordon (Duke) Keats: forward, Toronto Blue Shirts (1915-17), Edmonton Eskimos (1921-26), Boston & Detroit (1926-27), Detroit & Chicago (1927-28) Chicago Blackhawks (1928-29). Inducted 1958.

Leonard (Red) Kelly: defenseman, center, Detroit Red Wings (1947-60), Toronto Maple Leafs (1960-67). Inducted 1969.

Ted (Teeder) Kennedy: forward, Toronto Maple Leafs (1942-55 and 1956-57). Inducted 1966.

Dave Keon: center, Toronto Maple Leafs (1960-75), Hartford Whalers (1979-82). Inducted 1986.

Elmer Lach: center, Montreal Canadiens (1940-54). Inducted 1966.

Guy Lafleur: right winger, Montreal Canadiens (1971-85), NY Rangers (1988-89), Quebec Nordiques (1989-91). Inducted 1988.

Edouard (Newsy) Lalonde: forward, Montreal Canadiens (1910-11 and 1912-22), NY Americans (1926-27). Inducted 1950.

Jacques Laperriere: defenseman, Montreal Canadiens (1962-74). Inducted 1987.

Jack Laviolette: defenseman, Montreal Nationals (1903-07), Montreal Shamrocks (1907-09), Montreal Canadiens (1909-18). Inducted 1962.

Hugh Lehman: goaltender, New Westminster Royals (1911-14), Vancouver Millionaires (1914-26), Chicago Blackhawks (1926-28). Inducted 1958.

Jacques Lemaire: left winger, center, Montreal Canadiens (1967-79). Inducted 1984.

Mario Lemieux: center, Pittsburgh Penguins (1985-94, 1995-97). Inducted 1997.

Percy LeSueur: goaltender, Ottawa Senators (1905-14), Toronto Shamrocks (1914-15), Toronto Blueshirts (1915-16). Inducted 1961.

Herbie Lewis: forward, Detroit Cougars (1928-30), Detroit Falcons (1930-33), Detroit Red Wings (1933-39). Inducted 1989.

Ted Lindsay: left winger, Detroit Red Wings (1944-58 and 1964-65), Chicago Blackhawks (1957-60). Inducted 1966.

Harry Lumley: goaltender, Detroit Red Wings (1943-50), Chicago Blackhawks (1950-52), Toronto Maple Leafs (1952-56), Boston Bruins (1957-60).

Mickey MacKay: forward, Vancouver Millionaires (1914-19 and 1920-24), Vancouver Maroons (1924-26), Chicago Blackhawks (1926-28), Boston & Pittsburgh (1928-29), Boston Bruins (1929-30). Inducted 1952.

Frank Mahovlich: left winger, Toronto Maple Leafs (1956-68), Detroit Red Wings (1968-71), Montreal Canadiens (1971-74). Inducted 1981.

Joe (Phantom) Malone: forward, Quebec Bulldogs (1908-09 and 1910-17), Waterloo (1909-10), Montreal Canadiens (1917-24), Hamilton Tigers (1921-22). Inducted 1950.

Sylvio Mantha: defenseman, Montreal Canadiens (1923-36), Boston Bruins (1936-37). Inducted 1960.

Jack Marshall: forward, Winnipeg Victorias (1900-01), Montreal Victorias (1901-03), Montreal Wanderers (1903-05 and 1906-07 and 1909-12 and 1915-17), Montreal Shamrocks (1907-09), Toronto Tecumsehs (1912-13), Toronto Ontarios (1913-14), Toronto Shamrocks (1914-15). Inducted 1965.

Fred Maxwell: forward, Winnipeg Monarchs (1914-16), Winnipeg Falcons (1918-25). Inducted 1962.

Lanny McDonald: right winger, Toronto Maple Leafs (1973-80), Colorado Rockies (1980-82), Calgary Flames (1982-89). Inducted 1992.

Frank McGee: forward, Ottawa Senators (1902-06). Inducted 1945.

Billy McGimsie: forward, Rat Portage Thistles (1902-03 and 1904-06), Kenora Thistles (1906-07). Inducted 1962.

George McNamara: defenseman, Montreal Shamrocks (1907-09), Halifax Crescents (1909-12), Waterloo (1911), Toronto Tecumsehs (1912-13), Ottawa (1913-14), Toronto Shamrocks (1914-15), Toronto Blueshirts (1915-16), 228th Battalion (1916-17). Inducted 1958.

Stan Mikita: center, Chicago Blackhawks (1958-80). Inducted 1983.

Richard (Dickie) Moore: left winger, Montreal Canadiens (1951-63), Toronto Maple Leafs (1964-65), St. Louis Blues (1967-68). Inducted 1974.

Paddy Moran: goaltender, Quebec Bulldogs (1901-09 and 1910-17), Halleybury Comets (1909-10). Inducted 1958.

Howie Morenz: forward, Montreal Canadiens (1923-34 and 1936-37), Chicago Blackhawks (1934-36), NY Rangers (1935-36). Inducted 1945.

Bill Mosienko: forward, Chicago Blackhawks (1941-55). Inducted 1965.

Frank Nighbor: center, Ottawa Senators (1915-29), Toronto Maple Leafs (1929-30). Inducted 1947.

Reginald Noble: forward, Toronto Arenas (1917-19), Toronto St. Patricks (1919-25), Montreal Maroons (1924-27), Detroit Cougars (1927-32), Detroit & Montreal (1932-33). Inducted 1962.

Buddy O'Connor: forward, Montreal Canadiens (1941-47), NY Rangers (1947-51). Inducted 1988.

Harry Oliver: forward, Boston Bruins (1926-34), NY Americans (1934-37). Inducted 1967.

Bert Olmstead: left winger, Chicago Blackhawks (1948-51), Montreal Canadiens (1950-58), Toronto Maple Leafs (1958-62). Inducted 1985.

Robert (Bobby) Orr: defenseman, Boston Bruins (1966-76), Chicago Blackhawks (1976-79). Inducted 1979.

Bernard Parent: goaltender, Boston Bruins (1965-67), Philadelphia Flyers (1967-71 and 1973-79), Toronto Maple Leafs (1970-72). Inducted 1984.

Brad Park: defenseman, NY Rangers (1968-76), Boston Bruins (1976-83), Detroit Red Wings (1983-85). Inducted 1988.

Lester Patrick: forward, Brandon (1903-04), Westmount (1904-05), Montreal Wanderers (1905-07), Edmonton (1907-08), Renfrew Cream Kings (1909-10), Victoria Aristocrats (1911-16 and 1918-22), Spokane (1916-17), Seattle Metros (1917-18), Victoria Cougars (1925-26), NY Rangers (1927-28). Inducted 1947.

Joseph Lynn Patrick: forward, NY Rangers (1934-43 and 1945-46). Inducted 1980.

Gilbert Perreault: center, Buffalo Sabres (1970-87). Inducted 1990.

Tom Phillips: forward, Montreal AAAs (1902-03), Toronto Marlboroughs (1903-04), Rat Portage Thistles (1904-06), Kenora Thistles (1906-07), Ottawa Senators (1907-08), Vancouver Millionaires (1911-12). Inducted 1945.

Pierre Pilote: defenseman, Chicago Blackhawks (1955-68), Toronto Maple Leafs (1968-69). Inducted 1975.

Didier Pitre: forward, Montreal Nationals (1903-05), Montreal Shamrocks (1907-08), Renfrew Millionaires (1908-09), Montreal Canadiens (1909-23). Inducted 1962.

Jacques Plante: goaltender, Montreal Canadiens (1952-63), NY Rangers (1963-65), St. Louis Blues (1968-70), Toronto Maple Leafs (1970-73), Boston Bruins (1972-73). Inducted 1978.

Denis Potvin: defenseman, NY Islanders (1973-88). Inducted 1991.

Walter (Babe) Pratt: defenseman, NY Rangers (1935-43), Toronto Maple Leafs (1942-46), Boston Bruins (1946-47). Inducted 1966.

Joe Primeau: defenseman, Toronto Maple Leafs (1927-36). Inducted 1963.

Marcel Pronovost: defenseman, Detroit Red Wings (1949-65), Toronto Maple Leafs (1965-70). Inducted 1978.

Bob Pulford: center, Toronto Maple Leafs (1956-70), LA Kings (1970-72). Inducted 1991.

Harvey Pulford: defenseman, Ottawa Senators (1893-1908). Inducted 1945.

Bill Quackenbush: defenseman, Detroit Red Wings (1942-49), Boston Bruins (1949-56). Inducted 1976.

Frank Rankin: forward, Stratford (1906-09), Eaton's Athletic Association (1910-12), St. Michaels' (1912-14). Inducted 1961.

Jean Ratelle: center, NY Rangers (1962-76), Boston Bruins (1975-81). Inducted 1985.

Chuck Rayner: goaltender, NY Americans (1940-41), Brooklyn Americans (1941-42), NY Rangers (1945-53). Inducted 1973.

Kenneth Joseph Reardon: defenseman, Montreal Canadiens (1940-42 and 1945-50). Inducted 1966.

Henri Richard: center, Montreal Canadiens (1955-75). Inducted 1979.

Maurice (Rocket) Richard: right winger, Montreal Canadiens (1942-60). Inducted 1961.

George Richardson: forward, 14th Regiment (1906-13), Queens University (1908-09). Inducted 1950.

Gordon Roberts: forward, Ottawa Senators (1909-10), Montreal Wanderers (1910-16), Vancouver Millionaires (1916-17 and 1919-20), Seattle Metropolitans (1917-18). Inducted 1971.

Larry Robinson: defenseman, Montreal Canadiens (1972-90), Los Angeles Kings (1990-92). Inducted 1995.

Art Ross: forward, Westmount (1904-05), Brandon (1906-07), Kenora Thistles (1906-07), Montreal Wanderers (1907-09 and 1910-14 and 1917-18), Halleybury Comets (1909-10), Ottawa Senators (1914-16). Inducted 1945.

Blair Russel: forward, Montreal Victorias (1899-1908). Inducted 1965.

Ernie Russell: forward, Montreal AAAs (1904-05), Montreal Wanderers (1905-08 and 1909-14). Inducted 1965.

Jack Ruttan: forward, Armstrong's Point (1905-06), Rustler (1906-07), St. Johns College (1907-08), Manitoba Varsity (1909-12), Winnipeg (1912-13). Inducted 1962.

Borje Salming: defenseman, Toronto Maple Leafs 1973-1989, Detroit Red Wings, 1990. Inducted 1996.

Serge Savard: defenseman, Montreal Canadiens (1966-81), Winnipeg Jets (1981-83). Inducted 1986.

Terry Sawchuck: goaltender, Detroit Red Wings (1949-55 and 1957-64 and 1968-69), Boston Bruins (1955-57), Toronto Maple Leafs (1964-67), LA Kings (1967-68), NY Rangers (1969-70). Inducted 1971.

Fred Scanlan: forward, Montreal Shamrocks (1897-1901), Winnipeg Victorias (1901-03). Inducted 1965.

Milt Schmidt: center, Boston Bruins, 1936-42 and 1945-55). Inducted 1961.

Sweeney Schriner: forward, NY Americans (1934-39), Toronto Maple Leafs (1939-43 and 1944-46). Inducted 1962.

Earl Seibert: defenseman, NY Rangers (1931-36), Chicago Blackhawks (1935-45), Detroit Red Wings (1944-46). Inducted 1963.

Oliver Seibert: forward, Berlin Dutchmen (1900-06). Inducted 1961.

Eddie Shore: defenseman, Boston Bruins (1926-40). Inducted 1947.

Steve Shutt: left winger, Montreal Canadiens (1973-1984), LA Kings (1985). Inducted 1993.

Albert Charles (Babe) Siebert: defenseman, Montreal Maroons (1925-32), NY Rangers (1932-34), Boston Bruins (1933-36), Montreal Canadiens (1936-39). Inducted 1964.

Joe Simpson: defenseman, Edmonton Eskimos (1921-25), NY Americans (1925-31). Inducted 1962.

Darryl Sittler: center, Toronto Maple Leafs (1970-82), Philadelphia Flyers (1982-84), Detroit Red Wings (1984-85). Inducted 1989.

Alf Smith: forward, Ottawa Senators, 1894-1908), Kenora Thistles (1906-07). Inducted 1962.

Billy Smith: goaltender: LA Kings (1971-72), NY Islanders (1972-89). Inducted 1993.

Clint Smith: forward, NY Rangers (1936-43), Chicago Blackhawks (1943-47). Inducted 1991.

Reginald Joseph (Hooley) Smith: forward, Ottawa Senators (1924-27), Montreal Maroons (1927-36), Boston Bruins (1936-37), NY Americans (1937-41). Inducted 1972.

Tommy Smith: forward, Ottawa Victorias (1905-06), Brantford Indians (1908-10), Cobalt Silver Kings (1909-10), Galt (1910-11), Moncton (1911-12), Quebec Bulldogs (1912-16 and 1919-20), Ontarios (1914-15), Montreal Canadiens (1916-17). Inducted 1973.

Allan Stanley: defenseman, NY Rangers (1948-55), Chicago Blackhawks (1954-56), Toronto Maple Leafs (1958-68), Philadelphia Flyers (1968-69). Inducted 1981.

Barney Stanley: forward, Vancouver Millionaires (1914-19), Calgary Tigers (1921-22), Regina Capitals (1922-24), Edmonton Eskimos (1924-26). Inducted 1962.

Jack Stewart: defenseman, Detroit Red Wings (1938-43 and 1945-50), Chicago Blackhawks (1950-52).

Nelson Stewart: forward, Montreal Maroons (1925-32), Boston Bruins (1932-35 and 1936-37), NY Americans (1935-40). Inducted 1962.

Bruce Stuart: forward, Ottawa Senators (1898-1902 and 1908-11), Quebec Bulldogs (1900-01), Montreal Wanderers (1907-08). Inducted 1961.

William Hodgson (Hod) Stuart: forward, Ottawa Senators (1898-1900), Quebec Bulldogs (1900-06), Montreal Wanderers (1906-08). Inducted 1945.

Frederick (Cyclone) Taylor: forward, Ottawa Senators (1907-09), Renfrew Cream Kings (1909-11), Vancouver Millionaires (1912-21 and 1922-23). Inducted 1947.

Cecil R. (Tiny) Thompson: goaltender, Boston Bruins (1928-39), Detroit Red Wings (1939-40). Inducted 1959.

Vladislav Tretiak: goaltender, Central Red Army (1969-84), Soviet National Team (1969-84). Inducted 1989.

Harry Trihey: forward, Montreal Shamrocks (1896-1901). Inducted 1950.

Brian Trottier: center, New York Islanders (1979-89), Pittsburgh Penguins (1990-94). Inducted 1997.

Norm Ullman: center, Detroit Red Wings (1955-67), Toronto Maple Leafs (1967-75), Edmonton Oilers (1975-77). Inducted 1982.

Georges Vezina: goaltender, Montreal Canadiens (1910-26). Inducted 1945.

Jack Walker: forward, Toronto Blueshirts (1912-15), Seattle Metros (1915-24), Victoria Cougars (1924-26), Detroit Cougars (1926-28). Inducted 1960.

Marty Walsh: forward, Ottawa Senators (1907-12). Inducted 1962.

Harry (Moose) Watson: left winger, St. Andrews (1915), Aura Lee Juniors (1918), Toronto Dentals (1919), Toronto Granites (1920-25), Toronto Sea Fleas (1931). Inducted 1962.

Ralph C. (Cooney) Weiland: forward, Boston Bruins (1928-32 and 1935-39), Ottawa Senators (1932-34), Detroit Red Wings (1933-35). Inducted 1971.

Harry Westwick: forward, Ottawa Senators (1894-98 and 1900-08), Kenora Thistles (1906-07). Inducted 1962.

Fret Whitcroft: forward, Kenora Thistles (1906-08), Edmonton (1908-10), Renfrew Cream Kings (1909-10). Inducted 1962.

Gordon Allan (Phat) Wilson: forward, Port Arthur War Veterans (1918-20), Iroquois Falls Eskimos (1921), Port Arthur Bearcats (1923-33). Inducted 1962.

Lorne (Gump) Worsley: goaltender, NY Rangers (1952-63), Montreal Canadiens (1963-70), Minnesota North Stars (1969-74). Inducted 1980.

Roy Worters: goaltender, Pittsburgh Pirates (1925-28), NY Americans (1928-37), Montreal Maroons (1929-30). Inducted 1969.

GLOSSARY OF HOCKEY TERMS

Art Ross Trophy: Awarded to the player who wins the scoring championship during the regular season.

Assist: A pass that leads to a goal being scored. One or two, or none, may be awarded on any goal.

Backchecking: Skating with an opponent through the neutral and defensive zones to try to break up an attack.

Backhand: A pass or shot, in which the player cradles the puck on the off- or backside of the stick blade and propels it with a shoveling motion..

Back pass: A pass left or slid backwards for a trailing teammate to recover.

Blocker: A protective glove worn on the hand a goaltender uses to hold his stick so that the goalie can deflect pucks away from the net.

Blue lines: The lines, located 29 feet from each side of the center red line, which demarcate the beginning of the offensive zone.

Boarding: Riding or driving an opponent into the boards. A two- or five-minute penalty may be assessed, at the referee's discretion.

Boards: Wooden structures, 48 inches high, topped by plexiglass fencing, that enclose the 200 feet by 85 feet ice surface.

Bodycheck: Using the hips or shoulders to stop the progress of the puck carrier.

Breakaway: The puck carrier skating toward the opposition's net ahead of all the other players.

Butt-Ending: Striking an opponent with the top end of the hockey stick, a dangerously illegal act that brings a five-minute penalty.

Calder Memorial Trophy: Awarded to the goaltender, defenseman or forward judged to be the best first-year, or rookie, player.

Central Scouting Bureau: An NHL agency that compiles statistical and evaluative information on all players eligible for the Entry Draft. The information, which includes a rating system of all players, is distributed to all NHL teams.

Charging: Skating three strides or more and crashing into an opponent. Calls for a two-minute or five-minute penalty at the referee's discretion.

Conn Smythe Trophy: Awarded to the top performer throughout the Stanley Cup playoffs.

Crease: A six-foot semicircular area at the mouth of the goal that opponents may not enter. Only the goaltender may freeze the puck in this space.

Crossbar: A red, horizontal pipe, four feet above the ice and six feet long across the top of the goal cage.

Crosschecking: Hitting an opponent with both hands on the stick and no part of the stick on the ice. Warrants a two-minute penalty.

Defensemen: The two players who form the second line of defense, after the goalie. Defensemen try to strip opponents of the puck in their own zone and either pass to teammates or skate the puck up-ice themselves to start an attack. When retreating from the opponent's zone, defensemen move back toward their zone by skating backwards, facing the oncoming opponents.

Deflection: Placing the blade of the stick in the path of a shot on goal, causing the puck to change direction and deceive the goaltender. A puck may also deflect off a player's skate or pads.

Delay of game: Causing the play to stop by either propelling the puck outside the playing surface or covering it with the hand. Warrants a two-minute penalty.

Delayed penalty: An infraction, signaled by the referee's upraised right hand, but not whistled until the offending team regains possession of the puck. During the delay, the other team can launch a scoring attack, sometimes by replacing their goaltender with a skater. If the team scores during the delay, the penalized player does not sit out his penalty.

Elbowing: Striking an opponent with the elbow. Calls for a two-minute penalty.

Entry Draft: An annual event, at which all 26 NHL teams submit claims on young players who have not signed professional contracts. The talent pool consists of players from the Canadian junior leagues, U.S. high schools and universities and European elite and junior leagues.

Faceoff: A play that initiates all action in a hockey game, in which the referee or a linesman drops the puck onto a spot between the poised stick blades of two opponents. Marks the start of every period, also occurs after every goal and every play stoppage.

Fighting: Players dropping their gloves and striking each other with their fists. Calls for a five-minute penalty and ejection for the player who instigated the fisticuffs.

Forechecking: Harassing opponents in their own zone to try to gain possession of the puck.

Forwards: Three players—the center and the left and right wingers—comprise a hockey team's forward line. The forwards are primarily attackers whose aim is to score goals.

Frank J. Selke Trophy: Awarded to the player judged the best defensive forward in the NHL.

Goal: A goal is scored when the puck completely crosses the red goal line and enters the net.

Goals-Against-Average (GAG): Average number of goals a goaltender surrenders per game. Determined by multiplying the total number of goals allowed by 60 and dividing that figure by the total number of minutes played.

Goaltender: A heavily padded player who protects his team's goal.

Hart Memorial Trophy: Awarded to the player judged the most valuable to his team during the NHL regular season.

Hat Trick: One player scoring three goals in one game. A player who scores three consecutive goals in one period is said to have scored a 'natural' hat trick.

High sticking: Carrying the stick above the shoulder level. Calls for a faceoff if a player strikes the puck in this fashion. Calls for a two- or five-minute penalty if a player strikes an opponent with his stick.

Holding: Using the hands to impede the progress of an opponent. Two-minute penalty.

Hooking: Using the blade of the stick to impede an opponent. Two-minute penalty.

Icing the puck: Shooting the puck from one side of the center red line so that it crosses the opponent's red goal line. Calls for a play stoppage and a faceoff in the offending team's zone.

Interference: Using the body or stick to impede an opponent who is not in possession of the puck or was the last one to touch it. Two-minute penalty.

James Norris Memorial Trophy: Awarded annually to the player who is judged to be the best defenseman in the NHL.

Kneeing: Using the knee to check an opponent. Two-minute penalty.

Lady Byng Trophy: Awarded to the player who best combines playing excellence with sportsmanship.

Linesmen: Two on-ice officials responsible for calling offside, icing and some infractions, such as too many men on the ice. Linesmen drop the puck for faceoffs excluding those after a goal has been scored.

Neutral zone: The area of the ice surface between the two blue lines and bisected by the center red line.

Neutral-zone trap: Also called the delayed forecheck. A checking system designed to choke off offensive attacks in the neutral zone and enable the defensive team to regain possession of the puck.

Offside: A player who crosses the opposition blue line before the puck does is offside. Play is stopped when this occurs and a faceoff is held outside the blue line. A player also is offside if he accepts a pass that has crossed two lines (e.g. his team's blue line and the center red line). When this occurs, play is stopped and a faceoff is held at the point where the pass was made.

Original Six: In common usage, it refers to the six NHL teams in the pre-1968 expansion era: Toronto Maple Leafs; Montreal Canadiens; Boston Bruins; New York Rangers; Chicago Blackhawks; Detroit Red Wings.

Overtime: During regular-season play, teams play a five-minute, sudden-death overtime period if the score is tied at the end of regulation time. Teams play as many 20-minute sudden-death overtime periods as is necessary to reach a final result during the entire playoff schedule. Sudden-death means the game is over as soon as a goal is scored.

Penalty: A rules infraction which results in a player serving a two- or five-minute penalty in the penalty box, or in expulsion from the game. The penalized player's team must play one man short while he serves a minor or major penalty, but is not so handicapped if the player is assessed a ten-minute misconduct. The player cannot play until his time is up, but the team continues at full on-ice strength. A player assessed a game misconduct penalty cannot play for the rest of the game.

Penalty kill: A four- or three-man unit of players assigned to prevent the opposition from scoring while a teammate serves a two- or five-minute penalty.

Penalty Shot: Called when an attacking player, on a breakaway, is illegally prevented from getting a shot on goal. The puck is placed at center ice and the fouled player skates in alone on the goaltender.

Period: A 20-minute segment, during which time the clock stops at every play stoppage. A hockey game consists of three stop-time periods.

Playing Roster: A team may only dress 18 skaters and two goaltenders for each NHL game.

Plus-Minus: A 'plus' is credited to a player who is on the ice when his team scores an even-strength or shorthanded goal. A 'minus' is given to a player who is on the ice when an opponent scores an even-strength or shorthanded goal. A player's plus-minus total is the aggregate score of pluses and minuses. It is a barometer of a player's value to his team.

Point man: A player, usually a defenseman, who positions himself along the blue line near the boards and orchestrates an attacking team's offensive zone strategy. Often teams try to isolate the point man for a shot on goal.

Pokecheck: A sweeping or poking motion with the stick used to take the puck away from an opponent. Perfected by Frank Nighbor of the Ottawa Senators teams in the 1920s.

Power play: A situation in which one team has one or two more players on the ice than the other team, owing to penalties assessed. It provides the attacking team with an excellent opportunity to create quality scoring chances.

Puck: A vulcanized rubber disk, three inches wide and one inch thick. Game pucks are kept on ice before and during a game, which hardens them even more and helps them slide more quickly.

Rebound: A puck bouncing off the boards, the goaltender or the goalposts. A rebound gives an attacker a second chance for a dangerous shot on goal.

Red line: The red, center line dividing the ice surface in half. In junior and professional hockey, the red line is used to determine icing calls and offside passes. It is not used in U.S. college hockey.

Referee: The chief on-ice official at a hockey game. The referee calls all penalties except too many men on the ice and controls the flow of the game.

Roughing: Excessive pushing and shoving that has not escalated to the level of fisticuffs. Two-minute penalty.

Rink: A surface 200 feet by 85 feet on which a game of hockey is played.

Save: Occurs when a goalie uses his blocker, goalie stick, catching glove or pads to prevent a puck from entering the goal.

Scout: A man or woman who travels to junior, college and high school games, evaluating players who will be available in the Entry Draft. NHL teams also have pro scouts, who evaluate the play of opposing teams.

Shift: The period of time—usually 35-45 seconds—that a player spends on the ice playing the game. Normally a player will play several shifts each period. Some players log as much as 30 minutes in ice time in any given game.

Shot On Goal: Any deliberate attempt by a player to shoot the puck into an opponent's net that, without the intervention of the goaltender, would have scored a goal. Therefore, a shot that hits a goalpost or the crossbar and bounces away, is not a shot on goal.

Shutout: A game result in which the opponent does not score a goal, usually owing to excellent work by the goaltender.

Slap shot: Shooting the puck by swinging the hockey stick through the disk, in a manner similar to a golf swing, except with the hands several inches apart on the stick.

Slashing: Swinging a stick at an opponent. Two-minute penalty.

Slot, The: The area in the offensive zone directly in front of the crease, extending back between the two faceoff circles, about halfway toward the blue line. Teams work hard to create scoring opportunities inside this area.

Spearing: Using a stick as a weapon, jabbing it, like a spear, into an opponent. Five-minute penalty, with expulsion at the discretion of the referee.

Stanley Cup: A silver trophy, originally donated by Lord Stanley, Earl of Preston in 1893 to be emblematic of Canadian hockey supremacy. Since 1926 only NHL teams have competed for the trophy.

Stickhandle: Manipulating the puck back and forth, or any direction, with the blade of the stick in order to deceive an opponent and carry the puck up the ice.

Tip-In: A goal that results when one player shoots on net and a teammate, positioned near the crease, uses his stick to redirect the puck past the goaltender.

Vezina Trophy: Awarded annually to the player judged to be the best goaltender in the NHL.

Wrist shot: Shooting the puck by sweeping the stick along the ice, snapping the wrists on the follow-through.

Zamboni: The box-like, motor-powered vehicle used to resurface the ice in all NHL arenas. The machine collects the snow that builds up during a period of play and lays down a fresh coat of water, providing a smooth ice sheet to begin each period.

INDEX

Main entries indicated in **bold**